FOUNDATIONS OF
PERSONAL FINANCE

8th Edition

Sally R. Campbell
Winnetka, Illinois

Publisher

The Goodheart-Willcox Company, Inc.

Tinley Park, Illinois

www.g-w.com

Goodheart-Willcox Publisher Brand Disclaimer: Brand names,
company names, and illustrations for products and services included in this text are
provided for educational purposes only and do not represent or imply endorsement
or recommendation by the authors or the publisher.

Library of Congress Cataloging-in-Publication Data

Cambell, Sally R.
    Foundations of personal finance / Sally R. Cambell. – 8th ed.
        p. cm.
    Rev. ed. of: The confident consumer. c2004.
    Includes index.
    ISBN 978-1-60525-089-2
1. Finance, Personal. 2. Consumer education. I. Cambel, Sally R.
    Confident consumer. II. Title.
HG179.C32 2010
332.024--dc22
                                                2009039160

Cover image: Gettyimages RF

Introduction

Foundations of Personal Finance serves as a guide to the U.S. economic system and an introduction to the global economy. It will help you understand the system and how it affects you as a consumer, producer, and citizen. It will also help you make the most of the future opportunities that come your way in the global economy.

The text outlines the key characteristics of the free market system and the challenges of globalization. It describes your financial activities as worker, consumer, manager, and shopper. Mastering these decision-making functions lays the foundation for personal financial competence through all the stages of your life.

To manage personal finances, you need to define the economic goals you want to achieve and the steps you can take to achieve them. *Foundations of Personal Finance* explains how to identify your most important needs and wants and how to manage your resources to reach your goals. It can help you make the best use of all your resources to raise your standard of living and create financial security in your future.

As you use this book, you will learn how to make financial decisions related to routine spending for food, clothing, and personal needs. You will learn where to find reliable information about consumer products and services, government policies, and economic conditions. You will find out what to consider when making big spending decisions for items such as cars, housing, and home furnishings. You will also learn what is important to know when you use credit, buy insurance, and invest your money. In addition, the text identifies the tools you can use to protect your consumer interests as you carry out your financial transactions in the marketplace.

You will find a section on planning your future. These chapters will describe the education and job training that will prepare you to take your place in the work world. Finally, you will look at your role as a citizen of the world and custodian of the environment.

Foundations of Personal Finance is straightforward and easy to read. Each chapter begins with learning objectives and new terms to understand. Each chapter ends with review questions, critical thinking questions, and activities to help you study effectively and organize what you learn. The case studies provided throughout the text will help you relate the material to lifelike situations. You will also find features on careers; real-life connections to the text content; and links to history, math, and science.

About the Author

Sally R. Campbell is currently a freelance writer and consultant in consumer economics. She develops educational materials, including teacher's guides, curriculum guides, textbooks, and student activity materials.

She was formerly the editor and assistant director of the Money Management Institute of Household International where she wrote educational materials related to money management, consumer information, and financial planning.

Sally has a master's degree in education from St. Louis University and has completed the Certified Financial Planning Professional Education Program of the College for Financial Planning. She taught consumer education in the St. Louis public schools.

Welcome to Foundations of Personal Finance

Foundations of Personal Finance is designed to help you succeed. Each of the following features will assist you in mastering the concepts presented in the textbook.

Reading for Meaning provides tips to improve reading comprehension and understanding. Review the tip before you read each chapter.

Key Terms appear in bold, highlighted type in the text where they are defined.

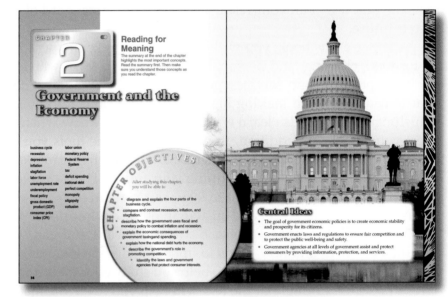

Chapter Objectives outline skills you will build while studying the chapter.

Central Ideas present the main concepts discussed in the chapter.

Real Life Connections features apply chapter concepts to real-life situations.

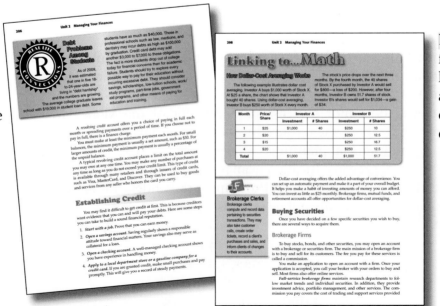

Linking to... features connect key topics to the academic areas of history, math, or science.

Economics in Action features discuss economic principles in evidence today.

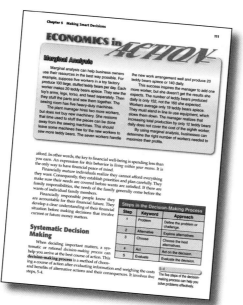

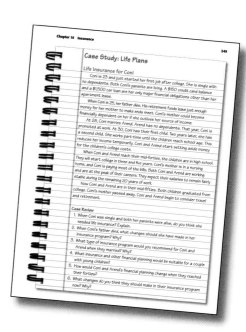

Case Studies bring financial concepts to life through realistic scenarios and follow-up questions.

Chapter Summary covers the main ideas of the chapter.

Review questions reinforce important concepts and help you recall, organize, and use the information presented in the text.

Critical Thinking activities expand chapter concepts and challenge you to use problem-solving skills. Thought-provoking questions motivate you to seek further information or exchange thoughts and opinions with classmates.

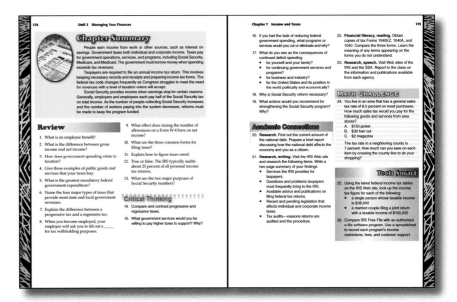

Academic Connections activities increase personal finance knowledge while developing academic skills. Academic areas include history, math, reading, research, science, social studies, speech, and writing. Activities may involve individual or team work.

Math Challenge helps you develop critical math skills related to personal finance.

Tech Smart encourages the exploration of financial concepts through high-tech means.

Student Organizations

You may be familiar with many student organizations at your school. Some exist specifically to help you and other young people learn the skills they will need in the work world. These organizations are known as Career and Technical Student Organizations (CTSOs). Joining one or more of these organizations can benefit you in many ways.

Reasons to Join

A CTSO related to your career interests can help you develop the skills you will need to succeed in your career. As part of an organization, you will have access to in-depth, profession-related knowledge. You will be working with peers who share similar values and goals. Staff, organization leaders, and teachers can provide you with valuable insights you will need on your career path. The friendships and networking connections you nurture now can also be beneficial throughout your career.

No matter what career you choose, a CTSO will help you acquire and develop abilities you will need for career success. Qualities such as leadership, cooperation, creativity, responsibility, and fairness will help you advance in any job. Skills in planning, communication, and teamwork will make you an essential employee.

Some CTSOs are directly involved in the subject of personal finance. They include FCCLA, DECA, FBLA, BPA, and SkillsUSA.

Family, Career and Community Leaders of America (FCCLA)

FCCLA is a student organization that promotes personal growth and leadership development through family and consumer sciences education. As the only in-school student organization with the family as its focus, FCCLA is an ideal companion to personal finance and other courses in your school's family and consumer sciences program.

Involvement in FCCLA offers the opportunity to

- participate in activities and events at local, state, and national levels
- develop leadership and teamwork skills
- help others through community service projects
- prepare for future roles in your family, career, and community

STAR Events—Students Taking Action with Recognition

Students compete in events that test their leadership and career preparation skills. Students participate in cooperative, individualized, and competitive events. Topics include career investigation, entrepreneurship, job interviewing, and life event planning.

For additional information, visit the organization's web site at www.fcclainc.org.

DECA

An Association of Marketing Students

DECA is an organization for students interested in marketing, management, finance, entrepreneurship, and business administration. DECA provides teachers with classroom activities related to developing career skills and business leadership traits. Community service is also emphasized. Competitive events allow students to demonstrate what they have learned and measure their progress.

More information can be found at www.deca.org.

Future Business Leaders of America (FBLA)

FBLA is an organization that helps students develop confidence as they prepare for business management careers. Students participate in activities and competitions that help them develop leadership skills and make connections in the business world.

Visit the Web site at www.fbla.org.

Business Professionals of America (BPA)

BPA focuses on developing skills that will aid those seeking careers in the professional business workforce. Problem-solving, leadership, technology, and citizenship are just some areas emphasized. The workplace Skills Assessment Program helps students measure their readiness for careers in office administration, business technology, and related areas.

The Web site can be found at www.bpa.org.

SkillsUSA

SkillsUSA is an organization of students preparing for careers in trade, technical, and health services. Students may compete in the SkillsUSA Championships at the local, state, and national levels. SkillsUSA emphasizes not only those qualities necessary to begin a successful career, but also the importance of lifelong education and training.

Check out the organization's Web site at www.skillsusa.org.

Explore Careers Through Foundations of Personal Finance

Your career decisions have a lasting impact on your personal and financial goals. *Foundations of Personal Finance* challenges you to plan for the future—and provides the information you need to make sound decisions.

Chapter 21, *Planning for Your Career,* explains how to develop a career plan based on your personal interests, aptitudes, abilities, values, and goals. You will learn about important resources for exploring careers, including the career clusters. The chapter also helps you determine the education and training needed to meet your career goals.

Chapter 22, *Entering the Work World,* discusses preparing résumés and cover letters and attending job interviews. You will also learn skills that lead to career success and explore entrepreneurship opportunities.

Look for the career clusters icons throughout the text to learn about occupations related to chapter content. The career clusters—16 general groupings of occupational and career areas—are a helpful resource for exploring careers. Each chapter features three occupations and highlights typical job duties and working conditions. More than 60 occupations are featured throughout the textbook.

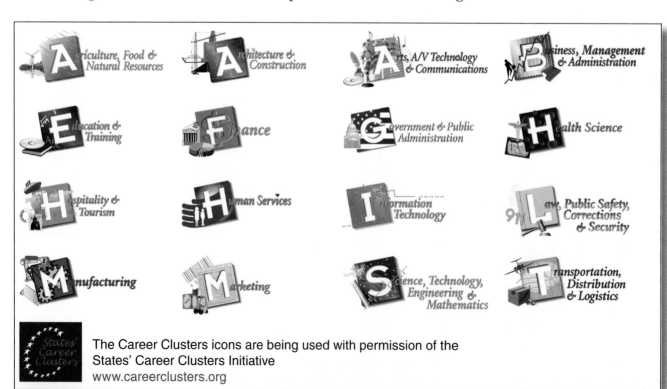

Agriculture, Food & Natural Resources

Architecture & Construction

Arts, A/V Technology & Communications

Business, Management & Administration

Education & Training

Finance

Government & Public Administration

Health Science

Hospitality & Tourism

Human Services

Information Technology

Law, Public Safety, Corrections & Security

Manufacturing

Marketing

Science, Technology, Engineering & Mathematics

Transportation, Distribution & Logistics

The Career Clusters icons are being used with permission of the States' Career Clusters Initiative
www.careerclusters.org

Featured Occupations

CONTENTS

Unit 3
Managing Your Spending   310

FEATURES

Linking to...

ECONOMICS in ACTION

REAL LIFE CONNECTIONS

Case Studies

Unit 1
The Economic System

In This Unit

You make many economic choices each day. When you spend money, you make economic choices. If you do without spending today to save for tomorrow, you make economic choices. How you spend your free time—working to earn money, studying to boost your grades, or just hanging out with friends—involves making economic choices. Over time, these choices will largely determine your overall quality of life. You can influence the economic choices of government by participating in the political system and making yourself heard. As you will see, the choices you make connect you to millions of other people in the U.S. and around the world.

CHAPTER 1

What Is Economics?

9 needs
15 wants
5. goods
13 services
3. economic system
14 traditional economy
8 market economy
4 free enterprise
13 system
consumer
11 producer
8 marketplace
command economy

8 mixed economy
12 resources
13 scarcity
9 nonhuman resource
6 human resource
14 trade-off
10 opportunity cost
11 profit
7. innovation
14 technology
13 supply
2. demand

CHAPTER OBJECTIVES

After studying this chapter, you will be able to

- **distinguish** between needs and wants.
- **compare** different types of economic systems.
- **define** scarcity in terms of needs and wants.
- **analyze** a decision in terms of trade-offs and opportunity cost.
- **explain** the role of the profit motive in the economic system of the U.S.
- **evaluate** how competition among producers influences the price of goods in a market economy.
- **interpret** the relationship between supply and demand.

vocab

command economy - system in
which a central authority,
usually the government, controls
economic activities.
consumer - a buyer and user
of goods and services
demand - quantity of a product
or service consumers are
willing to buy.

PERSONAL FINANCE

Chapter # 1

Mr. Dan Corona

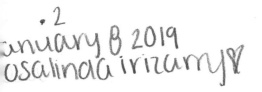

• 2
anuary 8 2019
osalinda irizarry

Create a document and name the file **personalfinancechapter1**. This document will be graded not just on content, but also on how it looks. Remember, that when producing a document, it must be pleasing to the reader's eye. Then from the chapter define the 24 vocabulary words and number them 1 – 24 if you want credit. Next, answer all the questions on this page and add them to your document, you can type the questions and answers, or just the answers. Do it the way that best helps you to study for the test. All the vocabulary and questions will be on the test.

1. As defined by this textbook, what type of world do we live in? economic
2. Items that we use every day are items and materials that are generated by what?
   _____
3. Looking back to earlier times the family was relatively self-sufficient, the family was considered to be the _____.
4. As families formed communities and moved away from an agricultural base, life became more complex. They became _____ who looked beyond the family to meet their many needs.
5. And as we all know physical items are considered _____, while work performed is called _____.
6. And as defined by the textbook, _____ include work done by a carpenter, plumber, or accountant.
7. There are four basic economic systems in our world, every nation has one, name the four types of economic systems, _____, _____, _____, _____.
8. Recently, some traditional economies have begun to develop a new approach to economics. They have come to see the advantages Of _____ and other advances in the modern world.
9. In a system where privately owned businesses operate and compete for profits with limited government regulation or interference, we know this as a _____ or _____.
10. The activities and decisions of consumers determine in large part what goods and services businesses will produce and sell. A market economy offers many _____ for businesses to grow and profit.
11. In this type of system, a _____, the needs and wants of consumers are not generally a driving force in the decision making process.
12. A command economy is most likely to be found in a _____ or _____ form of government.
13. All economic systems attempt to resolve the problem of unlimited needs and wants and _____.

14. _____ is a type of human resources, it is a set of personal qualities that helps an individual create, operate, and assume the risk of new businesses.

15. _____ can be measured in terms of dollars, time, enjoyment, or something else of value.

16. All societies are faced with scarcity and must make choices. The problem of _____ applies to individuals, families, businesses, and organizations. Governments also make economic choices that affect everyone.

17. You can gain a better understanding of how the U.S. economy works by studying the basic qualities of a _____.

18. The promise of earning money _____ the worker, shop owner, manufacturer, and investor to engage in economic activity.

19. Three key principles of private ownership, free choice, profit motive, and _____, come together to create a dynamic ever changing economy.

20. The laws of supply and demand work together. When demand and supply are relatively balanced, the market is said to be in _____.

Central Ideas

- Economics is the study of how people use scarce resources to satisfy their unlimited needs and wants.

- In a free enterprise system, market forces allocate the resources.

You live in an economic world. Money changes hands every time you buy a snack, rent a movie, ride a bus, turn on a light, text a message, or see a doctor. Economic wheels turn to keep schools open, maintain streets and parks, and provide police and fire protection. Your home receives electricity, your television receives broadcasts, and your favorite stores are stocked with items you want to buy. Every day, you use and depend on items generated by the U.S. economy.

Did you ever wonder how all these events happen? You will learn in this chapter about the powerful forces that link you to the nation's goods and services. You will also learn how these forces work and the important role you play.

Economic Systems

In earliest times, families were relatively self-sufficient. The family was the basic economic unit. It provided members with food, shelter, protection, hides for wearing and staying warm, and other needs. **Needs** are items a person must have to survive. Needs differ from **wants**, which are items a person would like to have but that are not essential to life.

As families formed communities and moved away from an agricultural base, life became more complex. No longer were families so self-sufficient. They became consumers who looked beyond the family to meet many of their needs. They began to trade with one another. Artisans and tradesmen became expert in their work.

As individuals and communities provided specialized labor, a wider variety of goods and services flourished. **Goods** are physical items such as food and clothing, while **services** refer to work performed. Examples of services include work done by a carpenter, plumber, or accountant. The interdependence of providers and users of goods and services marked the beginning of an economic system. An **economic system** is the structure in which resources are turned into goods and services to address unlimited needs and wants.

Types of Economic Systems

Every nation has an economic system. Economists have defined four basic types—traditional, market, command, and mixed economies.

Traditional

The **traditional economy** is a system in which economic decisions are based on a society's values, culture, and customs. Today this type of economy exists mostly in underdeveloped countries or nations governed by strong cultural, religious, or tribal leadership.

In these areas, change comes slowly. People tend to stick with what they know and do as they have always done. For example, if you lived in a traditional economy and your parents raised sheep, chances are that you would too. You would likely grow your own food and make your own

Economists

Economists study how society distributes resources, such as land, labor, raw materials, and machinery, to produce goods and services. They may conduct research, collect and analyze data, monitor economic trends, or develop forecasts.

1-1

In traditional economies, change comes slowly from generation to generation.

clothing. You would probably have little interest in doing something new or different from what your friends and family do, 1-1.

In recent years, some traditional economies have begun to develop a new approach to economics. They have come to recognize the advantages of technology and other advances in the modern world. There is a desire both to keep the old and to accept some of what is new.

Market

A **market economy** is a system in which privately owned businesses operate and compete for profits with limited government regulation or interference. It is also called a **free enterprise system** or *capitalism*.

In a market economy, consumers are important and businesses react to their demands. A **consumer** is a buyer and user of goods and services. A **producer** is an individual or business that provides the supply of goods and services to meet consumer demands. The activities and decisions of consumers determine in large part what goods and services businesses will produce and sell. A market economy offers many opportunities for businesses to grow and profit. It also offers hard-working individuals with education and training the incentives and opportunities to develop their talents and succeed in fields of their choice.

In economic terms, the **marketplace** or *market* is not a physical place like a mall or a grocery store. It is an arena in which consumers and

Case Study: Living in a Market Economy

Anita and Juan Search for Housing

Anita and Juan are in their mid-twenties and plan to marry in six months. They decide to buy their first home in the city and move to the suburbs once they have school-age children. They see two new one-bedroom apartments in their price range, but prefer a higher-priced loft apartment. The loft is a little over their spending limit, but the high ceilings, wood floors, and interesting floor plans tempt them. The units also have new kitchens and laundry equipment. Their real estate agent says the loft should have an excellent resale value when they decide to sell and move in a few years.

Case Review

1. How are housing costs determined in a market economy? Why are they likely to be higher than in a command economy?

2. What would happen to housing costs in a market economy when the supply is severely limited? How would prices change when there are more sellers than buyers?

3. How do you see the supply and demand for housing in your area? Would you rather be a buyer or a seller?

producers meet to exchange goods, services, and money. The term *market* may refer to all goods and services in an economy or to a limited number of goods in a selected segment. For example, there is a market for children's clothes, for luxury cars, and for electronics. There also is a global market that encompasses trade among all the nations of the world.

Command

A **command economy** is a system in which a central authority, usually the government, controls economic activities. A central authority decides how to allocate resources. It decides who will produce what. It decides what and how much to produce and sets the prices of goods and services.

In this type of system, the needs and wants of consumers are not generally a driving force in the decision-making process. Consumers do not have broad freedom of choice. They often cannot decide for themselves how to earn and spend income. A command economy often exists in socialist and communist forms of government.

Case Study: Living in a Command Economy

Mariya's and Sasha's Apartment

Mariya and Sasha plan to marry after they find a place to live. Now they each live in a small apartment with family members. Mariya works in a factory an hour away. Sasha works in the same factory and lives an hour away in another direction.

Every Sunday Mariya and Sasha go to a place where people gather to find living space. Hundreds of people carry handmade signs advertising living quarters to trade or living space wanted.

When housing agreements are made, the authorities must approve them. The parties involved must show their registration cards to prove they had permission to live in the country. In addition, the agreement cannot violate living space restrictions for different categories of people.

After several months of searching, Mariya and Sasha make an agreement with a man who plans to move from town to the country. He wants the U.S. equivalent of $300 for his one-room apartment. This is most of their savings, but Mariya and Sasha consider it a bargain. They do not see the apartment right away, but they know it is in a fairly new building not far from their workplace. More important, it will be theirs.

Case Review

1. How might a severe housing shortage affect you over the next 10 years?
2. Housing costs in command economies are controlled by the state and are very low compared to those in the United States. To what extent would you be willing to sacrifice privacy, quality, and availability of housing to cut housing costs by 70 to 80 percent?
3. Why is housing likely to be more limited in a command economy than in a market economy?

Mixed

Most economies are mixed. A **mixed economy** is a combination of the market and the command systems. For example, a mixed economy may function through a marketplace, although the government or central authority regulates the prices and supply of goods and services. Government may regulate certain industries such as utilities and airlines.

Although the U.S. economy is technically a mixed economy, in this textbook and elsewhere it is labeled a market economy. Compared with other mixed economies, the U.S. has minimal government involvement. The government's limited role in the U.S. economy is varied and important. That role will be covered in detail in the next chapter.

The Challenge of Scarcity

All economic systems attempt to resolve the problem of unlimited needs and wants and limited resources. Here the term **resources** refers to any input used to generate other goods or services. The challenge of stretching resources to cover needs and wants is called **scarcity**. Individuals, families, companies, and nations are all limited in the resources available to meet needs and wants. Deciding how to deal with scarcity is the basis for the study of economics.

Over your lifetime, your needs and wants will never end. There are many reasons for this. The most obvious is that you outgrow your current needs and wants and develop new ones. For example, as your feet grow bigger, you need larger shoes. Another reason is your needs and wants change as you grow mentally and emotionally. See 1-2.

Also, fulfilling one want often creates new ones. For example, if you buy a new music system, you will want music to play on it. You may want headphones and a shelf to hold your equipment. When your music system becomes outdated, you will want a new improved model.

Scarcity forces people, businesses, and governments to make choices in the use of resources and the needs to be met. There are two basic types of resources that are considered.

- **Nonhuman resources** are external resources, such as money, time, equipment, and possessions.

- **Human resources** are qualities and characteristics that people have within themselves.

Human resources include qualities that make workers more productive, such as good health, skills, knowledge, and education. *Entrepreneurship* is a type of human resource, too. It is a set of personal qualities that helps an individual create, operate, and assume the risk of new businesses.

Consumers have unlimited needs and wants for different goods and services. These include food, clothes, housing, medical care, cars, and spending money. Since resources are limited while wants are unlimited, it is necessary to choose which wants to satisfy.

For example, suppose you must choose between seeing a movie and going bowling because you do not have time for both. You may need to choose between a new pair of gym shoes and a pair of boots if you do not have money for both. Families may have to choose between buying a new car and taking a family vacation, or between buying a home and starting a business. Economic choices are endless.

Scarcity applies to government in the same way. The needs of citizens far exceed the resources of the government. That is why it is necessary to make choices. Local governments may need to choose between raising

taxes and cutting services. The federal government makes the same types of choices.

Trade-Offs and Opportunity Cost

Making choices involves evaluating two or
more options and selecting just one. Making
choices entails trade-offs. A **trade-off** is the item
given up in order to gain something else. For
example, there is a trade-off when you spend
$50 to buy a jacket. The trade-off is the other
ways you could have spent the $50, including
saving it for a future purchase.

Making a choice results in a trade-off,
and a trade-off results in an *opportunity cost*.
Opportunity cost is the value of the best option
or alternative given up. If you turn down an
after-school job because you have to be at soccer practice, there is an opportunity cost. The
opportunity cost of playing soccer may be the amount you could have
earned working. On the other hand, the opportunity cost of working
instead of playing soccer could be the pleasure and enjoyment of playing
a sport you love.

1-2

Clothes can be both a need
and a want.

Opportunity cost can be measured in terms of dollars, time, enjoyment, or something else of value. The opportunity cost of a decision often
varies from one person to the next. It depends on what the person who
made the decision values.

For example, if spending time with your family is most important to
you, missing family meals may be the opportunity cost of going to soccer
practice. If getting good grades is most important to you, losing time to
study may be the opportunity cost.

Opportunity cost applies to economic choices of families, businesses,
and governments as well as individuals. Weighing opportunity cost is a
valuable decision-making tool. You will read more about decision-making
tools in Chapter 5.

Scarcity and Economic Systems

All societies are faced with scarcity and must make choices. The problem of scarcity applies to individuals, families, businesses, and organizations. Governments also make economic choices that affect everyone.

At the local level, governments make many choices in allocating limited
resources. For example, a local government may need to choose between
using funds to build a public swimming pool or to repave the streets.

The federal government makes the same types of choices. For example,
the government may have to decide between investing in oil drilling and
investing in new energy sources. Major political and economic decisions
center on how to divide limited national resources given unlimited national

ECONOMICS in ACTION

More Tools to Evaluate Economic Choices

Marginalism is the added value versus the additional cost of one more unit or item. For example, suppose you buy two pairs of jeans at $65 and consider a third pair. Will the added pair bring as much satisfaction as the first two? As you buy more jeans, the per-unit price stays the same, but the "marginal" or extra value of one more pair decreases.

You can also approach economic choices through a *cost-benefit analysis*, which is similar to marginalism. The *cost-benefit principle* states that you should take an action or make a purchase only if the benefit is at least as great as the cost. For example, using the jeans example, suppose you see a casual jacket that complements the first two pairs of jeans. With the jacket and those jeans, you could coordinate several outfits. A third pair of jeans, on the other hand, would not benefit your wardrobe to the same degree as the jacket.

These principles apply to economic decisions of individual consumers, businesses, and governments. You'll read more about them in Chapter 5.

needs. These needs may include crime control, health care, environmental protection, education, national defense, and aid to the poor and homeless.

The scarcity of resources leads to three problems for all societies:

- what and how much to produce
- how to allocate resources in producing goods and services
- how to divide the goods and services produced

The way a society solves these problems defines its economic system. If these decisions are made by the country's religious leader, the nation's economic system is probably a traditional economy. If a central planning authority decides, the economic system is probably a command economy. In the U.S. free enterprise system, these decisions are made primarily by market forces.

How the U.S. Economy Works

A circular flow of goods, services, and money takes place within the economy, as shown in the circular flow model in 1-3. The blue outer circle shows the flow of consumer goods and services from producers/sellers to consumers/workers. It also shows the flow of the resources (labor, land, capital, and entrepreneurship) from consumers/workers to producers/sellers.

The orange circle shows the flow of payments for goods and services from consumers/workers to producers/sellers. It also shows the flow of payment for resources from producers/sellers to consumers/workers.

This model is a good snapshot of how consumers and producers interact in the economy. However, it does not show the whole picture. For example, producers and sellers can also be consumers. Businesses buy the goods and services that other businesses produce. In the next chapter, you will see how the government fits into this picture.

You can gain a better understanding of how the U.S. economy works by studying the basic qualities of a market economy. These are discussed in the following sections.

Four Qualities of a Market Economy

Four unique qualities—private ownership, profit, free choices, and competition—characterize a market economy. The dynamic combination of these qualities explains many aspects of the inner workings of the U.S. economy. A study of the law of supply and demand helps to complete the picture.

Consumer goods and services

Payment for goods and services

Producers/ sellers

Consumers/ workers

Payment for labor, land, and capital

Labor, land, and capital

1-3

This chart shows the circular flow of goods, services, and money between producers/ sellers and consumers/ workers.

Private Ownership and Control of Productive Resources

Productive resources include the human and nonhuman resources used to produce goods and services. In the U.S. economic system, citizens and businesses own and decide how to use these resources. Businesses invest in the equipment, labor, and land needed to produce goods and services. They exercise the right to own private property. Individuals and businesses can buy and sell property; they can use it or give it away. This includes personal property such as clothes, cars, and electronics. It also includes real estate and business enterprises.

The Profit Motive

The promise of earning money inspires the worker, shop owner, manufacturer, and investor to engage in economic activity. For businesses and investors, **profit** is the total amount of money earned after expenses are subtracted from income. The profit motive drives businesses to produce goods and services to meet consumer demand.

For individuals, profit comes in the form of income. Individuals sell their productive resources, such as labor, ideas, land, and capital. In return, they receive income or a return on their investments. This is what brings people into the workforce and investors into the stock market.

If there were no opportunity to earn profits, the U.S. economy would falter. Individuals would be less motivated to work. Investors would not invest in businesses and provide the money needed to turn resources into goods and services. Businesses would not grow and try to increase sales. All businesses, from the corner grocery to a worldwide corporation,

Business, Management & Administration

Business Development Managers
Business development managers plan strategies to improve a company's performance and competitive position. They analyze, interpret, and evaluate various types of data in order to make sound business decisions.

1-4

All businesses, such as this neighborhood florist, must earn a profit in order to stay open.

Entrepreneurs

Entrepreneurs are people who organize, operate, and assume the risk for a business venture or enterprise. Successful entrepreneurs have business management skills, marketing knowledge, and an understanding of the demand for the product or service they provide.

depend on profits, 1-4. It is a positive number. The *profit motive*, or the desire for profit, drives both individuals and businesses to produce.

Free Economic Choice

In the United States and other market economies, consumers are free to make many choices. This is good news for you. Free choice opens the doors of opportunity in many areas. Both individuals and businesses have the right to freely decide how they will earn, spend, save, invest, and produce. You choose

- what you will buy
- where you will buy it
- how much you are willing to pay
- whether you will use cash or credit
- whether you will spend or save

Businesses respond to consumer choices by producing and selling the goods and services consumers want. In the economy, the combined choices of individual consumers make the greatest impact. Your decision to buy a new cell phone will not greatly impact the manufacturer's bottom line. However, if thousands of others buy it, the company will make money.

You are also free to choose how to earn your money. There is a vast menu of job possibilities in a free market economy. Your future income will depend on the career choices you make and the abilities and skills you develop. If you are willing to work hard and get the training and education required, you can succeed in a market economy. This is not always true in a command economy, where a central authority controls much of the opportunity.

A free market economy is also ideal for starting your own business. The path of the entrepreneur is not an easy path, but it is open to anyone with a sound idea and the willingness to take risks and work hard. Take a look at the stories of those who founded well-known corporations such as McDonald's, Microsoft, and Walmart. Almost all of them started with an idea that greatly appealed to consumers.

Competition

Economic competition occurs when two or more sellers offer similar goods and services for sale in the marketplace. Each seller tries to do a better job than the other in order to attract more customers, make more sales, and earn more profits. Businesses compete with each other in many ways. They compete in the areas of price, quality, features, service, and new products.

In a market economy, **innovation** is the engine that sparks growth and prosperity. Innovation is the process of creating something—new or improved products and new ways to do things and solve problems.

Research and development (R&D) is the key to realizing the potential of innovation. It is an investment in the future. In simple terms, the innovator comes up with a new idea, explores its practicality, and turns it into a new product or service. Businesses, universities, and government agencies all participate in research and development, both independently and in cooperation with each other.

The U.S. invests more money in research and development than any other country in the world. This is one reason America is among the most prosperous nations. The same is true of businesses. Those that invest the most in research and development tend to be the most competitive and successful.

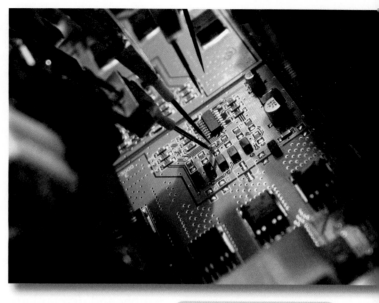

1-5

New technology is constantly being developed, tested, and marketed to consumers.

Technological advances are a major force in the creation of new products and services. **Technology** is the application of scientific knowledge to practical uses and product development, 1-5. Computers, cell phones, and fuel-efficient cars are examples of technological advances.

The companies providing the best products and services at the lowest prices generally achieve the highest sales and profits. Ideally, this results in higher quality at lower prices for consumers. Competition encourages competence and efficiency in the production and sale of goods and services.

Electronic products are a good example. Consider the development of personal media players that started out as simple audio players. Today you can use these players to view videos, text, photos, and lyrics. You can listen to and record FM radio, store data, and tell time. You get voice recording and computer interface. All these functions are contained in a player about the size of a credit card. You are getting more for your money with each new innovation. Most of this innovation was driven by competition and the profit motive.

There is also competition in the job market. The highest incomes go to the educated, trained, and skilled workers who produce the goods and services in greatest demand. This demand increases the competition among workers. They try to update their skills and education in order to qualify for better jobs, so they can then earn higher incomes and better benefits. This, in turn, improves a company's ability to compete.

Laws of Supply and Demand

These key principles—private ownership, free choice, profit motive, and competition—come together to create a dynamic, ever-changing economy. Individuals and families are free to act in their own best economic interests in the marketplace. By doing this, they make the economy work better for everyone.

Remember the economic challenges common to all societies? In short, the challenges are: what and how much to produce, how, and for whom. The U.S. economic system addresses these questions largely by letting the forces of supply and demand operate in competitive markets. **Supply** is the

Linking to... Math

Graph Reading

A candy company sells 5,000 candy bars a day when they are priced at $1 each. When the company raises the price to $1.25, it sells 4,500 a day at the higher price.

Draw a graph and plot the coordinates. Approximately how many candy bars would they sell per day if they were priced at $1.50 each?

amount of a product or service producers are willing to provide. **Demand** is the quantity of a product or service consumers are willing to buy. Both supply and demand are closely connected to price.

For example, suppose you own a gym shoe company. When you price them at $80 a pair, you sell 1,000 pairs. At $40 each, you sell 3,000 pairs.

When the chart's coordinates are plotted on a graph and connected, they form a line called the *demand curve*. Price and demand move in opposite directions, so the curve has a negative slope. This illustrates *the law of demand*—the higher the price of a good or service, the less of it consumers will demand.

As a producer, you want to sell your goods for the highest possible price. If you think you can get $80 for each pair of sneakers, you would want to produce more. If you think you can only get $20 a pair, you would want to produce less.

When the chart's coordinates are plotted on a graph and connected, they form a line called the *supply curve*. Price and supply tend to move in the same direction, so the curve has a positive slope. This illustrates the *law of supply*—the higher the price of a good or service, the higher the quantity supplied by producers.

Equilibrium

The laws of supply and demand work together. When demand and supply are relatively balanced, the market is said to be in *equilibrium*. Equilibrium is the approximate point at which the supply and demand curves intersect, 1-6. It is the price at which the quantity supplied equals the quantity demanded. This is when the market is operating at maximum efficiency.

Equilibrium is more of an idea than a reality. Markets are usually not in equilibrium. Changes in supply or demand trigger price adjustments. When a price for a product is set too high, products stack up on store shelves. When a price is set too low, there are shortages.

What conditions might cause price to increase? Prices rise when the demand for an item is greater than the supply, or when demand rises and supply remains the same. For instance, airline ticket prices are highest during peak travel times. Seasonal foods become more expensive when the season ends and they become less plentiful. Food prices also rise when crops are lost to severe weather.

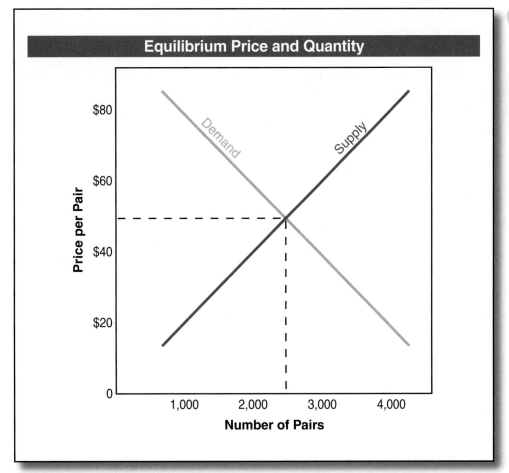

Equilibrium Price and Quantity

Price per Pair: $80, $60, $40, $20, 0

Number of Pairs: 1,000, 2,000, 3,000, 4,000

Demand

Supply

1-6
The demand curve shows how much people will buy (x-axis) at different prices (y-axis). The supply curve shows how much product will be produced (x-axis) at different prices (y-axis). Equilibrium, $50, is the point at which the demand and supply curves intersect.

What conditions might cause price to decrease? Prices fall when the supply for an item is greater than the demand, or when supply rises and demand remains the same. For instance, at the end of winter, the demand for coats and gloves drops. Stores drop prices and hold end-of-season clearance sales.

The Market's Answer to Scarcity

To a large extent, demand in the marketplace determines *what* and *how much is produced*. Demand is expressed by the spending choices of consumers, businesses, and governments. These choices, to a large degree, determine what and how much producers will bring to the marketplace. In many cases, consumer demand leads to new and improved products.

Businesses generally own and control productive resources. They determine the right mix of productive resources when they make products and deliver services to meet consumer demands. They determine *how to produce goods and services*.

The forces of supply and demand in the job market largely determine *how to divide the goods and services produced*. Those who can offer the skills, knowledge, materials, or capital needed for production receive income or profits. In job markets, those who have the qualifications to perform the work most in demand generally earn higher incomes and can buy more of the goods and services they need. This helps determine how production is divided.

Chapter Summary

You and other consumers carry out economic activities every day. These activities range from spending money to participating in the economic life of your community and government.

Needs and wants are unlimited, while the resources used to satisfy them are limited or scarce. Economists have defined four types of economic systems. Most economies, including that of the U.S., are mixed.

People, families, and governments make choices involving trade-offs and opportunity costs. These two concepts refer to what you give up when you choose one item over another.

In the economy of the U.S., the laws of supply and demand serve to answer the problem of scarcity. In the act of balancing supply and demand, the system determines what to produce, how, and for whom. Consumers play an important role in creating demand. Producers strive to meet demand and earn a profit doing it. The competition for profits in this system leads to the development of new and improved products.

Review

1. What are the four types of economic systems?

2. Why is the economic system of the U.S. a mixed economy?

3. Describe the concept of scarcity and how it applies to individuals, families, and government.

4. Why are human needs and wants unlimited?

5. What is the difference between human resources and nonhuman resources?

6. What three challenges caused by scarcity must all societies face?

7. What are the four basic concepts that drive the economy of the U.S.?

8. Why is innovation important in encouraging competition?

9. What is the relationship of trade-offs and opportunity cost?

10. Why would the U.S. economy falter if there was no opportunity to make a profit?

11. How do the laws of supply and demand relate to the prices of goods and services in the marketplace?

Critical Thinking

12. What can you gain by learning more about the economic system?

13. How do you and your family decide what needs and wants to satisfy? What trade-offs have you made in the marketplace? What were the opportunity costs of your trade-offs?

14. Suppose you started a service business such as babysitting or dog walking. Describe how you would assess the demand for your service.

15. Demonstrate the concept of scarcity in your own life. Make a list of items you want and need over the next five years of your life. What resources will you use to get what you want and need? Will you be able to satisfy all your wants? What compromises or trade-offs will you have to make? What will be some of the opportunity costs of your choices?

16. Interpret the following quote: "One person's wage increase is another person's price increase."

Academic Connections

17. **Social studies.** Invite an economist or another qualified authority to speak on the role of profits and competition in the U.S. economy.

18. **Reading, research.** Create a bulletin board of newspaper and magazine articles and advertisements illustrating different economic concepts in action.

19. **Research, writing, social studies.** Research a country that has a command economy to discover how industries develop and grow. Write a report of your findings.

20. **Writing.** Search the Internet for information on entrepreneurship at sites such as the U.S. Small Business Administration Teen Business Link (www.sba.gov/teens), National Foundation for Teaching Entrepreneurship (www.nfte.com), or Junior Achievement (http://studentcenter.ja.org). Gather information and write a "Do's and Don'ts" manual for a startup business.

MATH CHALLENGE

21. Justin graduates from high school in one month. He already has an offer for a full-time job that would pay $25,000 a year. He is also considering going to college for the next four years. Tuition is $8,000 a year. Room and board is $10,000 annually. If he works, he will not be able to make more than $3,000 a year doing part-time and summer work.
    A. What is the opportunity cost of attending college?
    B. What is the total cost of college?
    C. How many years would it take for college graduate Justin to catch up with the earnings of high school graduate Justin? On average, college graduates earn double what high school graduates earn.

Tech $mart

22. Use the Internet to research the economic system of each of the following countries. Write a report, including footnotes to the bibliography of your sources.
    - China
    - Cuba
    - Brazil
    - Congo

CHAPTER 2

Government and the Economy

Reading for Meaning

The summary at the end of the chapter highlights the most important concepts. Read the summary first. Then make sure you understand those concepts as you read the chapter.

business cycle

recession

depression

inflation

stagflation

labor force

unemployment rate

underemployment

fiscal policy

gross domestic
product (GDP)

consumer price
index (CPI)

labor union

monetary policy

Federal Reserve
System

tax

deficit spending

national debt

perfect competition

monopoly

oligopoly

collusion

CHAPTER OBJECTIVES

After studying this chapter, you will be able to

- **diagram and explain** the four parts of the business cycle.

- **compare** and contrast recession, inflation, and stagflation.

- **describe** how the government uses fiscal and monetary policy to combat inflation and recession.

- **explain** the economic consequences of government taxing and spending.

- **explain** how the national debt hurts the economy.

- **describe** the government's role in promoting competition.

- **identify** the laws and government agencies that protect consumer interests.

Central Ideas

- The goal of government economic policies is to create economic stability and prosperity for its citizens.

- Government enacts laws and regulations to ensure fair competition and to protect the public well-being and safety.

- Government agencies at all levels of government assist and protect consumers by providing information, protection, and services.

The U.S. economic system is called a market or a free enterprise system. Compared with many other nations, the United States government plays a small role in the economy. However, the economy could not function without certain types of government participation.

For example, government provides the legal and institutional environment that permits and encourages economic activity. Government protects individual liberties and private property rights and enforces contractual agreements. It provides the political stability and the *rule of law* that are necessary for economic prosperity. This is what enables individuals and businesses to carry out productive economic activities.

Government plays these specific roles in the operation of our economy:

- It sets economic policies in an effort to create stability and prosperity.

- It makes tax and spending decisions in response to economic conditions.

- It controls the money supply.

- It regulates business and economic activity to ensure fair business practices and to protect public well-being and safety.

The following section explores these government functions in greater detail.

Economic Conditions Monitored by the Government

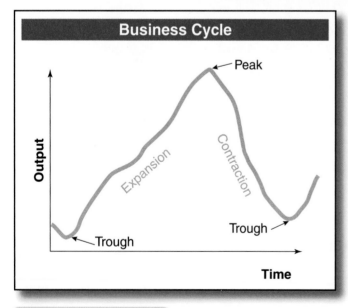

2-1

One business cycle consists of the time from one trough to the next.

The U.S. economy fluctuates between periods of economic growth and slowdown. This is true of economies in other industrialized nations as well. The term **business cycle** describes these ups and downs, 2-1. Some economists prefer the term *business fluctuations* because there are not predictable patterns to the ups and downs. The business cycle has four parts.

- *Expansion* is a period when business activity is growing.

- *Peak* is the height of expansion and lasts until growth begins to slow.

- *Contraction* is a period of slow or no growth.

- *Trough* occurs when a contraction stops.

Each period can last months or even years. For example, the longest economic expansion in modern U.S. history occurred during the 1990s and lasted 10 years. However, the average length of an expansion is about three years. Economists use measurements, or *indicators*, to figure out how the economy is doing and to try to predict its direction.

The following sections describe the most serious problems of a troubled economy.

Recession and Depression

When the business cycle starts a downward trend, people fear a **recession**, which is an extended period of slow or no economic growth. Technically a recession exists if negative growth lasts two quarters or more. (The business year is divided into four three-month quarters.) A recession is marked by

- high unemployment

- a decline in retail sales

- lowered average personal incomes

- decreases in consumer spending

- reduced spending by businesses on plants, equipment, and expansion

Overall economic activity declines. People lose their jobs and businesses fail. It may also be difficult to obtain a mortgage for a home, or to start a new business. When a recession goes on for several years, which is rare, the economy is said to be in a **depression**.

During the Great Depression of the 1930s, one out of four workers was unemployed. Pay cuts were common among those who had jobs. People lost their savings and investments. There was mass hunger, homelessness, and migrations of people across the country looking for work. It lasted for almost ten years. More recently, in 2008, the economy went into a recession and again many people lost their jobs and homes, businesses failed, and the value of savings and investments fell dramatically.

Inflation

Inflation is an overall increase in the price of goods and services. It threatens the nation's prosperity because it decreases the value of a dollar. Due to inflation, today's dollars buy less than last year's dollars.

For example, in 2006, a family that made an income of $65,000 could buy $65,000 worth of goods and services. However, in 2009, they would need $69,434 to buy the same goods and services. That extra $4,000 is the impact of inflation. The CPI Inflation Calculator at the Web site of the U.S. Department of Labor's Bureau of Labor Statistics calculates the cost of inflation. It is at http://data.bls.gov/cgi-bin/cpicalc.pl.

According to government data, the U.S. inflation rate is fairly low compared with the rates of other countries. For example, in 2008, the estimated rate of inflation in the U.S. was 4.2 percent. However, in India it was estimated at 7.8 percent. In Russia, it was about 14 percent, and in Iran it was 28 percent. Inflation is especially hard on individuals and families who live on fixed incomes. Income stays the same over the years, while costs climb. There are several types of inflation.

Demand-Pull Inflation

This type of inflation occurs during the recovery and peak periods of the business cycle. When the economy is growing, consumers are more likely to be employed and have spending money. Spending increases at a faster rate than supply. Put another way, there are too many dollars chasing too few goods. According to the laws of supply and demand, as demand goes up, so do prices.

Cost-Push Inflation

This type of inflation is triggered by an increase in the price of a widely used good. For example, when the price of oil rises, consumers pay more for fuel to power their cars and heat their homes. Many other goods and services—from food and flowers to building materials and airfares—increase in price as well. This is because so many businesses require fuel to operate and bring goods to market. Petroleum is also an ingredient in many products, particularly plastic.

Stagflation

Stagflation describes a period of slow growth (economic stagnation) and high inflation. The best-known episode of stagflation took place during the 1970s. Oil producers raised oil prices that triggered inflation as the costs of many goods and services rose. This occurred at a time of slow growth and high unemployment.

Impact of Unemployment and Underemployment

A nation's prosperity and stability depend on full use of its productive resources, including the labor force. This is one of the goals government seeks to achieve through its economic policies. The **labor force** is composed of people, age 16 and over, who are employed or looking for and able to work.

The **unemployment rate** is the percentage of the labor force that is out of work and seeking employment. That percentage fluctuated between 4 percent and almost 10 percent over the past 30 years, 2-2. Unemployment figures are closely tied to business fluctuations. The highest unemployment rates occur during periods of contraction.

Unemployment hurts workers and their families. When the family breadwinner is unemployed, the entire family suffers. Some families must move because they lose their homes or cannot afford to make rent payments. Some people go into debt and lose health benefits that are usually provided through an employer. Unemployment is also associated with health problems such as stress-related illnesses, depression, and substance abuse. There are several types of unemployment that economists consider.

Government & Public Administration

Labor Economists
Labor economists study changes in the supply and demand for labor. They analyze reasons for unemployment, identify factors that influence the labor market, and collect data on wages. Labor economists usually work for the government.

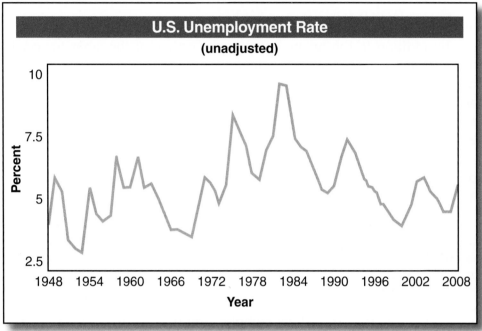

2-2
The U.S. Department of Labor keeps track of the civilian unemployment rate.

Bureau of Labor Statistics

Frictional Unemployment

This is short-term unemployment that affects people who are between jobs. These are people who have moved or changed jobs or careers. They can often find employment by matching their qualifications to available jobs. Some workers will be temporarily unemployed even in a strong and growing economy.

Structural Unemployment

Structural unemployment tends to be long-term, difficult to correct, and the most damaging to both workers and the economy. It refers to unemployment among workers who drop out of the labor force or do not enter. There may be a mismatch between their skills and available jobs. Often the old jobs were moved to cheaper labor markets or eliminated by new technology.

Cyclical Unemployment

Cyclical unemployment is tied to the business cycle. It occurs when the economy slows or is in a recession. Workers are laid off. When the economy moves into the recovery phase, workers are rehired.

Seasonal Unemployment

Finally, there is *seasonal unemployment* that is related to jobs that depend on seasonal activities. This includes the extra workers hired for the holidays, for vacation season, and for crop harvesting. Seasonal jobs end when the short-term demand for workers ceases.

Underemployment

In addition to the unemployed, a percentage of the labor force will be *underemployed.* **Underemployment** refers to workers who are employed only part time or who are "over qualified" for their jobs. They are the skilled workers who hold jobs requiring few skills. Some of these workers are underemployed by choice, but most cannot find work at their skill or educational level.

Continuing prosperity and stability require the workforce and other productive resources to be employed at full capacity. This is one of the goals government seeks to achieve through its economic policies.

Factors Affecting Economic Policies

The economy is incredibly complex and difficult to understand and predict. The primary and difficult challenge for government is to soften the ups and downs of the economy. Government policies are intended to increase growth and employment and to keep inflation low. Another goal of government, covered in Chapter 4, is to ensure the proper balance of trade in world markets.

Fiscal Policy

Fiscal policy refers to the federal government's taxing and spending decisions. Government often uses fiscal policy to stimulate the economy in periods of recession and high unemployment. Fiscal policy can also slow economic activity in periods of inflation or rising prices. The government's taxing and spending decisions are made in Congress. They are driven by economic indicators and analysis of the economy.

Gross Domestic Product

The economy is described in terms of many indicators. The best measure of economic growth is the gross domestic product (GDP). The **gross domestic product** measures the value of all goods and services produced by a nation during a specified period. The real GDP is the GDP adjusted for inflation.

The GDP includes the following:

- *personal consumption expenditures*—consumer spending
- *gross private domestic investment*—money businesses invest in buildings, equipment, technology, innovation, and inventory
- *net exports of goods and services*—the value of the goods and services exported minus the value of goods and services imported from other countries
- *government consumption expenditures and gross investment*—government spending

improvements, and the purchase of durable goods. Furniture, appliances, and cars are called **durable goods** because they have lasting value. Savings such as these increase your financial well-being as long as you do not spend beyond your ability to pay.

Saving and the Economy

In a market economy, the money you and other consumers transfer to financial institutions is pumped back into the economic system, 3-2. It is loaned to businesses and other consumers to pay for business growth, building construction, and the purchases of homes. Savings used this way help generate more jobs, greater productivity, and a growing economy. Therefore, the health of the economy is closely related to the *savings rate*, or the amount of money people save.

Borrowing to Spend

Each time you use a credit card or charge account or take out a cash loan, you are borrowing. These are forms of *consumer credit*. This is a tool that lets you buy now and pay later. There are good reasons to borrow. Borrowing is sometimes the only way consumers can pay for major purchases, such as a house, car, or college education. Saving enough money to pay for these large expenditures all at once is difficult. Credit can also help you pay for unexpected expenses, such as a large medical bill.

In most cases, you pay a fee for using credit. Credit is costly in another way, too. When you use credit, you spend future income. This means part of your future earnings must be used to pay what you owe. The use of credit reduces future income. People who do not monitor and control their borrowing can get into serious financial trouble. Chapter 9 discusses both the sound and risky uses of credit.

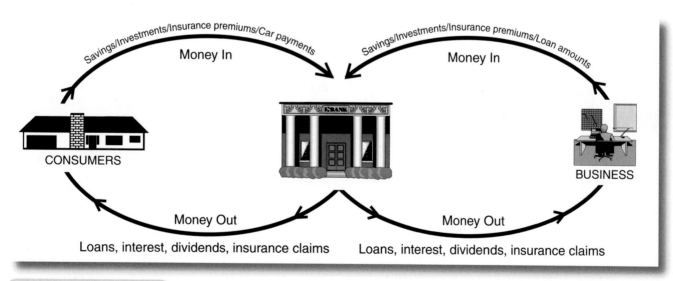

3-2

This diagram shows the flow of money in and out of financial institutions—banks, credit unions, and insurance companies.

Borrowing and the Economy

Consumer borrowing has two important effects on the economy. It increases the amount of money in circulation, and it increases the demand for consumer goods and services. For example, when you borrow, you have more money to spend. As you and other consumers use borrowed money, you increase consumer demand in the marketplace.

When the economy is in a recession, the use of credit can help increase consumer demand. Consumer spending, whether with cash or with credit, stimulates the production of goods and services. This is why the Federal Reserve System may lower interest rates and encourage the use of credit during a recession. It helps stimulate growth.

Consumer borrowing can have a negative impact on the economy when the supply of money increases faster than the supply of goods and services. This causes prices to rise, and inflation is the result.

Another reason for the cautious use of credit is its long-term effect. Unfortunately, the overuse of credit carries the seeds of an eventual economic downturn because the credit used today must be repaid with tomorrow's dollars. That means tomorrow's dollars will be paying today's debts rather than supporting future demand. Using credit increases immediate demand, but it decreases future demand. Economic prosperity is threatened if many people are deeply in debt.

Insuring Against Financial Risks

Insurance is a risk-management tool or a way to protect yourself against certain financial losses. When you buy insurance, you and other buyers pay a fee to own an insurance policy. A policy is a document that

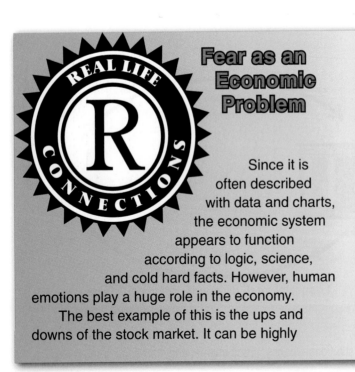

REAL LIFE CONNECTIONS

Fear as an Economic Problem

Since it is often described with data and charts, the economic system appears to function according to logic, science, and cold hard facts. However, human emotions play a huge role in the economy.

The best example of this is the ups and downs of the stock market. It can be highly volatile, fluctuating with consumer confidence and anxiety. The feelings and behavior of consumers can cause economic upturns and downturns. When consumers are optimistic about the economy, they spend more money, which boosts the economy. When they are feeling anxious or pessimistic, they curtail their spending, which depresses the economy.

The U.S. economic system is built on faith and trust. For example, millions of people put their money into banks because they trust that it will be safe there. The banks make money by taking in deposits and lending to businesses and other consumers. If anything should happen to frighten large numbers of depositors, they can demand their money and a bank failure can result.

outlines the specific terms, the risks covered, and the payments that must be made.

You share financial risks related to life, health, and property. For example, suppose you and 5,000 others buy health insurance. If you must go to the hospital for an illness, the insurance premiums of those who do not need to be hospitalized will help pay your expenses, 3-3. Insurance companies invest the insurance payments of all policyholders. These payments and their earnings are used to pay the bills of policyholders who suffer financial losses. The number of people who suffer losses at any given time is much smaller than the number of policyholders in the insurance pool. Many types of insurance are available. They will be covered in detail in Chapter 10.

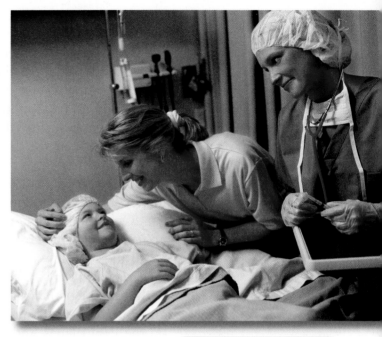

3-3
Health insurance will help pay this patient's medical bills.

Insurance and the Economy

Insurance strengthens the overall economic stability of the nation. It spreads financial risks and stabilizes income in the face of serious financial losses. Social insurance programs contribute to social stability. These government programs include Social Security, Medicare, Medicaid, unemployment insurance, and workers' compensation. They provide income, medical care, and other services to citizens who are retired, ill, disabled, or unemployed.

In addition, insurance companies invest billions of dollars of insurance payments in business enterprises each year. This investment contributes significantly to the strength of the economy. Personal insurance needs are covered in detail in Chapter 10.

Investing for the Future

When you have saved enough money to provide for emergencies and some goals, you will want to think about investing your money. An **investment** is an asset you buy that increases your wealth over time, but carries the risk of loss. An **asset** is an item of value you own, such as cash, stocks, bonds, real estate, and personal possessions. Consumers invest money to improve their financial position and increase their future economic security. The purpose of investing is to make more money than you invest. Investments include financial instruments such as stocks, business ownership, valuable items, and real estate.

Investments usually give consumers a greater return on their money than savings. However, the risk of loss is greater for investments than for savings accounts. The desire for profit motivates people to invest. Investors hope to eventually sell their investments at a higher price than they paid for them. However, there is the chance that they will lose part or all of their investment. That is why it is important to do careful research before you invest. Greater detail on investing your money will be covered in Chapter 12.

Investment and the Economy

Consumer investments pay for a large share of business growth and activity. Businesses use the money to help purchase new plants and equipment. Investments also help pay for the research and development of new technology and the marketing of new products and services. Economic development and growth are directly related to the investments and savings of individuals as described in the following example.

If an airline company wants to expand its service, it can issue new stock for sale to the public. When investors buy the stock, the company gets the money it needs to buy new planes. Companies building the planes create jobs. Operating the planes creates more jobs, better service for consumers, and a profit for the airline.

If the company continues to make a good profit, the price of its stock may rise. This encourages more investors to buy stock in the company with the hope of making a profit. Investors make money on the investment and workers receive more job opportunities. The company makes money on the new planes and consumers benefit from more flights and better service. Investment dollars start this type of chain reaction in businesses of all types, 3-4. The benefits of investment ripple through the economy.

3-4

This diagram shows how consumers and business work together through consumer investments to keep the economy going.

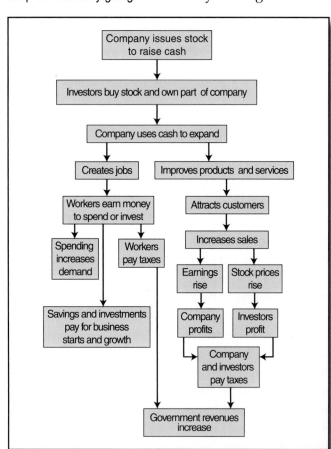

Paying Taxes for Government Services

In the previous chapter, you learned that the government provides many of the goods and services that citizens want and need. These include the military, highways, the judicial system, schools, and parks. Tax revenues pay for the many government departments, agencies, and programs and the services they provide.

Local, state, and federal governments levy different types of taxes. They include

- **income tax**—a tax on the earnings of individuals and corporations. It is levied by the federal government and most state governments.

- **sales tax**—tax added to the price of goods and services you buy.

- **property tax**—a tax that is paid on real estate owned by individuals and corporations.

In the U.S., voters indirectly decide what they want to "buy" from government. They decide the level of taxes they will pay for their purchases. For example, citizens vote for more taxes every time they vote for a new school, more police protection, or a new highway. They vote for higher taxes every time they vote for a

Consumer Preferences

Some products are imported because they are specialties of particular countries or regions. These products can be made just as efficiently in the importing country. However, the foreign-made products offer style and performance qualities that consumers prefer. This has been the case in high-fashion clothing from European designers, high-performance automobiles from Japan and Germany, and a variety of electronic products primarily from Asia.

Comparative Advantage

If a nation could produce all the goods and services its citizens and businesses need, there are still advantages to trade with other nations. An economic concept called *comparative advantage* explains why. **Comparative advantage** is the benefit to the party that has the lower opportunity cost in pursuing a given course of action. The opportunity cost of a choice is the value of the best option or alternative given up.

The following example explains how this works. Suppose a doctor and a nurse staff a small medical office. The doctor sees 20 patients a day. Each appointment is billed at $100. The nurse is paid $250 per day to run the office.

The doctor is more efficient than the nurse at both treating patients and running the office. Can the doctor save money by firing the nurse and doing both jobs? Looking at opportunity costs provides an answer. Without a nurse, the doctor has less time to see patients. There would be five fewer patients seen. The doctor's fees, which total $2,000 at 20 patients, would be reduced by $500.

For the doctor, the opportunity cost of managing the office is $500. However, the nurse is paid half that amount. It makes financial sense for the doctor to treat more patients and hire a nurse to manage the office.

When individuals, businesses, or nations specialize in the activities for which their opportunity costs are lowest, everyone benefits. Countries tend to export what they produce most efficiently. They import the goods and services produced more efficiently in other countries. When nations trade with each other, consumers gain more choices and lower prices.

One of the reasons for comparative advantage is an economic concept called **economies of scale**. The cost of producing one unit of something declines as the number of units produced rises. The costs of production are spread over more units. If a business can sell more of a product by expanding into overseas markets, it can take advantage of economies of scale.

U.S. Trade

The U.S. is a dominant power in global economic markets. According to the U.S. Bureau of Economic Analysis and the U.S. Census Bureau, the U.S. exported an estimated $1.83 trillion worth of goods and services in 2008. During that same year, the U.S. imported $2.52 trillion worth of goods and services.

With less than 5 percent of the world's population, the U.S. produces over 20 percent of the world's total output. In recent years, the people and businesses of the U.S. have sold between 10 and 12 percent of their total output in world markets.

The U.S. is the world's largest importer and a major market for more than 60 countries. Millions of people across the globe depend on the U.S. for their livelihoods. When the U.S. economy falters and consumers close their wallets, factories on the other side of the world shut down and workers lose their jobs.

The U.S. was once the world's largest exporter of manufactured goods. However, this is no longer true. According to the U.S. Census Bureau's Foreign Trade Division, the U.S. imported about $338 billion worth of goods from China in 2008. This is almost five times the worth of U.S. goods exported to China. This has created a trade imbalance that you will read more about in the following pages.

The U.S. imports more manufactured goods than it exports, 4-3. However, it exports more services than it imports, 4-4. The U.S. has a trade surplus in services and a trade deficit in goods. Top U.S. trading partners for both imports and exports are listed in 4-5.

U.S. Commerce		
Category	**Imports**	**Exports**
Industrial Supplies	Crude oil	Organic chemicals
Consumer Goods	Automobiles, clothing, medicines, furniture, toys	Automobiles, medicines
Capital Goods	Computers, telecommunications equipment, motor vehicle parts, office machines, electric power machinery	Transistors, aircraft, motor vehicle parts, computers, telecommunications equipment
Agricultural Products	Cocoa, coffee, rubber	Soybeans, fruit, corn

4-3

The U.S. has a trade deficit for goods, meaning it imports more than it exports.

U.S. Service Exports
Financial services—investing and insurance services
Information services—computer consulting, data processing
Other services—architectural design, construction, engineering, legal, advertising, marketing, accounting, management, technical training, travel, tourism, entertainment, and transportation services

4-4

These are just a few examples of U.S. service exports.

The more education and professional and technical skills you develop, the more opportunities and security you will gain.

- **Consider science- and math-related occupations.** The U.S. currently imports workers to fill many jobs that require science and math backgrounds. There is a great need for workers who have solid foundations in these subject areas, 4-13.

- **Keep your skills sharp.** After you enter the work world, keep the door to education open. Stay informed about trends in your field. Take advantage of retraining and educational opportunities on and off the job. Go back to school to learn new skills.

- **Learn a foreign language.** Fluency in almost any foreign language will become a key asset in the work world. Those who become proficient in Chinese (Mandarin) and other Asian languages, Russian, or Arabic will open doors to job opportunities around the world.

- **Learn about world affairs.** Regularly read newspapers, magazines, and Web sites that report extensively on international affairs and foreign policy issues. Seek out books about areas of the world that interest you. Tune in to radio and television programs broadcast from other countries.

- **Travel or live abroad.** Enroll in a student exchange program. Spend a summer working, studying, or doing volunteer work abroad. Visit relatives and friends who live in other countries. Learn about other cultures while having the adventure of your life. As the world grows more interconnected, global issues will become more important to everyone.

4-13
Workers who have education and training in science and technology fields will have better job opportunities in the future.

The citizens of every nation will become in a sense citizens of the world. Common interests will include policies governing the use and sharing of resources, environmental concerns, and controlling terrorism. Other issues include broad access to necessary medicines and health care services, alleviating poverty, and educating citizens for life in a global society.

As the globe grows smaller, the United States will have to decide whether it will become more involved with other nations in a variety of areas. Nations will need to cooperate with one another in addressing issues such as the environment, poverty, terrorism, AIDS, and disaster recovery. Peace keeping in areas of conflict will continue to call for international cooperation.

The future is likely to hold both more cooperation and more competition in global markets. There will need to be international agreements on the use of world resources. You will also likely see a continued increase in the exchange of ideas and developments in the fields of science and technology.

Chapter Summary

Economic globalization is the increasing economic interconnectedness among governments, businesses, and citizens of the world. Goods and services, money, labor, technology, and ideas all move rapidly across national borders. International trade plays an essential role in economic systems. It influences supply and demand, prices, competition, consumer choice, and government policies. It affects job opportunities and living standards.

As nations trade with each other, they export those goods and services they can produce efficiently and in abundance. They import goods and services they cannot produce efficiently or in adequate quantities to meet the nation's needs.

The exchange rate refers to the value of one nation's currency compared to another. The value of a currency goes up and down with the demand for it in world markets. The strength of a nation's currency affects its trading position in the world.

The balance of payments refers to the difference between a country's total imports and exports. When a nation imports more than it exports, it develops a trade deficit. If exports are greater than imports, a surplus develops. When a domestic industry cannot compete successfully with imports, there is a tendency to protect the domestic industry with some form of trade restraint. The goal of world trade organizations and agreements is to promote fair trade among nations for the benefit of all.

Review

1. What is economic globalization?

2. What is the role of specialization in trade between nations?

3. How does comparative advantage affect trade with other nations?

4. What are migrants and what role do they play in globalization?

5. What is the role of multinational corporations in globalization?

6. What is the difference between outsourcing and offshore outsourcing?

7. Why does the value of the dollar go up and down in relation to other currencies?

8. Explain the difference between a trade deficit and a trade surplus.

9. List two advantages and two disadvantages of free trade.

10. What is protectionism? What forms can it take?

11. List three ways international trade affects you.

Critical Thinking

12. How does the current value of the dollar affect U.S. trade with other nations?

13. Discuss the current U.S. account deficit and its consequences. What steps can the country take to reduce this deficit?

14. What are some of the immediate advantages and disadvantages of free trade?

15. If you were to lose your job to offshore outsourcing, what steps would you take to find a new job and recover financially? What do you think your employer and the government could and should do to assist you?

16. Outline what young people can do today to prepare for working in a global economy and to protect themselves against future job dislocations. What can you do personally?

Academic Connections

17. **Social studies, speech.** Trace the history of trade agreements over the past 50 years and present an oral report on your findings.

18. **Research, writing.** Write a paper on the European Union's origin and goals. Also discuss the EU's position in world trade. Include problems the EU nations experienced in converting to a single currency, and the advantages it has created in trade with other nations and in tourism.

19. **Social studies, research, writing.** List at least three trade agreements of the U.S. with other nations. Research and discuss the pros and cons of these agreements.

20. **Speech.** Debate international trade, with teams taking sides for and against open markets. Discuss some of the problems and disputes that have arisen among nations over trade policies.

MATH CHALLENGE

21. You want to buy two books published only in the U.K. The cost of the books is £17.98. The current exchange rate is $1 = £0.60797.
    A. What is the cost of the books in U.S. dollars? (Round up to the nearest cent.)
    B. Shipping from the U.K. is £9.97. What is the total cost of your purchase including shipping in U.S. dollars?

Tech Smart

22. Research current exchange rates for various currencies against the U.S. dollar. Include the British pound, Japanese yen, Indian rupee, Canadian dollar, Mexican peso, Chinese yuan, and the euro.

23. Using the Internet, look up and compare the U.S. economy with that of three other nations. Compare the following factors: type of government, gross domestic product (GDP), income per capita, literacy rate, significant natural resources, growth and inflation rates, annual exports and imports, and cost of living.

Unit 2
Managing Your Finances

In This Unit

Achieving financial security requires lifetime planning. You can start by identifying the values and goals that are most important to you. By planning, acting, and evaluating, you can manage your income and assets to create an effective money management plan. This, along with other financial tools discussed in this unit, can help you acquire and manage your financial resources throughout your lifetime.

CHAPTER

5

Making Smart Decisions

Reading for Meaning

Examine the photograph shown here and the list of key terms. What clues do they convey about the chapter topics you will study?

management

values

value system

ethic

goal

priority

standard

cost-benefit
  principle

marginal benefit

marginal cost

decision-making
  process

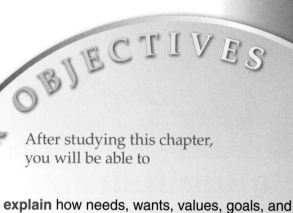

CHAPTER OBJECTIVES

After studying this chapter, you will be able to

- **explain** how needs, wants, values, goals, and standardsserve as guides to consumer decisions.
- **identify** personal goals to guide your decisions.
- **prioritize** your goals.
- **identify** the resources available to you.
- **plan** the use of resources available to you.
- **use** the decision-making process.
- **apply** management principles to help you achieve important goals.

Central Ideas

- Careful decisions and wise use of resources can help you achieve your financial goals.

- Reviewing the success or failure of past decisions helps you make better decisions.

Managers

Managers perform a broad range of duties. They coordinate and direct the many support services that allow organizations to operate efficiently. Specific duties vary in degree of responsibility and authority.

You are the manager of your life. Many factors depend on how well you do your job. For example, by managing your time, you accomplish more of what you want to do, 5-1. By managing your financial resources, you control the dollars that pass through your hands.

Management is the process of organizing and using resources to achieve predetermined objectives. It involves identifying resources, setting goals, making decisions, solving problems, and evaluating results. Developing good management skills can help you achieve all the goals you set for yourself.

The Personal Side of Consumer Choices

Some people always seem to know what they want and where they are going. They seem to know what is important and what is not worth serious attention. This sense of direction and purpose is often a key factor separating the people who achieve what they want from those who do not. Developing this sense of direction and purpose requires a clear understanding of personal needs, wants, values, goals, and standards.

Importance of Needs and Wants

As discussed in chapter 1, *needs* are those items you must have to survive. Examples include your basic physical needs for food, clothing, and shelter. Psychological needs include feelings of safety, security, love, acceptance, approval, and success.

Wants, on the other hand, are items you would like to have. They are not essential for life. For instance, you may want to buy a new cell phone or a completely new wardrobe. However, you can survive without achieving these wants.

Importance of Values

Values are a person's beliefs about what is important and desirable. They influence the way you live and think as well as your decisions, actions, and behavior. Values differ among people. Some of the important values for many people are a loving family, loyal friends, good health, a meaningful career, financial security, and inner peace. Do you support these values? Which other values are important to you?

Values govern and direct your life even if you are unaware of them. Identifying and choosing your values will give you a sense of control.

5-1
When you determine how to spend your time, you are managing your life.

Case Study: Making Decisions

What Do You Value?

As long as Reyna can remember, her family has been short of money. Her only spending money is what she earns from babysitting. Most of her clothes come from her older sister. She believes that having money is just about the most important thing in life. She intends to have plenty of it when she grows older and tries to be part of the "rich crowd" at school. Reyna thinks people who have money are really better than others.

Terrence has little respect for money because his family has always had plenty. He expects to attend one of the better universities in the country after high school graduation. His grades are good, and his family can afford any college he chooses. He doesn't really want to go, but he knows it will be easier than fighting his family about it. He believes there are more important things in life than money, but doesn't know where to search for them.

Carlos is 25 and works in a service station. He wants to marry Angelique, but Angelique's father says she is accustomed to having what she wants. He wonders if Carlos is ready for the financial responsibilities of marriage and supporting a family. Carlos wonders if he should find a better-paying job, or if he would be happier with someone who has values more similar to his own.

Case Review

1. What is most important to Reyna? to Terrence? to Carlos?
2. In what ways do you think Reyna, Terrence, and Carlos might change their views about money in the future?
3. How do their views differ from your own? To what extent do you agree with each of them?

Some people need to make a list of everything important to them before they know what their values are. When you give the list some thought, you will probably find that your family, friends, education, and life experiences all influence your list of values. As you meet new people and have new experiences, what is important to you may change. As life unfolds, your values may change, too. Some become more important and others less so.

As you continually make different decisions, you eventually create a *value system*. A **value system** guides your behavior and provides a sense of direction in your life. For example, good school performance may score

high in your value system. If so, you will try to participate in class, complete your homework, and prepare for exams. If loyalty to friends is high in your system, you will help your friends when they need you. If popularity ranks higher than loyalty, you may find it difficult to stand by an unpopular person or cause.

Importance of Ethics

A closely related concept is ethical behavior. An **ethic** is a moral principle or belief that directs a person's actions. Ethics often conform to accepted standards of right and wrong. Ethical behavior involves honesty, fairness, reliability, respect, courage, tolerance, civility, and compassion. These and other qualities make people's lives with each other peaceful and safe.

Ethical behavior is expected from businesses and government, as well as from individuals. The opposite of ethical behavior is *unethical behavior.* Unethical behavior is usually considered wrong and may even be illegal. Unethical behavior includes stealing office supplies from an employer, surfing the Internet on company time, and returning used merchandise to a store. Other examples include a business that releases toxic waste into the environment and government officials who use their office for financial gain.

Importance of Goals

A **goal** is an objective you want to attain. Usually goals are closely related to values. For example, if health and fitness rank high on your list of values, you may set goals to establish a personal fitness program, avoid drugs, and eat nutritious foods. If you rank education high, some type of career preparation program would become an important goal. This goal might motivate you to begin a savings program to pay for advancing your education. You might also commit extra hours to homework in preparation for further schooling.

Linking to... History

Crisis of Ethics

Unethical behavior played a large role in the financial crisis of 2008/09. Some consumers lied about their income so they could qualify for large mortgage loans. Eager to make money from loans, some financial institutions encouraged consumers to take on too much debt. Other business people sold investments that were riskier and worth less than investors were led to believe. Many corporate leaders collected large salaries while their companies went bankrupt or received taxpayer money to stay in business.

Much of this behavior could be described as unethical. It was driven by the desire for financial gain at the expense of others.

You can set goals for almost anything in life, and there are different types of goals. You may set "to be" goals, "to do" goals, and "to have" goals.

"To Be" Goals

These goals are related to personality and character. You might want to be smart, popular, entertaining, reliable, laid-back, or competitive. This group of goals also includes career choices. You may want to be a teacher, an airline pilot, a scientist, or an artist, 5-2.

"To Do" Goals

These goals cover the endless list of things you might want to accomplish. You may want to learn to play the piano or speak a foreign language. You may decide to go to college, travel, or get a job as soon as possible. You may want to see a particular movie or make the basketball team. Perhaps your goal is to clean out your closet and organize your life. These are all "to do" goals.

5-2
Career choices, such as becoming a health care professional, are "to be" goals.

"To Have" Goals

These goals are easy to identify and continually change. You may want a new watch, a car, your own phone, a personal media player, or concert tickets. These goals include the endless list of routine purchases such as socks and toothpaste. These goals also include higher-priced items for which you need to plan and save.

Timing of Goals

Financial goals can also be classified by their time schedules. *Short-term goals* are those that you want to reach within the next weeks or months, but within a year. For instance, saving enough money to buy a new coat may take several months. *Medium-term goals* are those that may take one to three years to achieve. These may include buying a new bike or musical instrument. *Long-term goals*, such as completing school, starting a career, getting married, or buying a house, may take several years to achieve.

Evaluating Goals

No one has enough resources to reach all of his or her goals at one time. You can get the most from your resources by planning how and when to use them. You will gain more control over your life and achieve the goals most important to you.

It is helpful to not only identify your goals, but to also rank them in order of importance. This helps you direct your time, energy, and money to the goals that are most important to you. As you set and rank your goals, ask yourself the following key questions:

Is the goal realistic and possible? Getting all As is a realistic goal for some, not for others. Buying a car in two years is possible for some, but not everyone. The important thing is not to let the impossible stand in the way of the possible. Make an effort to set realistic goals for yourself. What are some possible goals? Which are most important to you?

Can you break the goal into smaller goals? Many goals, especially medium- and long-term goals, can be challenging. You can tackle them by breaking them down into smaller, more-achievable goals. For example, saving $500 for summer camp may sound impossible. There are only five months until the money is due. However, you can focus on the smaller goal of saving $100 each month or even $25 each week. You will be even more motivated if you reward yourself for each milestone achieved.

Can progress toward the goal be measured? Progress toward a goal should be measurable in dollars, grades, hours, points, or something else. Otherwise, you cannot judge your progress. For example, if your goal is to get an A or B in a class this semester, you can measure your progress weekly by tracking your grades for homework, quizzes, and exams. If your goal is to buy something, such as a laptop computer, you measure progress by the number of dollars you save. Seeing progress motivates you to continue working hard.

What will the goal cost in time, money, and effort? After thinking it through, you may decide that some objectives are not worth what it takes to achieve them. For example, if you want to start a new business, a careful look at the time and the risks involved might change your mind.

Will you still want the goal by the time you are able to reach it? For instance, a high school senior may want a scooter for getting to and from school. If it requires a year or more of savings, the need may vanish by the time the money is available. The need for a car may become more important.

It pays to set worthwhile, realistic goals. Attaining them can give you a sense of satisfaction and accomplishment. On the other hand, working toward unrealistic goals can cause frustration. Aiming at the impossible can prevent you from reaching what is possible.

Interdependent and Conflicting Goals

People generally have several goals at one time. Goals may be *interdependent*. This means you have to achieve one goal in order to reach another. For instance, you need to finish high school before going to college. You need to complete training before starting a career. You need to complete driver education before getting a driver's license.

Goals sometimes conflict with one another. For example, Alfonso has $800. He wants to buy a used car and take a one-week trip with his friends. He does not have enough money for both. Alfonso must decide which of these *conflicting* goals he values more.

Judy also has conflicting goals. She wants to be on the girl's basketball team, which practices each day after school. At the same time, she wants to keep her part-time job after school. Judy cannot reach both her goals. She must decide which is more important to her.

Life is full of conflicting goals and difficult choices. When your goals conflict, your priorities and values will help you choose wisely.

Establishing Priorities

A **priority** is a goal or value that is given more importance than other goals and values. To *prioritize* is the process of ranking several items in their order of importance. It is helpful to identify what is important to you and rank each item from most to least important. This helps you direct your time, energy, and money to whatever you most want to achieve—your priorities.

Whenever you decide one thing is more important than another, you are making a priority judgment. If you think it is important to enjoy your work, you may choose a job you like over a higher-paying job that does not appeal to you. When you think about your own priorities, what would you put at the top of your list?

Case Study: Making Decisions

A Matter of Priorities

Maurice wants the male lead in the school play. The problem is that rehearsal is held for two hours every weekday afternoon for the next three months. If he gets the lead, he must quit his after-school job at a service station. If he quits now, the station manager probably wouldn't hire him for full-time summer work. Maurice desperately needs the income to help his family pay medical bills.

Since he is a senior, this is Maurice's last chance to be in a high school production. The best actors in the spring play are sometimes chosen for Summer Theater. This often leads to a career in drama, which Maurice has always wanted.

Case Review

1. What is the trade-off if Maurice decides to keep his job?
2. What is the opportunity cost if he decides in favor of the play?
3. What other alternatives might Maurice have?
4. How would you resolve Maurice's goal conflict if this were your decision?

Some values and goals are related to money and financial matters. These can have a major impact on the choices you make in the marketplace and in your personal life. The case studies about Reyna, Terrence, and Carlos present three different viewpoints about the importance of money. Reading them may help you understand how values, goals, and priorities affect behavior and financial choices.

Standards of Quality and Excellence

A **standard** is an established measure of quantity, value, or quality. The word *standard* is used in many different ways. Electrical products must meet certain safety standards before they receive a seal of approval. People who want to work in professions such as law and medicine must meet certain skills and knowledge standards before they can enter those professions.

Individuals develop their own personal standard of living. This living standard is expressed by the "to be," "to do," and "to have" goals that each achieves.

You set standards for the way you want to live, what you want to do, and the goods and services you want to buy. These standards depend on your values and goals. They often vary from situation to situation. For instance, if a big, perfect picture is a top priority when you buy a television, you may only settle for the best. Your standards for a TV would be high. However, suppose you just want a small TV that fits the corner of a work space. Your standards would call for something smaller and less pricey.

What degree of quality do you seek as you work toward your goals? Do you strive for As and Bs in school, or are you satisfied with Cs? See 5-3.

Do you practice a piece of music until you can play it without any mistakes, or are you satisfied playing it reasonably well? The answers to these questions can reveal some of your standards. Having a clear understanding of your standards, priorities, and goals will help you make wise financial decisions.

Identifying Resources

Resources are tools you can use to reach goals. As discussed in chapter 1, there are two types of resources—human and nonhuman. *Human resources* are those resources you have within yourself. They include energy, knowledge, experience, skills, talents, motivation, imagination, and determination. Other people and their skills are also human resources.

Nonhuman resources are external, such as money, time, and equipment. It is easy to overlook some of these. People often do not see their possessions as resources or as a means to achieving goals. Consider the resource value of a computer, camera, car, time, and other things available for your use.

anufacturing

Quality Control Technicians
Quality control technicians ensure that manufactured products or services adhere to a defined set of standards. They follow plans or procedures to improve production or service.

5-3
If your goal is to graduate from college, then you may set high standards for the grades you achieve now.

Do not overlook public resources such as libraries, parks, recreational facilities, schools, and public transportation. Very often you can use public services to bring you closer to the goals you wish to achieve. For instance, can you think of ways to reach a specific goal by using a local library? the park district? public transportation?

Everyone has different amounts and types of resources. To be a good manager, you need to identify all the resources available to you. As you consider how to use your resources, keep the following tips in mind:

Resources are scarce. The amount of available time, energy, money, land, and other resources is limited. By planning, you can make the most of them.

Resources are manageable. You can manage resources to meet specific goals. For example, saving money or using credit lets you buy costly items you cannot purchase with a single paycheck. Planning your errands to follow direct routes and avoid backtracking saves time and fuel. Reading a book when you are on a bus or in a waiting room makes idle time productive.

Resources are related to one another. You can often combine several resources to reach a specific goal. For example, you might use both savings and credit to buy a big-ticket item, such as a car. In addition, one resource may be needed to produce or make use of another. You could use your talent and skills to get a job and earn money. Finally, you can use one resource to make up for the lack of another. For example, if you have plenty of time and little money, you can check several stores for the best values before buying.

Practicing good resource management will help you reach your goals. The following are some questions to consider:

- Which of your resources are plentiful and which are scarce?

- Can you combine several resources for more effective use of each?

- How can you use your human resources to make up for what you are missing?

Making Financial Decisions

Every day you make countless decisions—big, small, important, and unimportant. Some are so routine that you hardly use any thought at all. Think about today. Before you left home, you decided when to get up, what to wear, what to eat, when to leave home, and how to get to school.

Every day people face big and little problems. They make promises and cannot keep them. They are supposed to be in two places at the same time. They run out of money before payday. Instead of thinking and planning, they relied on one of the following:

- *Acting out of habit.* Do you automatically get your favorite foods for lunch every day? Do you sit with the same group for lunch? Do you shop in a few favorite stores?

- *Acting on impulse.* Have you bought a pair of shoes on sale, even if they did not really fit? Did you ever go to a movie you did not care to see just because your friends were going?

- *Failing to act.* Have you settled for unemployment by not applying for summer jobs until they were all taken? Have you earned a poor grade by not studying for an exam? Have you been broke when you needed money because you failed to save?

You have probably used all these ways at one time or another. For some choices, these methods work just fine. However, the financial decisions in your life carry lasting consequences. Given their importance, these decisions call for systematic choices.

Cost-Benefit Principle

Economics gives you tools to make wise choices. One of the most basic of these tools is the **cost-benefit principle**, or *cost-benefit analysis*. Cost-benefit analysis is a method of weighing the costs against the benefits of an action. It shows that you should take an action or make a purchase only if the benefits are at least as great as the costs.

For example, if you want to take a vacation in another state, you may need to decide whether to drive or fly to your destination. Suppose you determine that flying costs $350 more than driving. However, it also saves you eight hours of driving time. You would ask yourself: Is the benefit of saving eight hours worth the cost of $350? The choice depends on the value you place on time saved and on how much money you can comfortably spend. The choice will be different for different people.

This principle applies to economic decisions of individual consumers, businesses, and governments. Is the benefit worth the cost?

Marginal Analysis

Marginal analysis is a powerful decision-making tool. It takes into account the added benefit, versus the added cost, of one more unit of a product. The change in total benefit of using one additional unit is the **marginal benefit**. The change in total cost of using one more unit is the **marginal cost**.

For example, suppose you are hungry and buy a slice of pizza. It tastes so good, you buy another and another. Will the second piece bring as much satisfaction as the first piece? Probably not, because you are less hungry. The third piece will be even less satisfying. Eventually you stop eating. You would probably be willing to pay more for that first piece than for the second, more for the second than for the third.

Eventually you stop eating because you get little or no benefit since your stomach is full. The marginal benefit of using each additional unit of something tends to decrease as the quantity used increases. This is called the *law of diminishing marginal utility*. The law applies to thrill rides, ice cream, movie tickets, and many other experiences and purchases.

A Commonsense Rule

Even before applying laws of economics to help make financial decisions, one rule is obvious. People should not spend more than they can

ECONOMICS in ACTION

Marginal Analysis

Marginal analysis can help business owners use their resources in the best way possible. For example, suppose five workers in a toy factory produce 100 large, stuffed teddy bears per day. Each worker makes 20 teddy bears apiece. They sew the toy's arms, legs, torso, and head separately. Then they stuff the parts and sew them together. The sewing room has five heavy-duty machines.

The plant manager hires two more workers, but does not buy new machinery. She reasons that time used to stuff the pieces can be done away from the sewing machines. This should leave some machines free for the new workers to sew more teddy bears. The seven workers handle the new work arrangement well and produce 20 teddy bears apiece or 140 daily.

This success inspires the manager to add one more worker, but she doesn't get the results she expects. The number of teddy bears produced daily is only 152, not the 160 she expected. Workers average only 19 teddy bears apiece. They must stand in line to use equipment, which slows them down. The manager realizes that increasing total production by only 12 teddy bears daily does not cover the cost of the eighth worker.

By using marginal analysis, businesses can determine the right number of workers needed to maximize their profits.

afford. In other words, the key to financial well-being is spending less than you earn. An expression for this behavior is *living within your means.* It is the only way to have financial peace of mind.

Financially mature individuals realize they cannot afford everything they want. Consequently, they establish priorities and plan carefully. They make sure their needs are covered before wants are satisfied. If there are family responsibilities, the needs of the family generally come before the wants of individual family members.

Financially responsible people know they are accountable for their financial future. They develop a clear understanding of their financial situation before making decisions that involve current or future money matters.

Systematic Decision Making

When deciding important matters, a systematic or rational *decision-making process* can help you arrive at the best course of action. This **decision-making process** is a method of choosing a course of action after evaluating information and weighing the costs and benefits of alternative actions and their consequences. It involves five steps, 5-4.

Steps in the Decision-Making Process		
Step	Keyword	Approach
1	Problem	Define the problem or challenge.
2	Alternative	Explore alternatives.
3	Choose	Choose the best alternatives.
4	Act	Act on the decision.
5	Evaluate	Evaluate the decision.

5-4
The five steps of the decision-making process can help you solve problems effectively.

1. *Define the problem to be solved or the issue to be decided.* You need a clear idea of the challenge before you can find the best solution. What is the problem? Perhaps you never have time to exercise. Identifying this problem can lead you to set an achievable goal, such as finding an hour each day for exercise.

2. *Explore all alternatives.* Analyze possible solutions to your problem. If you need to find an hour to exercise, identify and cut back on time killers. Can you free up an hour by limiting your Internet surfing and TV watching? Can you rearrange your schedule to gain time? Is there an after-school activity you can drop, or can you combine some of your activities?

3. *Choose the best alternative.* After considering all alternatives, decide on which best fits your situation. It may be one alternative or some combination.

4. *Act on your decision.* You must carry out your plans. For example, if you decide to rearrange your schedule, write a plan for the new routine. Make every effort to follow it for a few days to see how it works. You may need to make some adjustments. If you decide to limit phone time, it may help to tell friends when you are taking calls and when you are not available. Find reminders and aids to help you stick to your new schedule.

5. *Evaluate your solution or decision.* Evaluation is an ongoing process. As you carry out your plan, evaluate your progress toward your intended goal. Is the plan of action working? How can you improve it? The evaluation process can help you stay on track and make future decisions.

Managing Resources to Reach Goals

Whether you run a big corporation, an average household, or your own personal affairs, you need management skills to get things done. Management skills put you in control. You make the decisions. You carry them out. You benefit from the right choices and occasionally suffer from the mistakes.

You have seen that decision making is an important part of management. However, management involves more than making decisions and solving problems. Management is a three-part process: planning, acting, and evaluating.

The Planning Phase

A job well planned is a job half done. This familiar saying points out the importance of the planning phase of management. Whether you want to reach a career goal or decide what clothes to wear, some forethought or planning helps. Deciding what to wear to school may involve very little conscious planning. Choosing what to wear to a wedding or a job interview takes more thought. Building an appropriate wardrobe for your lifestyle can be a major planning challenge.

The planning phase of management involves identifying goals, obstacles, and resources.

- Start with your goals. What do you want to get or achieve?

- Next, consider the obstacles. What stands between you and your goals? What must you overcome?

- Then list your resources. What can you use to overcome the obstacles and reach your goals? Include personal resources, such as energy, creativity, determination, special skills, and talents.

Two management plans are shown in 5-5. Listed under each goal are the obstacles and resources related to it. Try putting together a similar plan for achieving something you want such as a summer job, a racing bike, or a part in a school play.

Customer Service Representatives
Customer service representatives interact with customers to provide information. They respond to inquiries about products and service, and handle and resolve complaints.

The Action Phase

Planning is of little value without action. The action phase of management involves putting your resources to work to overcome the obstacles that stand between you and your goals. Success in this phase depends on two key characteristics—determination and flexibility.

Achieving Goals by Overcoming Obstacles		
Goal	**Obstacles**	**Available Resources**
To complete an English assignment on time	time limitations lack of interest in the topic difficulty getting started tough grading by the English teacher	two free hours after school each day the public library reference room knowledge of the topic and where to go for information detailed instructions from the English teacher writing and computer skills a computer determination to finish on time and get a good grade
To become president of the student body	the popularity of the other candidates difficulty in contacting all the voters limited time before the election lack of organization among the supporters	knowledge of the job and its demands experience in student government organizational skills public speaking skills reputation for leadership energy and enthusiasm for planning and running the campaign knowledge of what the voters want broad support from both student body and faculty friends who are willing to help run the campaign use of school computers and graphics programs the desire to win

5-5

Listing your goals, obstacles, and resources give you perspective on what you can accomplish.

Determination helps you stay focused on the final goal and stick with the project to the end. Determination is especially necessary when something happens to change your plans. For instance, when working on a tough math assignment, you may feel like giving up. With determination, you keep working until the problem is solved.

Flexibility helps you adjust to new and unexpected situations. It helps you find ways to revise and improve your plans.

Imagine that you have two goals for the weekend: earn money for a camping trip and write a book report. You have a babysitting job on Saturday and plan to spend Sunday afternoon on the book report. When you are called to babysit for much longer than expected, you revise your plans. You write the report while babysitting when the children are asleep. This frees up time for something else on Sunday. Flexibility can work to your advantage in all kinds of situations.

The Evaluation Phase

Evaluation is a continuous function. Through evaluation, you assess your progress as you go through all stages of the management process. Evaluation also improves your management skills for future projects. Ongoing evaluation can help you develop better ways of using resources to reach goals. Consider what worked and what did not in your planning. How can you do better next time? See 5-6 on the process of evaluation.

The Process of Evaluation		
Evaluating Plans	**Evaluating Actions**	**Evaluating Results**
What are the goals?	Is the plan working?	Were the goals achieved?
What obstacles stand in the way?	Is there steady progress toward the goals?	Was achieving the goals worth the effort and resources used?
What resources are needed?	Are resources being used to their best advantage?	Are results satisfactory?
Are the needed resources available?	Are top priority goals getting top priority attention?	What key factors contributed to reaching or failing to reach the goals?
Are the goals realistic, given the obstacles and resources?	Is there room for improvement in the original plans? What adjustments can be made?	What were the weaknesses in the plans and actions? What were the strengths?
Are the goals worth the effort and resources required to attain them?	Have new or unexpected developments created the need to change the original plans? What changes are needed?	How can future plans be improved?

5-6

Evaluation is an important part of effective management.

Making smart decisions will help you sucessfully manage your finances.

Chapter Summary

Knowing yourself may be the most important requirement when it comes to making intelligent choices. Competent consumers base decisions on personal needs and wants—on the values, ethics, and goals that are most important to them. Goals for spending and well-established priorities can guide you to choices that give lasting satisfaction.

Management involves using resources (what you have) to reach goals (what you want). It starts with identifying available resources. There are two types of resources—human and nonhuman. Resources are limited, manageable, and related to each other. The process of management also requires making decisions and solving problems.

Economic decision-making tools include cost-benefit analysis and marginal analysis. Perhaps a more important tool is commonsense. It reminds you to live within your means so you can enjoy financial well-being now and in the future.

When aiming at specific goals, a systematic decision-making process helps consumers make intelligent choices. It is a five-step process. Making the best use of resources in management is a three-step process. It calls for planning, acting, and evaluating.

Review

1. Name and describe the three types of goals that differ by the amount of time it takes to reach them. Give an example of each.

2. How are standards related to values and goals?

3. How does the cost-benefit principle apply to decision making?

4. Give an example of why marginal benefit and marginal cost should be considered in decision making by consumers. Do the same for producers.

5. List the five steps of the decision-making process.

6. What three factors should be identified in the planning phase of management?

7. What two key characteristics determine success in the action phase of management?

8. What are the two purposes of evaluation in management?

Critical Thinking

9. Why are values and goals different for different people? Why and how are values and goals likely to change throughout your life?

10. Why is it important to establish priorities to guide your consumer and life choices?

player, a car, travel, or college. However, as you experience college, work, and perhaps marriage and parenthood, your financial goals will evolve.

2. Estimate and Total Your Income.

Determine your budget period. The period—weekly, biweekly, or monthly—depends on when you receive most of your income. **Income** is any form of money you receive, such as an allowance, a paycheck, and gains from an investment. If you receive a weekly allowance, for example, it makes sense to budget on a weekly basis. If you receive a regular paycheck and pay monthly bills, it may be easier to work with monthly figures.

Estimate your income during a typical budget period. Using a work-sheet such as the one in 6-2, write your best estimate of how much money you normally receive from each income source. Total the estimates and write it at the bottom of the sheet. This is your estimated total income for a budgeting period.

3. Estimate and Total Your Expenses.

After figuring your income, the next step is figuring your expenses. An **expense** is the cost of goods and services you buy. It helps to classify your expenses as *fixed or variable* expenses.

Fixed Expenses. A **fixed expense** is a set cost that must be paid each budget period. Fixed expenses may include

- rent or mortgage payments
- tuition
- insurance premiums
- loan payments (auto, educational)

Estimating Income		
Week or Month of _____		
Income Sources	**Estimated**	**Actual**
Jobs		
Babysitting	$ 25	$
Yard work	$ 40	$
Part-time at Pizza Parlor	$ 200	$
Allowance	$ 40	$
Gifts	$ 10	$
Total Income	**$ 315**	**$**

6-2

Use a form similar to this one to estimate expected income. Review your estimates and fill in with actual figures to stay up-to-date on the amount you have to spend and save.

Budget Analysts

Budget analysts examine financial plans to make sure all factors have been considered and plans are realistic. They also review financial statements, evaluate economic and market trends, and write budget justifications.

These expenses tend to increase in number and amount as you move into adult years. As a rule, fixed expenses must be paid when due. Therefore, it is important to list them first.

Variable Expenses. A **variable expense** is a cost that changes both in the amount and time it must be paid. These expenses can often be pared down or cut. When people are short of cash, variable expenses are the first expenses they will scrutinize. Variable expenses include

- food
- clothing
- medical expenses
- entertainment

Most teenagers receive the basic necessities from their families and spend their money on *discretionary expenses.* These expenses do not involve basic needs. They include music, snacks, computer games, and movies. For adults, discretionary expenses often include vacations, gifts, expensive clothing, and other unnecessary goods and services.

Clothing can be both a necessary and a discretionary expense. For example, buying a basic coat to keep you warm during cold weather is a necessary expense. However, a pricey designer coat is a discretionary expense because a less expensive coat would do.

Using the worksheet in 6-3 as a guide, list the general categories for your fixed and variable expenses in the far left column. For example, write *Snacks, Clothes,* and so forth. Then write down how much you spend on each.

Estimating Expenses

Week or Month of _____

Expense Items	Due Dates	Estimates	Actual
Fixed Expenses			
Bus pass	_____	$ 15	$_____
Lunches	_____	$ 90	$_____
Savings	_____	$ 15	$_____
Variable Expenses			
Snacks	_____	$ 20	$_____
Movies/concerts/events	_____	$ 40	$_____
Clothes	_____	$ 50	$_____
CDs/music files	_____	$ 25	$_____
Gifts	_____	$ 20	$_____
Magazines	_____	$ 15	$_____
Grooming aids	_____	$ 25	$_____
Total Expenses	_____	$ 315	$_____

6-3

Make adjustments to your variable expenses when you are short of cash.

Building Savings into Your Budget

It is wise to include savings in your budget. Save a small amount regularly in a special fund. This way, you will have cash available if an unexpected expense arises. Everyone needs an *emergency fund* when unexpected expenses occur. These can include a hefty car repair bill, unexpected medical expenses, or a home repair cost. An emergency fund is also an important financial cushion to have in case of job loss or some other disruption to income.

With savings, you can plan ahead for major expenses and medium- and long-term goals. For example, to prepare for a camping trip, estimate how much money you will need and the time you have to get it. Suppose the trip will cost $360 and it is five months away.

- How much do you need to save per month? Divide $360 by 5, the number of months. If you save $72 each month, you will have enough.

- How much do you need to save per week? Divide $360 by 20, the number of weeks in five months. If you save $18 each week, you will have enough.

You can use this method to plan for any expense if you know the amount you need and when you need it.

In the future, when you have money left over after expenses, saving that money can increase your resources. Later chapters cover many more ways to preserve and increase your financial resources. Chapter 9, for example, discusses the use of credit to meet goals and manage the peaks and valleys of income and expenses. Chapters 11 and 12 discuss savings in more detail, as well as investments that can improve your financial circumstances.

Charitable Giving as an Expense

Many people voluntarily contribute money or items of value to charities. A charity usually refers to an organization that aids the poor, the homeless, the sick, and others in need. **Philanthropy** is the act of giving

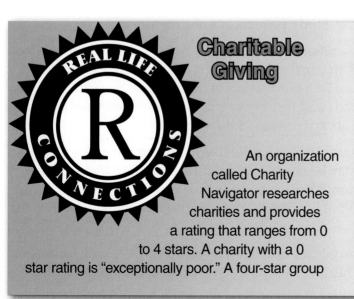

Charitable Giving

An organization called Charity Navigator researches charities and provides a rating that ranges from 0 to 4 stars. A charity with a 0 star rating is "exceptionally poor." A four-star group is "exceptional." You want to choose highly rated charities because they make the best use of your contributions. You also want to choose charities with programs that are growing.

By typing the name of a charity into www.charitynavigator.org, you can get a detailed report that tells you how much money it collects and spends. The group's "efficiency rating" is based on how much it spends on programs versus administrative costs and fund-raising. Charity Navigator gives the salaries of heads of charities. A "capacity rating" is based on the growth of revenue and programs.

money, goods, or services for the good of others. You may want to make charitable giving a regular expense in your budget. In addition to helping others, you often get a tax deduction.

Be watchful when giving to charities. Some groups pose as charities but use the funds they collect to enrich themselves. Other groups are genuine but use too much money for nonprogram costs. It pays to do some research before you give.

To determine how much you can give, consider your income, expenses, and outstanding debts. Until you have an income high enough to support charitable giving, you can always volunteer your time and energy.

4. Analyze Current Income and Spending.

Taking a close look at your record of income and spending is an important step in money management. It is easy to overestimate income and underestimate expenses. A detailed record of spending almost always turns up some surprises and some unnecessary spending. Inspect your record of income and expenses. Are your income figures accurate? Subtract your expenses from your income for each budget period. Do you come out even? Do you have money left over for goals?

If you have nothing left or if you are "in the hole," you will need to find ways to increase income or cut expenses. To increase income, explore these possibilities.

- Can you earn extra money by handling more responsibilities at home or for your neighbors? Can you go grocery shopping, wash windows, or reorganize closets and cabinets?

- Can you get a part-time job if you do not have one? Look for help wanted ads. Can you get ideas from family, friends, coaches, and counselors? Have you overlooked any job opportunities?

- If you have a job, can you negotiate an increase in wages? Can you work more hours without sacrificing the time you need for school-work and other important activities?

To reduce spending, study your record of expenses.

- Start with your discretionary expenses. Can you eliminate something? reduce the cost of an item? get something for free? For example, perhaps you can make a gift instead of buying one. You can cut back on music downloads and text messaging. You can read your favorite magazines at the library instead of buying them.

- Look at expenses you list under the fixed and variable categories. These expenses may be necessary, but can you reduce their cost by making substitutions? For example, maybe you can bring your lunch from home instead of buying it. Try a generic shampoo instead of an expensive brand.

- Can you cut any expenses unrelated to your priorities and goals? For example, if good health is a priority, you can stop buying soda and potato chips.

After you figure out how to stretch your income to cover your needs, you can move to step 5.

5. Prepare a Trial Budget.

At this point, it is time to bring together your goals, income, and expenses into some form of a plan. A plan reduces the temptation to spend carelessly. The form in 6-4 illustrates one way to organize a budget. You may wish to draft a similar form for your own financial planning.

Keep these records over a period of time so you can review your financial situation now and then. The important thing is to put your budget in writing and keep it up-to-date as you go along. The tips in 6-5 can make a budget work better.

Fill in the "Planned" column of the worksheet using the estimated calculations you made in 6-3. This is your trial budget.

6. Put Your Budget Into Action.

Once your budget is set up, you need to spend and save according to plans. Keep your budget handy and refer to it often. When the budget period ends, fill in the amounts for actual income and expenses. When an actual expense is greater than the amount you budgeted, identify the

Budget		
Week or Month of _____ October _____		
	Planned	**Actual**
Income	$ 315	$_____
Expenses		
Fixed Expenses	$ 120	$ 120
Bus pass	$ 15	$ 15
Lunches	$ 90	$ 90
Savings	$ 15	$ 15
Variable Expenses	$ 195	$ 195
Snacks	$ 20	$ 17
Movies/concerts/events	$ 40	$ 39
Clothes	$ 50	$ 55
CDs/music files	$ 25	$ 23
Gifts	$ 20	$ 20
Magazines	$ 15	$ 13
Grooming Aids	$ 25	$ 28
Total Expenses	$ 315	$ 315

6-4

You could use a form similar to this for your trial budget. Use your estimates of income and expenses, financial goals, and record of spending in making up your trial budget.

6-5

When planning a budget, keep these tips in mind.

Cash Flow Statement	
Week or Month of October	
	Actual
Income (Cash Inflows)	
Part-time jobs	$265
(Babysitting, yard work, pizza parlor)	
Allowance	$ 40
Gifts	$ 10
Total Income	**$315**
Expenses (Cash Outflows)	
Fixed expenses	$120
(Bus pass, lunches, savings)	
Total Fixed Expenses	**$120**
Variable expenses	$145
(Snacks, clothes, cell phone, grooming aids/makeup, movies/ concerts/events)	
Total Variable Expenses	**$145**
Total Expenses	**$265**
Net Cash Income	**$ 50**

6-6

A cash flow statement shows your actual income and expenses.

cause. Did you ignore the plan? Was there an unexpected expense? Was your estimate too low? If your estimate was too low, adjust your budget to better reflect actual costs.

7. Evaluate Your Budget Periodically.

From time to time, it is wise to review your money management plan to make sure it is working for you. You can expect your financial plans to change with significant events in your life. These include going to college, starting a new job, leaving home, getting married, having children, or changing jobs.

Consider these questions as you evaluate your budget.

- Is your financial plan working? Is your money doing what you want it to do?

- Are you reaching important goals?

- As you achieve goals, do you set new ones?

- Are you controlling your spending?

- Has your income or pattern of spending changed significantly?

- Are there changes in your life that call for adjustments in your financial planning?

When revisions are needed, make the necessary changes and update your budget. Recheck in a week or two to see if the new entries are an improvement. If you monitor your finances carefully, your income will work well for you over the years.

Preparing a Cash Flow Statement

A **cash flow statement** is a summary of the amount of money received as well as the amount paid out for goods and services during a specific period. A cash flow statement is also called an *income and expense statement*.

The cash flow statement shown in 6-6 appears very similar to the budget statement shown earlier. However, there are important differences. In the cash flow statement,

- income is called *Cash Inflow*

- expenses are called *Cash Outflow*

- the term *Actual* heads the column of figures instead of *Planned*

The cash flow statement goes beyond the budget to reflect actual money inflow and outflow for the month. Prepared at the end of the budget period, it shows real income and spending, not what was planned for the month.

To get accurate figures for the statement, record cash inflows and out-flows in an Income and Expense Log, 6-7. The log is also called a *personal spending diary*. Record any money you receive plus any you spend. For example, write "Snacks," "Clothes," and so forth to record expenses. Then write down how much you spend on each. Also report exactly how much money came in. Do this until you reach the end of your budget period.

With a cash flow statement in hand, you can prepare a budget for the next month more quickly. You will find that careful recording of cash inflows and outflows leads to more accurate budgeting.

Preparing a Net Worth Statement

It is wise to evaluate your total financial situation at least annually. A *financial* or *net worth statement* can help you do this accurately. A **net worth statement** is a written record of your current financial situation. Your **net worth** is the difference between what you own and what you owe. It measures your financial standing at a particular point in time.

This may not seem important now, but as you move into the adult world, your circumstances can change rapidly and tracking your finances can become complicated.

As you revise this statement, you see the progress you are making toward your goals. The net worth statement helps you chart your financial future. On it, you list *assets* and *liabilities* and subtract what you owe from what you own to determine net worth, 6-8.

Business, Management & Administration

Bookkeepers
Bookkeepers update and maintain accounting records. They calculate expenditures, receipts, accounts payable and receivable, and profit and loss. They may also handle payroll, make purchases, prepare invoices, and keep track of overdue accounts.

Income and Expense Log			
Date	**Item**	**Income**	**Expense**
9/10 Fri.	Bus fare—round-trip		$4
	Lunch		$5
	Snack		$2
9/11 Sat.	Babysitting	$20	
	Snack		$3.50
	School supplies		$17
	Movie ticket		$7
9/12 Sun.	Gift from uncle	$10	
	New sneakers		$34

6-7

Keeping a detailed log of your income and spending will help you develop a more accurate and realistic budget.

Net Worth Statement	
Assets	
Liquid Assets:	
Cash on hand	$_____
Cash in savings, checking, and money market accounts	_____
Cash value of insurance	_____
Other	_____
Total Liquid Assets	$_____
Investment Assets:	
Stocks and bonds	$_____
Mutual funds	_____
Individual Retirement Accounts	_____
Other	_____
Total Investment Assets	$_____
Use Assets: (market values)	
Auto	$_____
Home	_____
Furniture and equipment	_____
Other	_____
Total Use Assets	$_____
Total Assets	$_____
Liabilities	
Current Liabilities:	
Credit cards and charge account balances due	$_____
Taxes due	_____
Other	_____
Total Current Liabilities	$_____
Long-term Liabilities:	
Auto loan	$_____
Home mortgage	_____
Other	_____
Total Long-term Liabilities	$_____
Total Liabilities	$_____
Net Worth (total assets less total liabilities)	$_____

6-8

A net worth statement helps you determine your net worth at a given point in time.

Assets

An *asset* is an item of value you own, such as cash, stocks, bonds, real estate, and personal possessions. Assets are divided into three categories.

- *Liquid assets* include cash and savings that quickly and easily convert to cash.

- *Investment assets* include stocks, bonds, and invested funds that are set aside for long-term goals, such as the education of children or retirement needs.

- *Use assets* include a home, auto, personal possessions, and other durable goods that enrich your life through use.

Assets tend to change in value from year to year so you will want to list them at their *current* or *market value*. This is their estimated worth at the time you make your net worth statement.

Liabilities

A **liability** is a financial obligation that you currently owe or will owe in the future. Liabilities include unpaid bills, credit card charges, mortgages, personal loans, and taxes. These are divided into two categories:

- *Current liabilities* are items due soon, usually within the year. They include medical bills, taxes, and unpaid bills from credit cards and charge accounts.

- *Long-term liabilities* include obligations to be paid over a long period of time, such as a home mortgage or auto loan.

Your Net Worth

Subtract liabilities from assets to arrive at your net worth. If you own more than you owe, you have positive net worth. This means that you can meet your financial obligations. You may also have assets you can use to meet financial goals that go beyond your obligations.

Wealthy individuals will have assets far in excess of their liabilities. The term **wealth** refers to an abundance of assets that are accumulated over time. It includes investments, property, a business, and other items of value that contribute significantly to financial security and a high standard of living and giving.

If your net worth is a negative figure, your debts exceed your assets. You need to find ways to reduce expenses or increase income. Start with a careful look at expenses. Try to reduce or eliminate all the items that are not essential. Pay off credit debts and do not take on more credit obligations. Consider ways to increase income by working more hours or assuming more responsibilities on the job. A job change or additional training may also lead to higher income in some situations. In some families unemployed family members may be able to find work that pays. Take every possible measure to create a positive net worth.

Planning Family Finances

As you enter the adult world, your money management activities will expand. Teens eagerly await the day when they can afford to live on their own. Once independent, their eyes are opened to the many expenses they must handle that were previously paid by their parents. Managing finances well to remain independent becomes their number one challenge.

Often young adults who are newly independent try to hold down costs by sharing living expenses with one or more friends. After a period of living with others or on their own, many adults eventually form families. Their financial responsibilities increase dramatically. There are family as well as personal expenses to cover. Perhaps the most important factors affecting your adult budgeting decisions will be your age and the stage you occupy in the family life cycle.

Family life cycle refers to the stages a family passes through from formation to aging. Your goals and needs, as well as earning and spending patterns, will change with each stage. Becoming familiar with these patterns can provide you with a framework for your own financial planning. See 6-9.

Financial Aspects of the Family Life Cycle		
Stages in the Family Life Cycle	**Career and Income Characteristics**	**Typical Expenses and Obligations**
Beginning Stage		
Marriage Getting started as a couple Establishing a home	Finishing education Making career decisions Entering the workforce Low or no income, with gradual increases	Living expenses Tuition and/or repayment of education loans Auto loan payments and insurance Life, health, and other insurance Home furnishings Savings and retirement contributions Income tax
Expanding Stage		
Birth/adoption of first child The infant years	Increasing income and job responsibilities One or two full-time incomes Decreased income if wife leaves work for childbearing	Child care and baby equipment Education fund Increased insurance coverage Prenatal, birth, and postnatal health care Income taxes Retirement contributions

6-9

(Continued.)

Career and income characteristics along with typical expenses and obligations tend to follow a general pattern at different stages of the life cycle.

Developing Stage		
Toddler, preschool, and elementary school years: Children become primary focus	Job advancement likely Increasing income Increasing job responsibilities	Move to larger living space Additional home furnishings Property and income tax increases Increased living expenses Retirement contributions
Adolescent years: Involvement in school activities Preparation for launching stage	Continuing job advancement or possible career change Possible return of mother to the workforce Income still increasing	School expenses for extracurricular activities Savings and investments Savings for education Charitable contributions Travel Adolescents' spending Income and property taxes

Launching Stage		
Children leave home Parents adjust to "empty nest"	Heavier job responsibilities Peak performance years Income may peak as well Benefits may increase Retirement planning becomes a priority	Home improvements or new, smaller home Replacement furnishings Education and tuition costs Travel Retirement savings Income and property taxes Weddings of children

Aging Stage		
Parents focus on each other Children marry Grandchildren arrive Elderly parents may require care	Job responsibilities and earnings begin to level off Retirement and estate planning take form	Travel, recreation, and adult education Care for aging parents Increased savings and investments Gifts to help children get established Income and property taxes Long-term care insurance
Retirement years: Establishing new routines, interests, and hobbies Grandparenting	Part-time or volunteer work Social Security income Income from retirement savings Wills and estate plans are revised as needed	Health insurance Possible relocation to a retirement area Travel Health care and medications Taxes Long-term care

6-9

(Continued.)

Beginning Stage

From age 18 to the late 20s, young people are getting established on the job and in life. Those who marry begin the first stage of the family life cycle, called the *beginning stage.* Income for most young adults starts low and gradually increases with time on the job. Two-income couples enjoy the benefits of combined incomes. People who marry later may have established careers and higher incomes.

Expenses at this time are likely to include education, college loans, home furnishings, and insurance. The down payment on a home is often the largest single expense of young couples. Other major expenses include an auto, savings, or contributions to a retirement fund. Couples need to revise their savings and investment programs to meet their changing needs as they move to later stages in the life cycle.

Case Study: Making Plans

Looking Ahead

Maria and Tony plan to be married in six months. Maria is a nursery school teacher, and Tony is a welder. Their combined annual income is almost $60,000.

During their first few years of marriage, Maria and Tony plan to buy a house and some furniture. Tony owns a car. They both use credit cards, but have little debt.

After four to five years, they hope to start a family. Maria wants to work as a substitute teacher until their children reach school age. By then, Tony's income may be higher. His work benefits include health care coverage, and life and disability insurance.

Case Review

1. What expenses will this couple likely have in the first year or two of marriage?
2. What steps do Maria and Tony need to take now in order to drop to one steady income when children come?
3. What big expenses are likely to come with the purchase of a home? with their first child? with later children?
4. What contributions should Maria and Tony make for unexpected emergencies and expenses?

Expanding Stage

For adults under age 40, life is often characterized by job advancement, rising income, and increasing responsibilities. With the birth or adoption of the first child, couples enter the *expanding stage* with all its joys and responsibilities.

If one spouse leaves the workforce to raise children, income declines. At the same time, expenses increase. Child-related expenses include child care, children's clothing, baby equipment, toys, and medical expenses. With children may come the decision to move to a larger home, 6-10. This is a good time to review and expand insurance protection. An educational fund for children may be started. It is important to draw up a will, too.

Developing Stage

School-age children and adolescents bring a new set of circumstances for families. Family life tends to revolve around the children and their school life. Expenses include a larger clothing budget, sports and hobby equipment, lessons and tutoring, allowances, and savings for future education. Another expenditure for some is a second car.

During this stage, a spouse who left the workforce may return either to satisfy career goals or to supplement income. This may require at least a brief return to school to update education and skills. While income may still climb during parenting years, expenses grow as well. They include housing, insurance, taxes, education, savings, and retirement planning.

6-10
The arrival of children will call for major adjustments in financial planning.

Launching Stage

Parents in their 40s and 50s share another set of common experiences. Families enter this stage as the children leave home for college, jobs, or homes of their own. During these years, job advancements often bring higher incomes. Earnings may peak. It is also a time when some may seek a job or career change.

Many families at this stage need extra income to cover college expenses and retirement savings. Retirement planning is critical.

In some families, this is a time when aging parents become a concern. Those in this situation are often called the "sandwich generation." Parents find themselves "sandwiched" between college-bound teens and their own aging parents. Both financial and emotional demands are great when this happens.

Aging Stage

From the late 50s to retirement, people often need to adjust to new events. Earnings level off. Aging parents may require attention and assistance. Children have left home, creating the "empty nest." Many parents become grandparents. Married couples often renew their focus on each other. They may choose to travel or become more active in the community.

Individuals and couples often focus on retirement planning during these years. Empty-nest families may choose to move to a smaller home and simplify their lives for retirement. Those caring for elderly parents may face heavy health and nursing-care costs. Couples need to have reliable health insurance and consider buying long-term care insurance for themselves. At this stage, estate planning is important. It is also the time to review and revise wills.

For most people, this stage marks formal retirement. Some retirees seek part-time work or volunteer opportunities. For many, free time is a welcome luxury. It is a good time to downsize, live more simply, and conserve energy and income. Those in good health may travel more. Grandchildren are frequently important at this time of life.

Income and most living expenses usually decline during retirement years. Security and comfort depend on the financial planning that occurred in earlier stages. For those who have not planned, the retirement years can bring financial hardship as income drops. Serious spending cutbacks may be required, especially as medical costs rise. Retired adults need to review wills and estate plans. They should go over the provisions in each with their adult children.

Variations in the Cycle

Not every family follows the stages of the family life cycle in order, 6-11. The number of children and spacing between them can cause the cycle to vary from family to family. Some families skip, overlap, or repeat stages of the family life cycle. For example, couples that do not have children skip the expanding, developing, and launching stages. Parents with children in school could have more children. This would cause an overlap of the developing and expanding stages. Single parents who remarry may repeat stages with their new spouses.

As family conditions change, financial planning concerns change, too. For example, single individuals, childless couples, single-parent families, and divorced or separated people have these added considerations.

Singles and Childless Couples

Singles and couples with no dependents do not have the expenses related to childrearing, such as school and medical expenses. Both groups may spend more throughout the life cycle on travel, leisure, and other extras. Some may choose to give more to charitable causes. Both groups often feel a greater responsibility to help their aging parents.

Stages of the Family Life Cycle

Beginning Stage	Expanding Stage	Developing Stage

| Couple marries. | The first child is born. | Children start school. |

Launching Stage

Children begin moving away from home.

Aging Stage

Parents retire.

Variations in the Cycle

| A childless couple goes through the beginning and aging stages only. | A single parent in the expanding stage could repeat the beginning stage with a new spouse. | A couple with children in school could have another child, causing an overlap of the expanding and developing stages. |

A couple in the launching stage could adopt a child after an older child has left home, returning to the expanding stage.

In an extended family, a couple in the aging stage might not be alone after they retire.

6-11

Not all families proceed through all stages of the family life cycle in the same way.

Single-Parent Families

Females lead most single-parent families. Their income is typically less than that of two-parent families and single-parent families led by males. Saving and planning for future security is sometimes difficult as these families struggle to meet current expenses. Government and community services and assistance can be very helpful for single-parent families.

Case Study: Making Plans

The Single Life

At 28, Myra has no plans to marry and no children. She is a top-notch photographer and earns $50,000 annually. She also receives outstanding benefits through her job, including health, disability, and life insurance. Myra's parents are in good health and they both work. Her two brothers have jobs and families of their own. Myra lives in a rented apartment and is thinking about buying a home, something she has always dreamed.

Case Review

1. What changes in Myra's situation could alter her financial needs and plans?
2. Suppose one of Myra's parents becomes ill, resulting in financial problems. How could this affect Myra's financial plans?
3. Suppose Myra's brother and his wife die in an accident and Myra is named guardian of their children. How might this change her financial plans?
4. What are some financial steps Myra should take before purchasing a home? What steps should she take after becoming a homeowner? What additional expenses will home ownership bring?
5. What are some key differences in financial planning for those with and without dependents?
6. How does an individual's age relate to financial planning and decisions?

Separated and Divorced People

Separated and divorced people face a unique set of financial concerns. They may have the following expenses: legal fees, alimony, child support, and property settlement costs. The costs of establishing and maintaining two homes rather than one is another expense, especially if there are children. A divorce or separation may require additional furnishings and moving costs.

No matter what your situation will be, it is wise to begin a savings and investment program and to insure against financial risks early in your adult life. These two steps are the foundation of financial security in later life. Savings can cover unexpected expenses and emergencies and help to reach goals. Insurance protects against major disasters. With both, you can feel reasonably comfortable with your financial situation. Start with a personal savings plan. The longer you save, the more you will accumulate.

Financial Decisions in a Changing World

Besides the family life cycle, other important factors and forces will impact your life. These include economic, social, cultural, and technological forces. Individually and together, these factors will cause you to redefine your financial needs, priorities, and goals.

The Economy and Your Finances

When the economy is on the upswing, people are generally optimistic. Businesses make money, grow, and hire more workers. People who want work can find good jobs. Most consumers who want to can find a job. Their future income is fairly secure and they can pay their bills. If they plan carefully, they can even save and invest for the future. However, when the economy is plagued by problems, such as recession, inflation, or unemployment, managing your finances becomes even more important and challenging.

Recession, a period of slow or no economic growth, can have a major impact on personal money management. This is especially true for those who are out of work or whose incomes are stagnant. Recessions spread uncertainty and pessimism over the entire economy. Consumers spend less and save more if possible. Businesses cut back and unemployment rises.

ECONOMICS in ACTION

Severe Recessions Hit Home

When recessions hit the U.S. economy, the impact is felt in millions of homes across the country. Young adults struggle with finding work as businesses shed jobs and curtail growth. Financial institutions make fewer loans. Long-term goals, such as increasing one's education and buying a home, must be put on hold.

When people lose their jobs or have their hours reduced, entire families feel the pain. Many lose the health insurance that was provided through their jobs. Unemployment often pushes many families out of their homes.

Loss of income means lifestyle changes for almost everyone. There is less money and much more anxiety. Retirement savings drop with the stock market. People who were retired or nearing retirement are forced to work beyond their planned retirement age, if they can find work.

Inflation, or a period of rising prices, also relates to personal money management. As prices go up, the value of a dollar goes down. If income does not rise at the same rate that prices rise, buying power is reduced. Consumers cannot buy as much or save as much. Financial planning and saving can help consumers cope with challenging economic conditions.

Demographics and Your Finances

To some extent, the way you manage your money and your life in the years ahead will depend on *demographics*. **Demographics** refer to the statistical characteristics of the population. *Vital statistics* include records of births, deaths, and marriages. *Social statistics* include population breakdowns by age, sex, and race with geographic distributions and growth rates.

Other social-economic statistics concern education levels, income levels, employment, religion, crime, immigration, and ethnic representation. A current almanac is a good place to look for the latest demographic statistics. Recent demographic trends have an impact on the overall economy, and in turn, on the financial life of consumers. Consider some of the following trends and their economic implications:

- Couples are marrying and having children later in life.

- The percentage of single-parent families is growing, 6-12.

- The average age of the overall population is increasing.

- Educational requirements for jobs are rising and job markets are changing.

- Skilled workers are in greater demand.

- More young adults are living at home with their parents.

- The number of unmarried adults is increasing.

- More mothers are working away from home.

- The number of births to single mothers is increasing.

All these and other factors will affect your financial future.

6-12

The growing number of single-parent families is one demographic factor that has affected the economy.

Culture and Your Finances

Most urban areas include a variety of racial and ethnic groups. Each group makes an impact on consumer attitudes and buying habits, community services, schools, and many other consumer and family issues.

Relationships and marriages between people of different races, cultures, and religions are on the increase. This creates a blending of ethnic traditions, religious beliefs, languages, and concepts of "family." Cultural and ethnic traditions affect many everyday choices and routines. They may dictate the role each partner plays in the family, who makes financial and spending decisions, whether both partners work, how the family uses credit, and how the family manages its money.

Technology and Your Finances

New developments and discoveries in communications, medicine, science, and other areas change the way we live in the world. For example, medical advances may result in a longer, healthier life for you and others. New findings on healthful lifestyles include fitness routines, nutritious diets, and stress reduction. You now know how to improve your own health and quality of life. However, living longer makes financial planning even more critical. Your savings must sustain you over a longer life span.

Technology brings other changes in the way you live and deal with financial matters. For example, the Internet has altered the way people buy goods and services. You can buy everything from groceries to autos to movie tickets online. Information technology can bring you the latest information from around the world about consumer products, services, and issues. Money management software brings you up-to-the-minute tools for managing money and performing many financial tasks online. You can do your banking, bill paying, investing, and fund transfers online in your own home, 6-13. The Internet brings an international marketplace to your fingertips.

6-13

With a computer and an Internet connection, you can manage your finances almost anywhere.

Certified Financial Planners

Certified financial planners have met certification requirements issued by the Certified Financial Planner Board of Standards. They assess the financial needs of clients and use their knowledge of investments, tax law, and insurance to recommend the most beneficial financial options for their clients.

Advanced technology creates new markets and brings more and cheaper goods and services to consumers. It also creates new jobs in many fields. Unfortunately it also has fueled *offshore outsourcing* in some fields. This is the business practice of moving factories and jobs overseas and across borders to take advantage of cheap labor and business-friendly government regulations. As a result, many American workers must compete for jobs with lower-paid workers in other countries. This has caused layoffs and unemployment, especially among those who work in manufacturing and information technology industries. Today and in the future, the higher-paying jobs will require higher levels of education and training. Education has never been more important than in today's economy.

Working Through Financial Problems

You can often avoid financial trouble by living within your means and keeping debt under control. This involves taking responsibility for your life, including your financial choices and decisions.

Preparation will help you weather a crisis situation if it arises. Getting the best education and job training possible are ways to be prepared. With a good education and job skills, you are better able to find work and advance on the job. Staying current in your field through continuing education and training programs also helps. Usually higher earnings and greater job security result.

An emergency fund equal to several months' pay is another way to prepare for the unexpected. The amount of money needed in the fund differs from one person to another. However, it should equal your monthly income multiplied by the number of months you are likely to be out of work. In some cases, such as during a recession or if you work in a competitive field, the emergency fund should equal as much as eight to ten months of pay.

Preventive measures also help. Those discussed here and in other chapters include

- sound money management
- practical credit controls
- regular savings
- insurance protection
- reasonable caution in financial matters
- regular discussions of financial matters with household members old enough to understand the fundamentals of money management

Prevention, when possible, is the most painless way to deal with potential disasters.

Unexpected Crisis

There may be times when financial disaster strikes because of circumstances beyond your control. A **family crisis** is a major problem that

11. How do you think financial security, financial insecurity, and financial crises affect each of the following groups?
    A. Single individuals with no dependents and no sources of income other than their own earnings.
    B. Married couples with no children.
    C. Married couples with dependent children.
    D. Retired couples.

12. How would a financial crisis in your family affect you personally?

13. Cite an example of ways each of the following can influence personal and family money management and lifestyles.
    A. The economy.
    B. Demographics.
    C. Cultural and ethnic traditions.
    D. Technology.

Academic Connections

14. **Social studies.** Research local government agencies and community organizations that offer assistance to individuals and families who are facing financial hardships. Develop a brief directory of available services.

15. **Research, writing.** Choose one of the following topics. Write a three-page report using at least five reliable sources of information.
    - The role of savings in achieving financial security.
    - Dealing with financial crises.

16. **Research, speech.** Interview two couples: one that has been married less than 5 years and one that has been married more than 15 years. Ask the couples to list some of the adjustments people need to make in financial planning and decisions when they marry.

Math Challenge

17. Lena Chang, 23, lives alone in a rented apartment. She earns $2,300 a month after taxes and payroll deductions. She has a savings account containing $1,500. She also owns $2,000 in stocks and some jewelry worth about $1,000. Her largest asset is a car that could sell today for $10,000. She still owes $15,000 on a student loan.

    Her monthly expenses include
    - $250 savings
    - $750 rent
    - $250 student loan payment
    - $250 utilities
    - $200 gas, car insurance, and registration
    - $230 groceries
    - $50 donations to a charity
    - $350 extras such as entertainment, eating out, and clothing

    Create a net worth statement for Lena. Is her net worth statement positive or negative?

Tech Smart

18. Find the Web sites of three private charitable organizations that you may want to support someday. Check out each organization on www.charitynavigator.org for an evaluation of its effectiveness. What group does each organization serve? What types of contributions, besides money, might be needed?

19. Investigate online several available money management software programs and outline the key features of one of them. Discuss ways money management software could help you with financial planning and management over your lifetime.

CHAPTER 7

Income and Taxes

Reading for Meaning

Before reading a new section, study any charts and tables. This will increase your understanding of the material.

earned income

wage

minimum wage

piecework income

salary

commission

tip

bonus

compensation

employee benefit

gross income

payroll deduction

FICA (Federal Insurance Contributions Act)

net income

unearned income

interest

entitlement

Social Security

Medicare

disability

Medicaid

Form W-4

Form W-2

tax deduction

exemption

tax credit

CHAPTER OBJECTIVES

After studying this chapter, you will be able to

- **identify** different types of income and employee benefits.
- **relate** taxation to government spending.
- **list** goods and services government provides.
- **identify** different types of taxes.
- **identify** common tax forms.
- **describe** basic procedures for filing a tax return.
- **explain** the purposes and function of the Social Security system.

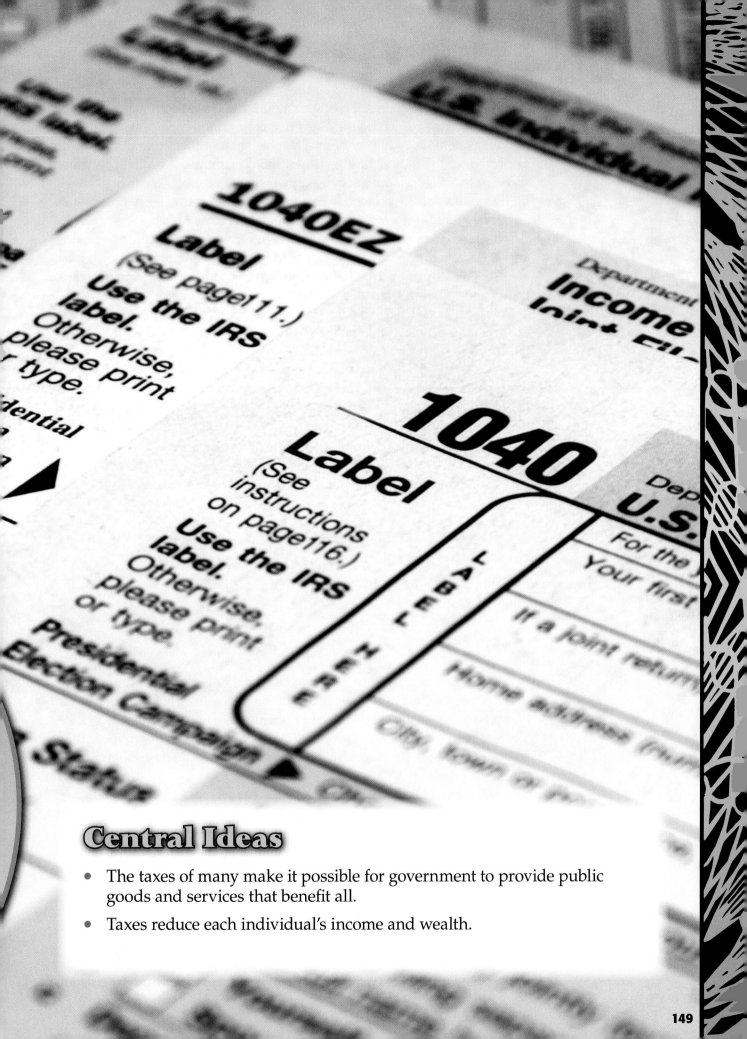

Central Ideas

- The taxes of many make it possible for government to provide public goods and services that benefit all.

- Taxes reduce each individual's income and wealth.

Income gives individuals spending money. Taxes give the various levels of government their spending money, which is called *revenue*. A major way for government to raise revenue is by taxing each person's income as well as items they buy or own. The government then uses that revenue to provide public goods and services that benefit all. As a teen, you use some of those goods and services now, such as schools, libraries, parks, highways, and police protection. As an older adult, you will use other types of public goods and services, such as Social Security benefits.

In this chapter, you will examine different types of income and taxes and the ways different levels of government use your taxes. The chapter also discusses procedures for paying income and Social Security taxes. Important issues related to tax legislation are outlined. Finally, you will learn about Social Security benefits and some of the concerns that may prompt changes both in Social Security benefits and the way we pay for them.

The Many Forms of Income

There are many ways to acquire income, but for most, employment is the primary way. A person can also receive income from sources other than work, and that income may likewise be subject to taxation.

Money Earned from Work

Earned income is the income you receive from employment. As you enter the workplace, you will learn that income from work can have the following forms.

Wages

A **wage** is payment for work and is usually computed on an hourly, daily, or piecework basis. A wage is paid on a schedule—often every week, every two weeks, or every month. For example, an hourly wage is a set amount paid for each hour worked. Eligible workers who put in more than 40 hours per week must recieve overtime pay at least 1½ times their hourly rate.

Many unskilled and beginning workers are paid the *minimum wage*. The **minimum wage** is the lowest hourly wage employers can pay most workers by law. Workers who frequently receive minimum wage include food preparers in fast-food restaurants, store salespeople, and workers at a car wash. Contrary to popular belief, most minimum wage workers are adults, not teens.

Piecework income is a wage based on a rate per unit of work completed. For example, garment workers may be paid by the number of garments completed. They must, however, receive at least the minimum wage.

Government sets and enforces the minimum wage through the Fair Labor Standards Act of 1938 (FLSA). Periodically, lawmakers pass legislation raising the minimum wage so it keeps pace with cost-of-living increases. See www.dol.gov to check the current minimum wage. Some states require a higher minimum wage than the federal wage. If there is both a state and a federal minimum wage, workers get whichever is higher.

Some employees are exempt from receiving the full minimum wage. For example, workers under the age of 20 who are receiving job training can be paid less. However, this is only during their first 90 consecutive days on the job. High school students enrolled in career education classes can sometimes be paid less than full minimum wage. Your state's department of labor can answer questions about wage requirements.

Salary

Salary is payment for work that is expressed as an annual figure. It is paid in periodic equal payments. The payment period is usually weekly, biweekly, or monthly. For example, the salary for a job may be listed as $50,000 a year. A worker does not receive a lump sum payment of $50,000. Instead, the salary is divided into equal payments at regular intervals during the year.

Salaried workers are expected to put in as much time as it takes to do the job. Therefore, teachers, managers, supervisors, and professionals are not paid overtime.

Commission

A **commission** is income paid as a percentage of sales made by a salesperson. Some people may work on a commission-only basis. Others may receive a combination of base salary plus commission. Salespeople who usually work on commission sell cars, real estate, insurance, and other goods and services.

For a salesperson on commission, making many sales means income goes up. If customers do not buy, income shrinks. For many salespeople, income varies from month to month and year to year. A good salesperson generally earns more in commissions than in salary.

Tips

A **tip**, or gratuity, is money paid for service beyond what is required. A customer leaves a tip as a reward for good service. Tips are also given as incentives for workers to provide good service. This money belongs to workers, not their employers. This form of income is common for waiters, taxi drivers, hairdressers, and other service-industry workers, 7-1.

7-1

Tips are a form of income and are subject to taxation.

In some cases, tip-earning employees are also entitled to a minimum wage. It is less than the standard minimum wage. However, if a worker's total earnings are below the standard minimum wage, the employer is required to pay the difference.

Bonus

A **bonus** is money added to an employee's base pay. It is usually a reward for performance or a share of business profits. Bonuses are incentives to encourage workers to perform better. Bonus income is usually based on worker performance, length of time with the company, or company performance.

Employee Benefits

Employee Benefits Specialists

Employee benefits specialists oversee programs available to employees. Such benefits include health insurance, parental leave, wellness, and retirement programs, among others. These specialists help employees take full advantage of the benefits paid completely or partly by their employer.

So far, this chapter has discussed forms of monetary compensation. **Compensation** is the payment and benefits received for work performed. Some of the most valuable forms of payment to workers are not monetary. An **employee benefit**, or *fringe benefit*, is a form of nonmonetary compensation received in addition to a wage or salary. Employee benefits offer important financial advantages.

The availability of employee benefits and other extras depends on the company and type of work. While these are not dollar-income items, they contribute significantly to the financial well-being of workers and their families. Common types of employee benefits include the following:

- paid vacation and holiday time from work
- paid sick leave
- life and health insurance
- retirement savings plan

Your employer can help you save money for the future. An employer-sponsored retirement savings plan is an investment program. One example is a 401(k) plan for corporate employees. Money is deducted from employee paychecks and placed into a savings fund before pay is taxed. Employers sometimes match employee contributions. However, with a few exceptions, money must stay in the account until retirement to avoid taxes and penalties. (Chapter 12 will present more information about these and other valuable financial resources.)

Business Profit Income

A growing proportion of the U.S. workforce is self-employed. Unlike employees, who perform services for their employer, the self-employed work for themselves.

This category of workers includes many entrepreneurs in the trades, such as plumbers, carpenters, and painters. Artists and consultants are often self-employed. A teenager who has a part-time job mowing lawns is self-employed.

The form of income they earn is called *profit* or *self-employment income.* One of the drawbacks of being self-employed is that you must arrange and pay for your own employee benefits. Some of these benefits, especially health care, are costly when purchased by individuals. Another disadvantage is that you must pay the entire cost of your Social Security and Medicare taxes instead of half the cost.

Payroll Deductions

The dollar figure on your paycheck is not the same as the dollar figure you are told when hired for a job. **Gross income** is wages or salary before payroll deductions. A **payroll deduction** is a subtraction from your gross income. Common payroll deductions are

Case Study: A Taxing Situation

Unmet Expectations

Alvira is a high school junior looking for a summer job. She loves animals. This led her to a local veterinarian. Luckily, the vet was looking for an office assistant. She needed someone to assist in handling the animals that came in for treatment, grooming, and boarding. Alvira would work 30 hours and earn $240 per week. She would get paid every two weeks.

Alvira's first paycheck was much lower than the $480 she expected. Her paycheck stub showed the following payroll deductions: $29.76 for FICA, $6.96 for Medicare tax, $62.10 for federal withholding tax, and $28.80 for state income tax. Alvira was shocked and disappointed to receive only $352.38. Still, she had the job she wanted and felt it was pretty good money anyway.

Case Review

1. Do these figures surprise you? What has been your experience with jobs and payroll deductions?
2. Do you think it is fair for Alvira to pay $127.62 in taxes every two weeks? Why or why not?
3. What benefits does Alvira receive from the money she pays in taxes? Does she receive any direct benefits? What services that she enjoys are paid by tax dollars?
4. What information from her paycheck stub will be important when Alvira files her income tax return?

- *Social Security tax, or* **FICA (Federal Insurance Contributions Act), and Medicare.** It is 7.65 percent of earnings. Employers pay half of the FICA taxes for each employee.

- *federal withholding tax.* It varies with employee earnings and eligibility for tax benefits.

- *state withholding tax.* It varies with employee earnings and from state to state.

- *city withholding tax.* Some cities charge income tax.

- *other benefits.* These may include health care, dental, vision care, and other insurance that employees purchase through their employers.

Net income, or *take-home pay*, is your gross income (plus bonuses, if you get them), minus payroll deductions. See the paycheck stub in 7-2. In a pay period, the worker earned a total of $1,113.73 in wages and overtime pay. This is gross income, but the worker's net pay is only $827.70. Net income is reduced by payroll deductions collected by the employer and sent to government authorities and insurance companies. Deductions can lower a paycheck by 20 percent or more.

By law, workers are required to pay Social Security and withholding taxes. These topics are discussed in greater detail later in this chapter.

Money Earned Outside Work

Earned income is earnings from employment. **Unearned income** is earnings from sources other than work. It includes

Town Department Store	**Employee** Kristy A. James **Pay Period** 3/8/XX to 3/21/XX **Pay Date** 3/27/XX **Check No.** 12341234			**SSN** 987-65-4321 **Net Pay** $827.70		
Earnings	**Hrs.**	**Current**	**YTD**	**Deductions**	**Current**	**YTD**
REGULAR	80.00	1113.73	5923.12	FICA	69.06	494.17
OVERTIME			1872.99	MEDICARE	16.15	115.58
				FED. TAX	116.17	880.89
				STATE TAX	52.40	347.68
				HEALTH	32.25	225.75
TOTALS	80.00	1113.73	7796.11		286.03	2064.07

7-2

This paycheck stub shows some of the common payroll deductions from income.

- interest paid on savings and bonds. **Interest** is paid by financial institutions, businesses, and government in exchange for the use of customers' money.

- earnings from investments or selling assets

- rent, or regular fees paid for the use of property

- Social Security and retirement account payments

- inheritance, awards, and gifts

- alimony

- unemployment compensation

Taxes on unearned income vary. Most sources are taxed. Some are taxed at higher rates than others.

The Importance of Taxes

The government generates revenue by taxing its citizens and businesses. Tax revenue is used to run the government. However, since its resources are limited, government must make choices. So, like individuals and families, government creates a budget for spending. The budget reflects the priorities and goals of the government and its people.

At present, most taxpayers spend a sizable share of their dollars to pay their income, Social Security, and other taxes. It is to your advantage to know what your tax dollars buy and how the tax system works.

Paying for government operations, facilities, and services is the primary purpose of taxes. The government provides goods and services that benefit the public. Examples include fire and police protection, schools, highways, airports, parks, and water and sewage treatment.

Besides providing goods and services necessary for society, legislators may raise or lower taxes to achieve one of the following goals.

Stabilizing the economy. The government may use taxes to promote economic stability, fight inflation, or slow a recession. (Chapter 2 discusses this in more detail.)

Addressing social challenges. Some tax dollars are used to provide services and opportunities for the aging and other populations in need. Food stamps, housing subsidies, and veterans' educational benefits are examples of such programs. A less obvious but very important way that government addresses social needs is by supporting an economy that raises the country's standard of living. Less government assistance is needed when people have the ability to improve their financial situation.

Influencing behavior. By removing taxes from some items and taxing others, government tries to change peoples' behavior. For example, the government allows taxpayers to deduct certain charitable donations. This lowers the donor's taxes and encourages giving. The government adds tax on alcohol and tobacco products, which increases their cost and discourages their use.

Federal Government Spending

Taxation is the primary source of revenue for both federal and state governments. Approximately 57 percent of all tax dollars goes to the federal government. In those years when the government spends more than it collects, it must borrow money. This is called *deficit spending*, and it increases the national debt. Sources of the federal government's revenue and expenditures are shown in 7-3.

Mandatory Expenses

Each year the federal government spends over 60 percent of its total budget on *mandatory expense* items. A mandatory expenditure is a commitment the federal government has made. It must pay these expenses. If there are not enough tax dollars to support it, the government must borrow the money to meet these commitments.

About 60 percent of mandatory expenditures are entitlements. An **entitlement** is a government payment or benefit promised by law to eligible citizens. The largest entitlement program is Social Security, followed by Medicare.

Social Security is a federal program that provides income when earnings are reduced or stopped because of retirement, serious illness or injury, or death. In the case of death, benefits are provided to survivors of the deceased. Benefits are funded by a payroll tax on workers' income and matching contributions from employers.

Medicare is a federal program that pays for certain health care expenses for older citizens and others with disabilities. A **disability** is a limitation that affects a person's ability to function in major life activities. Medicare is funded by payroll taxes and administered by the U.S. Department of Health & Human Services.

Medicaid is a government program that pays certain health care costs for eligible low-income individuals and families. It is administered by state governments. Funding comes from state and federal tax revenues.

Other entitlement programs include federal employee retirement benefits, veterans' pensions and medical care, nutrition assistance, unemployment compensation, and housing assistance. Any reductions or changes in these programs require new legislation.

Interest on the national debt is also a mandatory expense item. This interest must be paid, even if the government must borrow money to pay it.

Federal Government Dollars

Where they come from...
Revenues $2.5 trillion

- All other 4%
- Excise tax 3%
- Individual income tax 45%
- Social insurance tax 36%
- Corporate income tax 12%

Where they go...
Expenditures $2.9 trillion

- Other entitlement programs 10%
- Medicaid 8%
- Medicare 15%
- Social Security 21%
- Defense 21%
- Nondefense discretionary 17%
- Interest on national debt 8%

Congressional Budget Office, 2008 Budget

7-3

This chart shows where federal government revenues come from and where they go. When expenditures exceed revenues, the government must borrow money, creating an increase in national debt.

------------------------------------- Cut here and give Form W-4 to your employer. Keep the top part for your records. -------------------------

| Form **W-4** Department of the Treasury Internal Revenue Service | **Employee's Withholding Allowance Certificate** ▶ **For Privacy Act and Paperwork Reduction Act Notice, see page 2.** | OMB No. 1545-0010 **20XX** |

| 1   Type or print your first name and middle initial | Last name | 2   Your social security number |
| Kristy A. | James | 987 65 4321 |

Home address (number and street or rural route)	3 ☒ Single ☐ Married ☐ Married, but withhold at higher Single rate.
1027 Cedar Street	**Note:** *If married, but legally separated, or spouse is a nonresident alien, check the "Single" box.*
City or town, state, and ZIP code	4 If your last name differs from that on your social security card,
Franklin, IL 65432	check here. You must call 1-800-772-1213 for a new card. ▶ ☐

5	Total number of allowances you are claiming (from line **H** above **or** from the applicable worksheet on page 2)	5	2
6	Additional amount, if any, you want withheld from each paycheck	6	$
7	I claim exemption from withholding for 20XX, and I certify that I meet **both** of the following conditions for exemption:
	● Last year I had a right to a refund of **all** Federal income tax withheld because I had **no** tax liability **and**
	● This year I expect a refund of **all** Federal income tax withheld because I expect to have **no** tax liability.
	If you meet both conditions, write "Exempt" here . . . . ▶	7	

Under penalties of perjury, I certify that I am entitled to the number of withholding allowances claimed on this certificate, or I am entitled to claim exempt status.

Employee's signature
(Form is not valid unless you sign it.) ▶   *Kristy A. James*   Date ▶ *January 2 20XX*

| 8   Employer's name and address (Employer: Complete lines 8 and 10 only if sending to the IRS.) | 9   Office code (optional) | 10   Employer identification number |

Cat. No. 10220Q

7-5

Employees complete the Form W-4. It provides information employers use to determine how much federal tax to withhold from paychecks.

Each year, by the end of January, you will receive a **Form W-2** from each employer, 7-6. This is called a Wage and Tax Statement and is usually mailed to your home. It states the amount you were paid during the previous year. It also gives the amounts of income, Social Security, and Medicare taxes withheld from your income during the year.

You will receive a *Form 1099-MISC* if you received income from self-employment, royalties, rent payments, unemployment compensation, and other sources.

Preparing Your Return

You will need the following records and forms to prepare your return correctly:

- Form W-2 from each of your employers

- all 1099 forms

- other records of income, such as from tips

- Social Security number for yourself and household members

- copies of your tax returns from the previous year you filed

- forms and instructions from the IRS
  See 7-7 for other records you may need.

a Employee's social security number 987-65-4321				OMB No. 1545-0008	Safe, accurate, FAST! Use	IRS e~file	Visit the IRS website at www.irs.gov/efile.

b Employer identification number (EIN) XX-XXXXXXX	1 Wages, tips, other compensation 28956.98	2 Federal income tax withheld 3020.42

c Employer's name, address, and ZIP code Town Department Store 111 Broadway Avenue Franklin, IL 65432	3 Social security wages 28956.98	4 Social security tax withheld 1795.56
	5 Medicare wages and tips	6 Medicare tax withheld 419.90
	7 Social security tips	8 Allocated tips

d Control number	9 Advance EIC payment	10 Dependent care benefits

| e Employee's first name and initial   Last name   Suff. Kristy A.   James

1027 Cedar Street Franklin, IL 65432	11 Nonqualified plans	12a See instructions for box 12
	13 Statutory employee ☐ Retirement plan ☐ Third-party sick pay ☐	12b
	14 Other	12c
		12d

f Employee's address and ZIP code

15 State Employer's state ID number IL XX-XXXXXXX	16 State wages, tips, etc. 28956.98	17 State income tax 1362.40	18 Local wages, tips, etc.	19 Local income tax	20 Locality name

Form **W-2** Wage and Tax Statement   **20XX**   Department of the Treasury—Internal Revenue Service

Copy B—To Be Filed With Employee's FEDERAL Tax Return.
This information is being furnished to the Internal Revenue Service.

7-6

A Form W-2 shows how much an employee was paid during a year and what payroll deductions were taken.

Other Helpful Records for Filing Taxes

- Canceled checks and receipts for deductions or credits entered on your tax return
- Itemized bills and receipts for deductible expenses
- Bills and receipts for permanent home improvements
- Records of interest paid on home mortgages
- Real estate closing statements
- Investment records including purchase and sale dates, prices, gains, losses, and commissions

7-7

You need certain records, receipts, and documents to help you fill out tax return forms.

Choosing a Tax Form

When filing a tax return you will use one of three common forms: *1040EZ, 1040A,* or *1040.* These forms and many others are updated each year. They are available on the IRS Web site, or at public places such as libraries and post offices. The tax instruction booklet tells you which form to use.

Long form. Form 1040 must be used by taxpayers with an income over a certain amount or with itemized tax deductions. A **tax deduction** is an expense that can be subtracted from taxable income. *Itemize* means to list your tax deductions. You should use the long form when adjustments to income, itemized tax deductions, and tax credits can reduce your taxes.

You may want to consult a tax specialist to help you complete the forms and determine what expenses you can deduct.

Short form. Young workers usually use less complicated forms. Form 1040EZ and Form 1040A are relatively easy to complete and file, 7-8. These two forms may only be used by taxpayers whose income falls within certain limits and who choose not to itemize tax deductions.

Case Study: A Taxing Situation

A Time to Collect

Horace and Mandy Khan raised two children. Their youngest child left home last year. Horace is just turning 65 and Mandy is 62. Horace worked 42 years for the same company and can now retire with full pension. Mandy worked part time when the kids were young and full time for the last 10 years. They always paid Social Security taxes when they were working. With retirement near, they look to their Social Security benefits for part of their retirement income.

Horace's earnings over the past five years have been between $40,000 and $50,000 annually. Mandy earns between $25,000 and $30,000 each year. Horace's pension will pay him $2,000 each month. Mandy has no retirement plan through her employer.

Case Review

Contact your local Social Security office or go online to answer the questions.

1. Approximately how much can Horace and Mandy expect in Social Security retirement benefits each month?
2. Can Mandy collect anything for the Social Security tax she paid during her working years?
3. Will the Khans be required to pay income tax on their Social Security benefits?
4. How will monthly payments change if Horace dies? if Mandy dies?

- spouse of any age if caring for a retired worker's child under age 16 or disabled

Disability Benefits

A worker who becomes disabled before retirement age may receive disability benefits. Getting these benefits often involves an extensive application process. A worker must present concrete evidence that disability prevents him or her from earning a living. The Social Security Administration will review a worker's medical records and other information to determine eligibility. Monthly disability benefits may also be paid to a worker's family members.

Survivors' Benefits

If a worker dies, benefits may be paid to certain members of the worker's family. A single, lump-sum payment may also be made when a worker dies. This payment usually goes to the surviving spouse. Monthly benefits may be paid to these members of a deceased worker:

- unmarried children under age 18 (19 if full-time high school students) or over 18 if severely disabled, with the disability occurring before age 22

- spouse 60 or older (50 if disabled)

- spouse at any age who is caring for a worker's child under age 16 or disabled

- spouse 50 or older who becomes disabled

- parents who depend on the worker for half or more of their support

Benefits for Divorced People

An ex-spouse can be eligible for benefits on a worker's record under certain circumstances. This eligibility does not affect the amount of benefits the worker and the worker's family are entitled to receive. To qualify for benefits, an ex-spouse must satisfy these requirements:

- married to the worker at least 10 years

- at least 62 years old

- not eligible on his or her own or on someone else's Social Security record

Social Security benefits do not start automatically. When a person becomes eligible, he or she must apply for them at the nearest Social Security office. The Social Security administration calculates benefits and issues monthly payments. The administration also calculates possible future benefits based on current earnings. However, calculations cannot be exact for young workers far from retirement age.

It is a good idea to check your Social Security record every few years to make sure your earnings are being credited to your record. You can get a free postcard form at any Social Security office for this purpose.

Retirees need to contact the Social Security office in their area several months before retirement. This will give the office plenty of time to calculate benefits and begin payments as soon as retiring workers are eligible.

Social Security System Reform

The sound future of Social Security depends on responsible fiscal action today. People are living longer lives. By 2030, there will be almost twice as many Americans of retirement age as there were in 1999. Presently, about three workers pay Social Security taxes for every beneficiary. By 2030, there will be only two workers to every beneficiary. While the system has some reserves, benefit payments will exceed tax collection around 2013 unless Social Security reforms are enacted soon.

If benefit payments exceed tax collection, the Social Security trust fund will be depleted. There will be no money in the fund to support all the persons who have paid into it. Dealing with this problem will require increasing taxes, decreasing benefits, or both. In the 1980s, Congress called for taxing some retirees' benefits and raising the retirement age. This was done, but it was not enough. Among the other solutions proposed are plans to

- reduce the automatic cost-of-living allowance (COLAs) increases in benefits
- raise taxes on benefits to higher-income recipients
- cut benefits for higher-income recipients
- raise the retirement age again
- increase Social Security tax contributions
- invest Social Security trust fund surpluses in the stock market
- permit individuals to invest a portion of their Social Security taxes in personal retirement accounts

As policy makers work toward reform, it will be important to provide dependable benefits regardless of changes in the economy and financial markets. Benefits must continue for the retirees, people with disabilities, and low-income individuals who currently receive payments. One of every three people getting benefits in the current system is *not* a retiree.

Continued funding of the system will likely require increasing revenues and reducing benefits. It also will require fiscal responsibility, a curb on deficit spending, and a reduction of the national debt. It will be in your best interest to keep up with new developments in Social Security reform as it relates to both taxes and benefits. It is your money at both ends—paying and receiving.

Chapter Summary

People earn income from work or other sources, such as interest on savings. Government taxes both individual and corporate income. Taxes pay for government operations, services, and programs, including Social Security, Medicare, and Medicaid. The government must borrow money when spending exceeds tax revenues.

Taxpayers are required to file an annual income tax return. This involves keeping necessary records and receipts and preparing income tax forms. The federal tax code changes frequently as Congress struggles to meet the need for revenues with a level of taxation voters will accept.

Social Security provides income when earnings stop for certain reasons. Generally, employers and employees each pay half of the Social Security tax on total income. As the number of people collecting Social Security increases and the number of workers paying into the system decreases, reforms must be made to keep the program funded.

Review

1. What is an employee benefit?

2. What is the difference between gross income and net income?

3. How does government spending relate to taxation?

4. Give three examples of public goods and services that your taxes buy.

5. What is the greatest mandatory federal government expenditure?

6. Name the four major types of taxes that provide most state and local government revenues.

7. Explain the difference between a progressive tax and a regressive tax.

8. When you become employed, your employer will ask you to fill out a _____ for tax withholding purposes.

9. What effect does raising the number of allowances on a Form W-4 have on net income?

10. What are the three common forms for filing taxes?

11. Explain how to figure taxes owed.

12. True or false. The IRS typically audits about 25 percent of all personal income tax returns.

13. What are the two major purposes of Social Security numbers?

Critical Thinking

14. Compare and contrast progressive and regressive taxes.

15. What government services would you be willing to pay higher taxes to support? Why?

is discussed in Chapter 9, savings accounts in Chapter 11, and investment services in Chapter 12.

Types of Financial Institutions

In the past, financial institutions were more specialized. Each type of institution offered a distinct set of services to a specific set of customers. Deregulation, computer technology, and recent economic conditions have made these institutions more alike. Following are brief descriptions of financial institutions and their services.

Commercial Banks

A **commercial bank** is owned by stockholders and operated for profit. Its primary functions are to receive, transfer, and lend money to individuals, businesses, and governments. Commercial banks are often called full-service banks. They offer a wide variety of services.

These banks may be chartered by the federal government or by a state government. Federally chartered banks are called national banks and may use the word *national* in their names. These banks must comply with federal banking regulations. State chartered banks are regulated by state banking commissions.

The **Federal Deposit Insurance Corporation (FDIC)** is a U.S. government agency that protects bank customers by insuring their deposits. It also examines and supervises financial institution policies and operations. Its goal is to help maintain consumer and business confidence in the banking system. To do this, the FDIC insures bank deposits. This guarantees that depositors are protected if their bank fails or cannot repay deposits on demand. See 8-2.

In the past, the FDIC insured $100,000 of a customer's total deposits in a given bank. This amount has been temporarily increased to $250,000 until the end of 2013. Then, in 2014, it will revert to $100,000.

Suppose a depositor has $240,000 in savings and $10,000 in a checking account at the bank. All $250,000 would be returned by the FDIC to its owner if the bank were unable to pay. On the other hand, if the person has $256,000 in checking and savings deposits, FDIC insurance covers all but $6,000.

It is possible for that customer to have a separate type of account at the bank (such as a business account). In this case, the total of the customer's accounts is insured up to $250,000. If the person opens an account at another bank, the FDIC also insures this account for $250,000.

8-2
Accounts in commercial banks are insured by the FDIC.

ECONOMICS in ACTION

A Banking System Breakdown

The U.S. economy depends on the flow of money and the services financial institutions provide. When that flow stops, all parts of the economy are negatively affected. Such an event began in the fall of 2008.

Many financial institutions in the United States and around the world lost billions of dollars on risky real estate loans and other investments. Some of them, including banks and big Wall Street financial firms, failed. Other firms were weakened and taken over by stronger companies. Still others received funds from the federal government to help them stay in business.

Even with billions of dollars pumped into the banking system by the federal government, money did not circulate freely. Banks drastically reduced lending, triggering a downward spiral in the economy. Many consumers could not get loans for cars, homes, or other needs. Businesses could not borrow to expand, meet payrolls, or pay for inventories. They grew cautious and cut spending. Firms focused on survival by cutting spending as well as their workforce.

Unemployment grew to new highs. Even consumers who had jobs lost confidence and cut their spending. Demand for goods and services fell. Many businesses posted losses, and eventually some failed. The economy went into a serious recession.

Savings and Loan Associations

Savings and loan associations (S&L) are financial institutions that previously only made mortgage loans and paid dividends on depositors' savings. Today savings and loan associations offer most of the services commercial banks do. They may be state or federally chartered. There are two types of savings and loans.

- Mutual savings and loan associations are owned by and operated for the benefit of their depositors. These depositors receive dividends on their savings.

- Stock savings and loan associations are owned by stockholders. Like commercial banks, these companies operate for profit.

Credit Unions

A **credit union** is a nonprofit financial cooperative owned by and operated for the benefit of its members. Its services are offered only to members. Membership is available through affiliation with an employer, a union, religious organization, community organization, or some other group.

Since credit unions are not-for-profit organizations, they pay no federal income taxes. Members often run them, and operating costs may be relatively low. For these reasons, successful credit unions can lend funds to members at slightly lower rates than other financial institutions. They

3. amount of the check in numbers

4. amount of the check in words

5. reason for writing the check, after the word *Memo,* if you want a record

6. your signature, which should look like that on your bank signature card

For your own protection, write checks in dark ink. If you make a mistake, destroy the check and write a new check. Do not make corrections on the check.

When you write a check, record the check number, date, payee, and amount in your checkbook register. Subtract the check amount from your balance. Record a destroyed check by writing its number and the term *void.* When you make a deposit, also record the date and amount of the deposit and add it to your balance. If you follow these guidelines, you will always know how much money is in your account.

Balancing Your Checkbook

Once you open a checking account, you will generally receive a bank statement each month online or in the mail. A **bank statement** is a record of checks, ATM transactions, deposits, and charges on your account, 8-11.

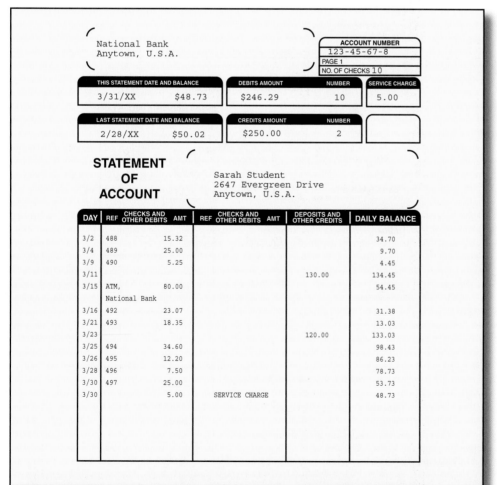

8-11

A bank statement is a record of all deposits, checks, charges, and other transactions involving your account during the statement period.

National Bank
Anytown, U.S.A.

| ACCOUNT NUMBER |
| 123-45-67-8 |
| PAGE 1 |
| NO. OF CHECKS 10 |

THIS STATEMENT DATE AND BALANCE		DEBITS AMOUNT	NUMBER	SERVICE CHARGE
3/31/XX	$48.73	$246.29	10	5.00

LAST STATEMENT DATE AND BALANCE		CREDITS AMOUNT	NUMBER	
2/28/XX	$50.02	$250.00	2	

STATEMENT OF ACCOUNT

Sarah Student
2647 Evergreen Drive
Anytown, U.S.A.

DAY	REF	CHECKS AND OTHER DEBITS AMT	REF	CHECKS AND OTHER DEBITS AMT	DEPOSITS AND OTHER CREDITS	DAILY BALANCE
3/2	488	15.32				34.70
3/4	489	25.00				9.70
3/9	490	5.25				4.45
3/11					130.00	134.45
3/15	ATM, National Bank	80.00				54.45
3/16	492	23.07				31.38
3/21	493	18.35				13.03
3/23					120.00	133.03
3/25	494	34.60				98.43
3/26	495	12.20				86.23
3/28	496	7.50				78.73
3/30	497	25.00				53.73
3/30		5.00		SERVICE CHARGE		48.73

This statement usually begins with a summary of your account. It will tell you the beginning balance, the total amount of checks and other payments, the total of deposits and credits, and the ending balance. The summary will be followed by a detailed listing of

- checks paid, with the date, number, and amount of each
- other items paid, such as withdrawals, fees, and bills you authorized the bank to pay for you
- deposits and credits, with the dates, descriptions, and amounts

Canceled checks or photocopies of checks paid from your account may be enclosed with the statement. The first step in balancing your checkbook is to compare the canceled checks with those recorded in your checkbook register. Compare the deposits in your register with those on the statement and any receipts you may have. Check ATM transactions and fees recorded in your register against those on the statement. If the statement shows any service charges, subtract these from the balance shown in your register. Contact your bank if the statement lists questionable fees or items of which you have no record.

Next, account for the checks, ATM transactions, and deposits you made that have not yet appeared on your statement. There is a worksheet on the back of most bank statements for this, 8-12. On the worksheet, follow these steps:

1. On the first line, write the closing balance as shown on the bank statement.

8-12

This type of worksheet and directions for balancing an account will appear on the back of most bank statements.

BALANCING WORKSHEET

MONTH _March_ , 20 _XX_

BANK BALANCE shown on this statement $ _48.73_

ADD+ $ _125.00_

DEPOSITS made but not shown on statement because made or received after date of this statement.

TOTAL $ _173.73_

SUBTRACT–

CHECKS OUTSTANDING ....∴ $ _68.40_

BALANCE...............$ _105.33_

The above balance should be same as the up-to-date balance in your checkbook.

CHECKS AND DEBITS OUTSTANDING (Written but not shown on statement because not yet received by Bank.)

NO.		
498	28	40
499	15	00
ATM	25	00
TOTAL	68	40

2. List all deposits you made that are not on the statement.

3. Add the amounts from steps 1 and 2. Write the total.

4. List by number and amount any checks and ATM withdrawals not included on the statement. Add these amounts together and enter the total at *Checks outstanding*.

5. Subtract the amount in step 4 from the amount in step 3 and enter the *Balance*.

The balance on your worksheet should match the current balance in your checkbook register. If they do not agree, go through the above steps very carefully to check your math. If the figures still do not agree or come close, you may want to contact your bank for help.

Special-Use Checks

In addition to personal checks, other types of checks can be used to transfer funds from payer to payee. Each serves a special purpose. They are available from most financial institutions, usually for a fee.

Cashier's Check

You buy a *cashier's check* from the bank and use it to make a payment to another person. A **cashier's check** is drawn by a bank on its own funds and signed by an authorized officer of the bank. The bank guarantees payment.

Certified Check

A **certified check** is a personal check with a bank's guarantee the check will be paid. When a bank certifies a check, the amount of the check is immediately subtracted from your account. A certified check is used to make a payment to a payee who does not accept personal checks.

Money Order

A **money order** is an order for a specific amount of money payable to a specific payee. People who do not have checking accounts may use money orders to send payments safely by mail. Money orders are sold in financial institutions, U.S. post offices, and other convenient locations.

Traveler's Checks

People who travel and do not want to carry large amounts of cash often use **traveler's checks**. They can be cashed at many places around the world. If the checks are lost or stolen, they can be replaced at the nearest bank or by the agency selling them. Keep a record of check numbers separate from the checks. You need identifying numbers to replace lost or stolen checks. Sign the checks only at the time you cash them.

Chapter Summary

Financial institutions aid the flow of money in the economy. For consumers they provide key money management services. These include checking, savings, and credit accounts. Most institutions also provide online banking, 24-hour ATMs, and other services to make banking more convenient.

A checking account is the first financial service needed by most consumers. Types of checking accounts include basic, lifeline, and interest-bearing checking accounts. Each meets different consumer needs. Shop around and ask questions before choosing a specific account and financial institution.

Managing a checking account involves certain basic skills—making deposits, writing and endorsing checks, and balancing your account each month.

You may also want to look into the variety of other financial services designed to help consumers manage their money. It pays to shop around for a financial institution offering the services and personal attention you need.

Review

1. What is the primary function of financial institutions in the economy?

2. Name and briefly describe three common financial institutions serving consumers.

3. Describe an electronic funds transfer (EFT) and how it relates to your financial transactions.

4. What are the conveniences of automatic teller machines (ATMs)?

5. What financial transactions can be handled with an online account?

6. When might you need overdraft protection or a stop payment order?

7. List four fees frequently connected with a checking account.

8. Name and describe the three types of checking accounts.

9. What is the purpose of endorsing a check?

10. Name and describe four special-use checks.

Critical Thinking

11. If a person prefers to pay for everything with cash, is a checking account needed?

12. If you had the choice of opening a checking account in a bank or a credit union, which would you choose? Explain your reasoning.

13. Describe three smart ways to use and manage an ATM machine and card.

14. When would a person probably use a cashier's check? a certified check? traveler's checks?

Central Ideas

- Credit is a powerful financial management tool.
- Serious financial problems result from the misuse of credit.

In a cash transaction, you hand over money in exchange for goods or services. Like cash, credit is a medium of exchange. **Credit** allows you to buy goods or services now and pay for them later. More specifically, it is an agreement between two parties in which one party, the **creditor**, supplies money, goods, or services to the other. In return, the receiving party, or the borrower or debtor, agrees to make future payment by a particular date or according to an agreed-upon schedule.

Credit is more costly than cash because fees are usually added to the amount owed. It is costly in another way, too. When you use credit, you spend future income. This means part of your future earnings must be used to pay what you owe. The use of credit reduces future income.

Governments, businesses, and consumers use credit. Credit plays an important role in personal economics. Used carefully and wisely, it can help people get more of the things they need when they need them. Misused credit can lead to financial disaster. It is important for your own financial well being to learn how to manage your credit dollars.

Consumer credit also plays an important role in the economy. It provides the extra buying power needed to support mass production and distribution of goods and services. Therefore, credit helps make more goods and services available to consumers at lower prices.

Understanding Consumer Credit

All credit is based on trust. The creditor believes there is a high likelihood the borrower can and will pay what is owed. For example, suppose you go out to eat with friends. One friend does not have enough money and asks to borrow some of yours. If you trust that friend and can spare the money, you will probably lend it, 9-1.

Credit also has an element of risk. When you lend a friend money, a DVD, or a shirt, you risk that he or she will not return it. An unpaid debt between friends can harm a friendship. If a friend does not pay you back, you will probably not lend to him or her again.

Although a car loan is more complicated, it also depends on the creditor trusting that the borrower will repay the debt. The creditor takes a risk, but that risk is minimized in several ways. Before the loan is made, the borrower must sign a **contract**, a legally binding agreement between the borrower and the creditor. The contract states the terms of the car loan. If the borrower **defaults**, or fails to pay the debt, the creditor can take the borrower to court and even take back the car.

9-1

People usually feel comfortable lending to friends they trust because they believe the debt will be repaid.

Borrowers must pay creditors for the cost of making credit available and for the risk involved in possible defaults. Payment takes the form of interest and other finance charges. This means that a borrower repays not only the **principal**, or amount borrowed, but also the finance charges stated in the contract. That makes buying with credit more costly than paying cash.

Before making credit available, a creditor reviews the borrower's financial history. Just as you may not lend money to someone who does not repay debts, creditors will not lend to a person with a poor credit reputation. Before making a loan offer, creditors already know the likelihood of the borrower defaulting on the loan. If risk of default is high, most reliable creditors will not lend. Less reputable creditors may lend, but with a much higher finance charge and unfavorable terms.

Reasons to Use Credit

You will find it smart to use credit in some situations, but not in others. Several advantages of using credit are listed here.

- *Use of goods and services as you pay for them.* Being able to wear a coat or drive a car as you pay for it can be a big plus. This is a common reason for using credit.

- *Opportunity to buy costly items that you may not be able to buy with cash.* Many people find it difficult or impossible to save enough to pay for a car or hospital bill in one payment. With credit, you can buy goods and services as you need them and pay for them over a

Linking to... History

Role of Credit in the Computer Industry

Consumer credit can help launch a new product. For example, when personal computers first hit the market, prices were high and sales were low. In 1981, around 750 thousand personal computers were being used in homes across the country. By 1991, the number had increased to almost 28 million.

Today, approximately 75 percent of U.S. households have personal computers and Internet access. Since 1980, personal computers improved dramatically. They are more powerful, efficient, and user-friendly. They are also smaller and less expensive. The vast array of software available continues to grow.

Most buyers used some form of consumer credit to pay for their personal computers in the early 80s. The use of credit made it possible for more people to buy. Increased consumer demand supported mass production and distribution while lowering unit production costs. Manufacturers passed on these savings to consumers in the form of lower prices. Growth in the computer industry also financed research and development.

Lower prices sparked even more sales. The industry grew rapidly, bringing exciting job opportunities. More people were hired to sell and service personal computers. New businesses emerged to produce, sell, and rent software and accessories for these computers.

In the case of personal computers, credit stimulated consumer demand and business growth. It helped maintain a healthy balance between supply and demand. Without consumer credit, the industry would have grown less rapidly. Prices would have stayed higher and sales lower. Fewer jobs would have been created and fewer people employed.

period of time. Borrowing is sometimes the only way consumers can pay for major purchases, such as a car.

- *Source of cash for emergency or unexpected expenses.* Even the best money managers face the unexpected. Credit can offer temporary help.

- *Convenience.* Credit eliminates the need to carry large amounts of cash. It provides a record of purchases. It usually simplifies telephone, mail, and Internet shopping as well as necessary returns and exchanges.

- *Sales.* Credit allows you to take advantage of sale prices on goods or services you need when you do not have enough cash at sale time.

- *Long-range goals.* Credit can help consumers make purchases that are part of a long-range financial plan, such as paying for education, furniture, or a vacation.

Drawbacks of Credit Use

To use credit wisely, you need to be aware of its drawbacks as well as its benefits. Consider the negatives when you are deciding how and when to use credit. Here are some disadvantages of using credit:

- *Reduction of future income.* By using credit, you spend future income. You thereby reduce the amount of money you can spend later.

- *Expense.* Using credit usually costs money. The more credit you use and the more time you take to repay, the more you will pay in finance charges. This reduces the amount you will have to spend for other goods and services.

- *Temptation.* Credit makes it easy to spend money you do not have. It can be difficult to resist buying what you cannot afford or can do without when you have ready credit.

- *Risk of serious consequences.* Failure to pay debts on time and in full can cause serious financial problems. You will read about these later in this chapter.

Cost of Credit

When you borrow $10 from a friend, you probably repay the friend an even $10. If you charge purchases or borrow cash in the marketplace, you usually pay finance charges. You pay these charges because it costs businesses money to grant you credit.

The creditors who do not have cash on hand borrow the money to make credit available. When they borrow, they must pay interest. Creditors with cash on hand lose the chance to invest it when they use their money to give you credit. In a sense, they are investing in you, and the interest you pay is their return on investment.

Creditors must also pay the costs of opening and servicing credit accounts. These costs include employees, facilities, and the materials needed to lend money, send out bills, and record payments.

When consumers fail to pay on time or in full, the creditors' costs go up. The expenses of collecting overdue debts and absorbing the losses of unpaid accounts add up quickly. As a result, the price of credit goes up for all consumers, even those who pay on time.

Case Study: Using Credit

The Credit Game

Chiyo graduated from college recently and has a steady job. She wants the convenience of charging purchases, so she opens a credit card.

Chiyo's first credit card bill is almost $600. Since she did not keep track of her charges, the bill is a surprise. Her paycheck is only $1,035 a month after deductions. After paying rent and other expenses, she has only $30 left to pay on her credit account each month.

Chiyo didn't need most of the credit card purchases. It takes her 24 months to pay off the debt. She pays over $118 in finance charges.

Damian looks at credit as a useful tool. He realizes the importance of establishing credit so he can get loans in the future. Besides, he doesn't think it is realistic to buy everything with cash.

Although Damian is happy to have his credit card, he is a little afraid of it. His family had some debt problems when he was younger.

Damian uses his credit card sparingly and keeps track of his charges. He limits his overall debt to an amount he can repay. He uses credit only for things he really needs. His first purchase is a pair of waterproof boots he buys on sale. Damian uses his credit card because he doesn't have enough cash. If he waited until payday, the boots would no longer be on sale. By using credit wisely, Damian saves $20.

Case Review

1. How does offering credit work in the interest of sellers?
2. How can the use of credit work for consumers? How can it create problems?
3. What advice would you give Chiyo for the future use of credit?
4. What did you learn from Damian's example?
5. How can consumers enjoy the benefits and avoid the problems of using credit?

Finance Charges

The finance charge is the total dollar cost of credit. It is the dollar amount paid for credit. A finance charge has two parts: interest and fees.

For example, a $1,000 loan may have a finance charge of $50, which is $10 in fees and $40 in interest. When you apply for credit, the interest you pay depends on the *annual percentage rate (APR)*, the amount of credit used, and the length of the repayment period. Here is how these factors work to determine the cost of credit.

Annual Percentage Rate

The finance charge you pay for the use of credit is expressed as a percentage. An **annual percentage rate (APR)** is the annual cost of credit a lender charges. The higher the APR, the more you pay. For example, the interest for a $500 loan repaid in 12 monthly payments would cost

- $50.08 at 18 percent
- $58.72 at 21 percent
- $67.36 at 24 percent

Amount of Credit Used

The more you charge or borrow, the more interest you pay. For example, the interest on a loan repaid in 12 monthly payments at an annual percentage rate of 18 percent would cost

- $50.08 for a $500 loan
- $110.01 for a $1,000 loan
- $220.02 for a $2,000 loan

Length of the Repayment Period

The more time you take to repay the money you borrow, the more interest you will pay. For example, the interest on a $500 loan at 1.5 percent per month (18 percent per year) would cost

- $50.08 if repaid in 12 monthly payments
- $99.44 if repaid in 24 monthly payments
- $150.88 if repaid in 36 monthly payments

Loan Officers

Loan officers work for financial institutions. They assist in gathering documentation that is needed for loan approval. They analyze and assess the creditworthiness of potential borrowers to determine if they qualify for a loan.

Types of Credit

There are many types of consumer credit and ways to categorize them. The following are widely used terms you should know.

Closed-End Credit

Closed-end credit refers to a loan that must be repaid with finance charges by a certain date. These loans are given for a specific purpose, and include car loans, student loans, and most home loans, 9-2.

Loans are granted by commercial banks, credit unions, finance companies, insurance companies, and credit card agencies. When you take out a loan, you sign a contract stating the amount of the loan, the interest rate, length of the loan, and other provisions of the agreement.

A **secured loan** requires collateral. **Collateral** is property that a borrower promises to give up in case of default. If you fail to pay as agreed, the creditor may take the property to settle the claim against you. You may pay lower finance charges on a secured loan because the creditor takes less risk when collateral is pledged. The car is collateral in an auto loan.

An *unsecured loan* is made on the strength of your signature alone. You sign a contract and promise to repay according to terms of the agreement. It is difficult to obtain a loan of this type unless you have a strong credit rating. If you have nothing to pledge as collateral, you still may be able to get a loan if you have a cosigner. A **cosigner** is a responsible person who signs the loan with you. By signing the loan, the cosigner promises to repay the loan if you fail to pay. Unsecured loans usually have higher interest rates than secured loans.

Most closed-end credit is offered in the form of installment loans. An *installment loan* lets you borrow a given amount of money and repay it with interest in regular installments. Finance charges vary with the size of the loan, the interest rate, and the repayment period. Interest rates vary with different lenders and with the collateral pledged.

9-2

Home loans are a type of closed-end credit that homeowners repay by a certain date.

Open-End Credit

Open-end credit allows the borrower to use a certain amount of money for an indefinite period of time. As long as the borrower makes payments on a schedule, pays any finance charges, and stays within the borrowing limit, he or she can continue to use the credit.

One example of open-end credit is a credit card. Retailers, merchants, banks, credit agencies, and other businesses that issue credit cards to consumers offer open-end credit. Terms may differ slightly with different creditors and in different states.

Two common types of open-end credit are regular charge accounts and revolving credit accounts. A *regular charge account* lets you charge goods and services in exchange for your promise to pay in full within 25 days of the billing date. You receive a bill or statement each month. If you pay on time, there is no finance charge.

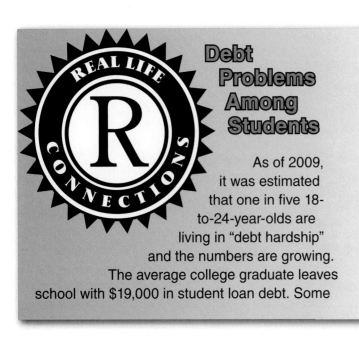

Debt Problems Among Students

As of 2009, it was estimated that one in five 18- to-24-year-olds are living in "debt hardship" and the numbers are growing. The average college graduate leaves school with $19,000 in student loan debt. Some students have as much as $40,000. Those in professional schools such as law, medicine, and dentistry may incur debts as high as $100,000 by graduation. Credit card debt may add another $3,000 to $7,000 to these obligations. The fact is more students drop out of college today for financial concerns than for academic failure. Students should try to explore every possible way to pay for their education without incurring excessive debt. They should consider savings, scholarships, low-tuition schools, work/study programs, part-time jobs, government aid programs, and other means of paying for education and training.

A *revolving credit account* offers you a choice of paying in full each month or spreading payments over a period of time. If you choose not to pay in full, there is a finance charge.

You must make at least the minimum payment each month. For small balances, the minimum payment is usually a set amount, such as $10. For larger amounts of credit, the minimum payment is usually a percentage of the unpaid balance.

A typical revolving credit account places a limit on the total amount you may owe at any one time. You may make any number of purchases at any time as long as you do not exceed your credit limit. This type of credit is available through many retailers and through issuers of credit cards, such as Visa, MasterCard, and Discover. They can be used to buy goods and services from any seller who honors the card you carry.

Establishing Credit

You may find it difficult to get credit at first. This is because creditors want evidence that you can and will pay your debts. Here are some steps you can take to build a sound financial reputation.

1. *Start with a job.* Prove that you can earn money.

2. *Open a savings account.* Saving regularly shows a responsible attitude toward financial matters. Your savings also may serve as collateral for a loan.

3. *Open a checking account.* A well-managed checking account shows you have experience in handling money.

4. *Apply to a local department store or a gasoline company for a credit card.* If you are granted credit, make small purchases and pay promptly. This will give you a record of steady payments.

If you have never used credit, you will need to establish a credit rating from scratch.

Your Credit Rating

Creditors decide whether or not to grant people credit based on their credit ratings. A *credit rating* is the creditor's evaluation of your willingness and ability to pay debts. It is measured by the three Cs:

- *Character*—based on your reputation for honesty and your financial history. The person who has a record of paying bills on time and of assuming financial responsibility will rate high on character.

- *Capacity*—your ability to earn money and pay debts. It is measured by your earning power and employment history.

- *Capital*—your financial worth. People with land, a home, cars, savings, or anything of value have capital. Capital gives a person a more favorable credit rating.

A **creditworthy** applicant is judged to have the assets, income, and tendency to repay debt.

The Credit Report

How do lenders get the information to evaluate a consumer's creditworthiness? They look at the application and whether the prospective borrower has a job. They may contact references listed on the application. An important factor is the length of the credit history. If you are unemployed or never have used credit, it may be difficult to get a loan or credit card.

Most lenders also turn to *credit reporting agencies*. A *credit reporting agency*, or credit bureau, is an organization that collects information about the financial and credit transactions of consumers. Businesses notify the credit reporting agencies when a consumer opens a new account, closes an account, or skips or makes late payments.

There are three major national credit reporting agencies: Equifax, Experian, and TransUnion LLC. Once you begin to use credit, you will automatically establish a record at a credit-reporting agency. These agencies sell credit reports to creditors.

A **credit report** is a record of a person's credit history and financial behavior. It includes every credit account ever opened and outstanding balances on current credit accounts. It also lists negative information such as *delinquent* or late payments and overdue taxes. The information on credit reports from the different agencies does not always match up. Carefully review your credit report and check key information in each section, 9-3. If you find errors, contact the credit reporting agency for instructions on filing a dispute.

Your credit report largely determines whether you can get credit when you need it. With a poor report, you will have trouble getting credit and may have to pay higher finance charges.

9-3

A credit report shows if a person has used credit wisely.

How to Read a Credit Report	
Section	**What to Check**
Personal Information	Verify your personal information, such as your name, address, phone number, date of birth, and Social Security number.
Credit Summary	This section summarizes your revolving and installment accounts and any home loans. Check the balances and your total amount of outstanding debt.
Account Information (also called *Credit Items)*	Make sure all accounts listed belong to you. This section may be lengthy, but it is important to check all details for accuracy, including payment history, balance, and account status. Late payments and accounts taken over by collection agencies appear in this section.
Public Records (also called *Negative Information or Items)*	Any bankruptcies, garnishments, or liens are shown here. Ideally, this section should be blank.
Inquiries (also called *Credit History Requests)*	Look over the list of creditors that recently viewed your credit report. Applying for a credit card, taking out a loan, submitting an apartment application, or applying for insurance can trigger inquiries.

Credit Scores

Creditors also evaluate creditworthiness by looking at *credit scores*. A credit score is a numerical measure of a loan applicant's creditworthiness at a particular point in time. It is generated primarily by credit reporting agencies.

Your credit score may differ from one credit reporting agency to another. Each agency has access to different information and uses different mathematical formulas to calculate scores. However, the scores for the same person are usually similar. A credit score is based on the following:

- *Bill paying.* You score high here if you have a record of paying your bills on time.

- *Debt-to-credit-limit ratio.* Your debt is the total of all you owe on credit cards, car loans, home loans, and so forth. Your credit limit is the total amount you are allowed under credit card maximums and your original loan amounts. A lower ratio is best.

- *Credit history length.* The longer you have used well-managed credit card accounts, the better.

- *Recent credit application.* Several applications for new credit accounts can have a negative effect on your credit score.

- *Different types of credit.* Having a mix of loans and credit cards is slightly favored over using only one type of credit.

The higher a credit score, the greater a person's creditworthiness. However, what is considered a good credit score varies. For example, the credit-reporting agency Experian uses a scoring system based on letters, such as the grades you receive in class, 9-4.

What one creditor considers a good score may not be good enough for another. What a creditor considers a good score today may be too low for that same creditor tomorrow. When credit is tight, creditors look for higher credit scores before granting a credit request. A person's credit score changes as his or her financial history and obligations change.

Credit Score Ratings

This is how Experian rated credit scores in early 2009.

- **A: 901 to 990.** Consumers in this group have a low risk of defaulting on loans and lenders offer them the best rates and terms.
- **B: 801 to 900.** Consumers in this group have managed their credit well and are offered good rates and terms by lenders.
- **C: 701 to 800.** Lenders may consider consumers in this group for loans, but often require more information.
- **D: 601 to 700.** Consumers in this group have a higher default rate. Lenders may give them credit, but only at a higher interest rate.
- **F: 501 to 600.** Consumers in this group have a high risk of defaulting on loans. Lenders will often deny them credit. If they get credit, they pay higher interest rates.

9-4

In early 2009, the U.S. average credit score, according to Experian, was 692.

Getting a Credit Card

Credit cards are most often used to buy goods and services on a time-payment plan. You pay for the purchase later, plus interest. Some credit cards may also be used to obtain cash. There are three common types of credit cards:

- *General-purpose cards,* such as Visa or MasterCard, are issued by banks, credit unions, and other financial institutions. You can use these cards around the world at the many places where they are accepted. Very often, you can also obtain cash at automated teller machines using these cards. They carry a credit limit and require minimum monthly payments. Finance charges and other fees vary.

- *Company or retail store cards,* issued by service stations, local merchants, or chain stores, permit you to charge purchases only with the merchant issuing the card. Normally, you have a credit limit and are required to repay a minimum amount each month. Finance charges vary.

- *Travel and entertainment cards* usually require you to pay the entire balance each month. Some cards allow you to pay over a longer period for travel- and vacation-related expenses such as airfare, tours, cruises, and hotel bills. On these balances, you usually pay a high interest rate and must make minimum monthly payments.

How Credit Cards Work

This example illustrates how a typical credit card is used. Valerie opens a revolving charge account at a local department store. She is issued a credit card. In May, she charges $85 on her credit card. This amount is more than she wants to pay in June when the bill comes. She decides to pay the minimum payment of $10. During June, she charges another $15 worth of merchandise.

In July, the bill totals $91.13. This includes the $75 unpaid balance from June, a 1.5 percent finance charge of $1.13, and $15 for new purchases.

Case Study: Using Credit

Ty's "Deal"

Ty is buying a motorcycle. He's so excited about his new bike that he closes the deal right away and finances with the seller.

He rides away on his new bike feeling great until he runs into his friend Sara. She explains how credit charges differ from lender to lender. The chart below compares Ty's deal with two other sources for a $2,000 loan financed over a 24-month period. Failing to shop for credit was an expensive mistake.

Comparing Credit Sources			
	Ty's Deal	Source 1	Source 2
Annual Rate	15%	10%	12%
Monthly Payment	$96.35	$92.01	$93.75
Total Payments (monthly × 24)	$2,312.40	$2,208.24	$2,250.00
Down Payment	$250.00	$250.00	$250.00
Total Paid	$2,562.40	$2,458.24	$2,500.00
Finance Charges (total payments less $2,000)	$312.40	$208.24	$250.00

Case Review

1. What should Ty have done before financing through the seller of the motorcycle?
2. How much money could Ty have saved by financing at a 10 percent annual rate?
3. How many months would you take to pay off a loan of this type? How would this affect your finance charges?
4. How much time would you be willing to spend looking for the best loan terms?
5. How would you have handled Ty's situation differently?

Now Valerie can continue to make minimum payments or pay her account in full.

Since Valerie's credit limit is $1,000, she can continue to charge merchandise until her unpaid balance reaches that limit. As her unpaid balance goes up, so will the minimum monthly payment and the finance charge.

Making minimum payments increases the cost of credit and the amount of time it will take to pay it off. Pay off the balance in full each month to avoid finance charges.

Shopping for a Credit Card

Shopping for credit is as important as shopping for the goods and services you buy with it. When you want to borrow cash or use credit to finance a purchase, shop around for the best credit terms. The more you borrow, the more you pay. The higher the annual percentage rate, the more you pay. The longer you take to repay, the more you pay in credit charges.

The Contract

When you apply for credit, you will be asked to fill out a credit application form like the one in 9-5. This form helps creditors evaluate your financial standing and credit rating.

Using credit involves certain responsibilities for you and the creditor. These are spelled out in credit contracts and agreements. The terms outlined in a written agreement are legally binding. They can be enforced in courts of law if you or the creditor fails to carry out the terms of the contract. It is very important to understand exactly what you are agreeing to do before you sign any contract.

Read the contract thoroughly. Be sure all blank spaces have been filled. None should be left open for someone to fill later. Make sure the annual percentage rate and the dollar cost are stated clearly and accurately. Ask questions if there are any terms you do not fully understand.

Study the contract to find out what action the creditor can take if you pay late or fail to make a payment. Also find out if you can pay in advance. If so, check to see if part of the finance charges will be refunded.

Contract Clauses to Avoid

Watch for an *acceleration clause* that allows the creditor to require full and immediate payment of the entire balance if you miss a payment or fail to abide by the terms of the contract.

For a home loan or an installment loan, find out whether the contract calls for a *balloon payment*. This is a final payment considerably larger than the regular monthly or periodic payments and it is required to retire the loan. If a balloon payment is required, find out the amount and your options if you are unable to make this final payment. Can you refinance? If so, under what terms?

Be wary of *add-on clauses* that allow you to buy additional items before paying in full for goods you have already purchased. The clause may allow

9-5

This application form helps creditors evaluate your credit worthiness. Note the questions on the form.

BELK CREDIT APPLICATION

EMPLOYEE NO.	DATE

Type of Account Requested:
□ INDIVIDUAL   □ JOINT

PLEASE TELL US ABOUT YOURSELF

FIRST NAME (TITLES OPTIONAL) | MIDDLE INITIAL | LAST NAME | AGE

STREET ADDRESS (IF P.O. BOX — PLEASE GIVE STREET ADDRESS) | CITY | STATE | ZIP

□ OWN   □ LIVE WITH RELATIVE | MONTHLY PAYMENT | YEARS AT PRESENT ADDRESS | HOME PHONE NO. | NO. OF
□ RENT   □ OTHER | $ | | ( ) | DEPENDENTS

PREVIOUS ADDRESS | CITY | STATE | ZIP | HOW LONG

NAME OF NEAREST RELATIVE NOT LIVING WITH YOU | RELATIONSHIP | PHONE NO. ( )

ADDRESS | CITY | STATE

NOW TELL US ABOUT YOUR JOB

EMPLOYER OR INCOME SOURCE | POSITION/TITLE | HOW LONG EMPLOYED YRS.   MOS. | MONTHLY INCOME $

EMPLOYER'S ADDRESS | CITY | STATE | TYPE OF BUSINESS | BUSINESS PHONE ( )

MILITARY RANK (IF NOW IN SERVICE) | SEPARATION DATE | UNIT AND DUTY STATION | SOCIAL SECURITY NO.

SOURCE OF OTHER INCOME (Alimony, child support, or separate maintenance need not be revealed if you do not wish to have it considered as a basis for repaying this obligation) | SOURCE | INCOME $ | □ MONTHLY □ ANNUALLY

AND YOUR CREDIT REFERENCES ARE

NAME AND ADDRESS OF BANK/SAVINGS AND LOAN □ CHECKING □ SAVINGS □ LOAN | PREVIOUS BELK OR LEGGETT ACCOUNT? □ YES □ NO
ACCOUNT NO.
HOW IS ACCOUNT LISTED?

List Bank cards, Dept. Stores, Finance Co.'s, and other accounts:

NAME	ACCOUNT NO.	BALANCE	PAYMENT
		$	$
		$	$
		$	$
		$	$

INFORMATION REGARDING JOINT APPLICANT

COMPLETE THIS AREA IF □ JOINT ACCOUNT IS REQUESTED □ YOU ARE RELYING ON SPOUSE'S INCOME OR CREDIT HISTORY TO OBTAIN CREDIT

FIRST NAME | MIDDLE INITIAL | LAST NAME | AGE | RELATIONSHIP | SOCIAL SECURITY NO.

JOINT APPLICANT'S ADDRESS IF DIFFERENT FROM APPLICANT
ADDRESS | CITY | STATE | ZIP

JOINT APPLICANT'S PRESENT EMPLOYER | ADDRESS | HOW LONG EMPLOYED YRS.   MOS.

BUSINESS PHONE ( ) | POSITION/TITLE | MONTHLY INCOME $

YOUR SIGNATURE PLEASE

Store Stamp Below

I have read and agree to the Terms and Conditions of the Belk Retail Charge Agreement as set forth on attached. Belk is authorized to investigate my credit record and exchange credit experience with other creditors and Credit Reporting Agencies. This information is given to obtain credit, and is true and complete.

FOR OFFICE USE ONLY
Letter _____
CB. RPT. _____
EMP. VER _____

Applicant's Signature   Date

DATE	EMP.	#CARDS	T/C	CR/LN.	APPROVED

Joint Applicant's signature
(required if joint applicant section completed)   Date

the seller to hold a security interest in the items purchased first until you pay for later purchases in full. For example, you buy a washer and dryer, but before paying for them you add a refrigerator. The seller can hold title to the washer and dryer until you also pay for the refrigerator.

Read credit contracts thoroughly with particular attention to possible fees, penalties, and consequences of failing to carry out all the terms of the agreement. Do not sign until you fully understand all the terms and the obligations you are assuming.

Disclosures

By law, credit card offers must include certain disclosures or credit terms, 9-6. Before accepting and using any of these cards, you need to read the fine print on any contract you sign and ask questions. Knowing the exact cost of credit can help you compare finance charges and find the best

Annual percentage rate (APR) for purchases	2.9% until 11/1/XX after that, 14.9%
Other APRs	Cash-advance APR: 15.9% Balance-Transfer APR: 15.9% Penalty rate: 23.9% See explanation below.*
Variable-rate information	Your APR for purchase transactions may vary. The rate is determined monthly by adding 5.9% to the Prime Rate.**
Grace period for repayment of balances for purchases	25 days on average
Method of computing the balance for purchases	Average daily balance (excluding new purchases)
Annual fees	None
Minimum finance charge	$0.50

Transaction fee for cash advances: 3% of the amount advanced

Balance-transfer fee: 3% of the amount transferred

Late-payment fee: $25

Over-the-credit-limit fee: $25

* Explanation of penalty. If your payment arrives more than ten days late two times within a six month period, the penalty rate will apply.

** The Prime Rate used to determine your APR is the rate published in the Wall Street Journal on the 10th day of the prior month.

Adapted from the brochure *Choosing a Credit Card*, Board of Governors of the Federal Reserve System

9-6

On credit card application forms, disclosures are usually shown in a box similar to this one.

deal. It also helps you decide how much credit you can afford to use. The application should include the following information.

Annual Percentage Rates

The APR must be disclosed. This is the finance charge on unpaid balances. There is usually one rate for purchases and a higher rate for cash advances.

The issuing companies often offer an attractive "introductory rate" that lasts only three to six months, after which you pay the considerably higher regular rate. In this case, it is important to check how long the introductory rate lasts and what the regular rate is.

In addition, know the terms of the rate. Can the credit card company raise the rate for any reason, such as missing a payment on this card?

Variable-Rate Information

Interest rates can be fixed or variable. A *variable interest rate* fluctuates with the ups and downs of the economy. It can start out low and reset to a higher rate. A *fixed interest rate* stays the same, although under certain conditions such as a late payment, it can change.

Grace Period

A **grace period** is the time between the billing date and the start of interest charges. You have that time to pay the full balance without interest.

In a few states, a grace period is mandatory on any new charges made each month. Interest may only be figured on outstanding balances from the prior month. There are no interest charges on credit card balances that are paid in full by the due date each month.

Method of Computing the Balance

It is important to understand how interest is calculated. If you pay less than the full amount owed each month, you will pay interest on the unpaid balance. Creditors compute interest charges in different ways. Their methods can result in very different actual finance charges, 9-7. You need to read the fine print on credit agreements and monthly statements to learn what methods are used to calculate interest. Creditors are required by law to provide an explanation.

Annual Fee

Find out whether you must pay an annual fee for the privilege of using the card. These fees can be as much as $50 or more. It pays to look for cards with low or no annual fees.

Other Fees

It pays to know what extras can be charged to your account and how you can avoid these charges. These may include fees for

- late payments

- exceeding your credit limit

- cash advances

- balance transfers

Shop around for the best credit card deal. You can compare cards, interest rates, fees, and features online as well as by contacting individual credit card issuers.

Rewards

You may want to find out whether there are any perks or rewards associated with using a certain credit card. These may include cash-back offers, no-interest introductory offers, credits for purchases of certain goods and services, and other incentives. You want to weigh the value of any rewards against the costs and fees associated with each card.

Subprime Credit Cards

Subprime credit cards are cards offered to people who have a poor credit history. Often they carry very high interest rates, large annual fees, sign-up fees, participation fees, late payment penalties, and other charges.

Bankruptcy

When financial circumstances are desperate, some debtors have little choice but to file for personal *bankruptcy*. **Bankruptcy** is a legal state in which the courts excuse a debtor from repaying some or all debt. In return, the debtor must give up certain assets and possessions. The *Bankruptcy Act* allows debtors to file "Chapter 7" or "Chapter 13" bankruptcy.

- *Chapter 7 Bankruptcy.* The court declares the person unable to meet financial obligations. Most debts are discharged or forgiven. This is also referred to as *straight bankruptcy*. The court then takes and sells the debtor's property and possessions. Proceeds from the sale are divided among the creditors. The law exempts certain assets and possessions: a small equity in a home, an inexpensive car, and limited personal property.

- *Chapter 13 Bankruptcy.* This plan permits debtors with regular incomes to pay all or a portion of their debts under the protection and supervision of the court. The court sets up a three- to five-year repayment schedule. It also establishes the monthly amount to be paid toward debts. Once the court accepts the debtor's petition, creditors may not take action against the debtor. This plan has three advantages over straight bankruptcy. The debtor fulfills credit obligations, keeps most of his or her own property and possessions, and maintains a reasonably sound credit rating.

Some types of debt cannot be wiped out by declaring bankruptcy. These include most student loans, alimony, child support, and many types of taxes.

The consequences of filing bankruptcy can haunt a debtor for many years. Once a court declares that people are bankrupt, a report stays in the credit records for 10 years. They may be denied loans or credit cards, or only be granted credit at inflated interest rates. They may be denied a job, a business loan, insurance, or housing by anyone who sees their credit report.

Bankruptcy, even for unavoidable reasons, often carries a stigma. People who file bankruptcy may be viewed as dishonest or untrustworthy. They may be considered irresponsible for not paying their debts. For these reasons, bankruptcy is a last resort.

The Easy-Access Credit Trap

You have probably heard the term **loan shark**. It refers to someone who loans money at excessive rates of interest. They usually use predatory lending tactics and offer easy-access credit. **Easy-access credit** refers to short-term loans granted regardless of credit history at high interest rates. Even people who are poor credit risks can get these loans if the practice is considered legal in their state. Easy-access credit includes the following:

- **Payday loan.** These are short-term, high interest loans that must usually be repaid on the borrower's next payday. Repayment is guaranteed by the borrower's personal check at the time of the loan or by access to the borrower's bank account. Payday loans carry extremely high finance charges, but some states have laws that limit them.

- **Pawnshops.** A pawnshop is a business that gives customers high-interest loans with personal property, such as jewelry, held as collateral. Some pawnshops offer payday loans, too.

- **Rent-to-own.** This is an arrangement in which a consumer pays rent for the use of a product and eventually owns it. The advantage is little or no initial payment. The disadvantage to the consumer is paying much more than the product's purchase price by the time the final payment is made.

- **Title loan**. A short-term loan is made using a borrower's car as collateral. The cost of these loans is high and the borrower risks losing his or her car.

Here is an example of how easy-access credit differs from legitimate sources of credit. Suppose you borrow $1,000 by using a credit card cash advance. The APR is 21.99 percent. That is equivalent to a monthly interest rate of 1.833 percent (APR divided by 12). If you repaid the money in a month, you would pay an $18.33 finance charge.

Contrast that to what you would pay if you borrowed from a payday loan company. Finance charges are often $15 or more for every $100 borrowed. At $15, you would pay $150 to borrow $1,000. To get the loan, you write a check for $1,150. You get $1,000 and must pay this back in two weeks.

If you do not have the money, like many borrowers, you can roll the loan over for another two weeks for an additional finance charge. You owe the lender another $150. After one month, you have paid $300 in fees. What is the annual equivalent of this interest rate? If you continued to roll over the loan for a year, the APR would be 350 percent, or $3,600!

Inform Creditors

If you have trouble paying your bills, notify creditors promptly. Many reputable creditors will work with you. They may help you by renegotiating repayment schedules, or setting up a repayment program you can handle. They may be willing to extend your repayment schedules to lower the size of your monthly payments. Of course this will cost you more in credit charges in the long run, but it may help you get through a difficult period.

The quicker you realize you are having financial problems, the quicker and easier it will be to correct them. It pays to tackle these problems before they get beyond your control.

Get Credit Counseling

With a sound financial spending and savings plan, some people can correct their own financial problems. However, when financial problems get out of control, it is time to look for outside help. Following are some possible options. Be cautious of "credit doctors" and for-profit credit repair clinics that promise to fix your credit rating for a fee. These companies promise what no one can deliver. Read on for more reliable options.

Debt Counselors

Debt counselors help clients resolve financial difficulties. They provide financial counseling about debt, credit, money management, budgeting, and housing issues.

One reliable source of help for people with credit problems is a *credit counseling service.* A credit counseling service is an organization that provides debt and financial management advice and services to people with debt problems at little or no cost. The National Foundation for Consumer Credit sponsors several hundred credit counseling services throughout the United States and Canada. The credit counseling services, with the support of local merchants and financial institutions, offer aid in two forms.

The service helps a debtor with a stable income work out a practical financial program for repaying debts, 9-10. The service also helps the debtor plan and control current expenses to avoid further debts.

When debtors are very deep in debt, the counseling service offers another alternative. It tries to arrange new repayment plans with creditors. If creditors agree, the debtor gives the counseling service a set amount from each paycheck, and the service pays the creditors. Credit counseling services of this type help about five of every six applicants.

9-10

Credit counselors help clients develop a plan to get out of debt.

Finding a Reputable Company

Unfortunately, some of the businesses that claim to be nonprofit credit counseling services are not. These include debt negotiation or debt adjusting businesses that charge high fees. The fees cause their clients to fall deeper into debt.

A company that charges high fees or demands that the debtor pay them rather than their creditors should be avoided. Debtors should pay little or nothing for the help they receive. Claims that are too good to be true indicate a problem. This might be a guarantee that they can make debt disappear or dramatically reduce total debt. Also be suspicious of those who claim an ability to remove accurate negative information from credit reports.

Consumers can contact their local consumer protection agency to get a referral to a reputable consumer credit counseling service. The U.S. Trustee Program of the Department of Justice maintains a list of credit counseling agencies approved for prebankruptcy counseling. The list is found on their Web site. It also is a good idea to check with the local Better Business Bureau or the state attorney general's office for reports of consumer complaints against specific companies.

Consumer Credit Legislation

Over the years a number of federal laws have been passed to protect consumers when they use credit. The key points of the most important credit legislation are outlined in the following sections.

Truth in Lending Law

The *Truth in Lending Law*, passed in 1969, requires creditors to tell consumers what credit will cost them before they use it. Under this law, credit contracts and agreements must include

- the amount financed or borrowed

- the total number, amount, and due dates of payments

- the finance charge in dollar amount and annual percentage rate

- all charges not included in the finance charge

- penalties or charges for late payment, default, or prepayment

- a description of any security held by the creditor

For merchandise purchased on time, creditors must provide additional information. This includes a description of the merchandise, the cash price and the deferred payment price, and the down payment or trade-in. The Truth in Lending Law also prohibits creditors from issuing credit cards you have not requested.

Equal Credit Opportunity Act

The *Equal Credit Opportunity Act*, passed in 1975, prohibits credit grantors from discriminating against consumers on the basis of sex, marital status, race, national origin, religion, age, or the receipt of public assistance. This means credit can be denied only for financial reasons and not for any of the factors listed above. When applicants are turned down, creditors must provide a written explanation of why credit was denied.

Fair Credit Reporting Act

Passed in 1971 and revised in 1977, the *Fair Credit Reporting Act* requires accuracy and privacy of information contained in credit reports. If you are refused credit because of information supplied by a credit reporting agency, this law gives you the right to

- receive the name and address of the reporting agency that sent the report

- find out from the reporting agency what facts are on file, the source of the information, and who has received the information

- require a recheck of any information you find to be false

- receive a corrected report if errors are found

- require the agency to send the corrected report to all creditors who received false information

Fair Credit Billing Act

The *Fair Credit Billing Act*, passed in 1975, protects consumers against unfair billing practices. It outlines the procedures to follow in resolving billing errors or disputes. The law requires creditors to send customers a written explanation of steps to take when questions arise concerning bills. The customer has 60 days after receiving a bill to notify the creditor of an error, 9-11. The creditor must answer within 30 days. Within 90 days, the creditor must either correct the bill or explain if it is accurate. Creditors may take no collection action on amounts in question until billing disputes are resolved. However, the customer must pay any amount not in question.

Electronic Funds Transfer Act

Electronic Funds Transfer (EFT) systems use electronic impulses to activate financial transactions instead of cash, checks, or paper records. The *Electronic Funds Transfer Act* protects consumers in these transactions by

- prohibiting the distribution of unrequested EFT cards. You receive a card only if you ask for it.

- requiring issuers of EFT cards to provide cardholders with written information outlining their rights and responsibilities for the card and its use.

- limiting to $50 the liability for unauthorized transfer. The cardholder must notify the issuer of card loss or misuse within two business days.

- requiring issuers to provide cardholders with printed receipts of EFT transactions.

- requiring issuers to promptly investigate and correct EFT errors.

9-11
Under the Fair Credit Billing Act, customers have a certain amount of time to resolve billing disputes.

Fair Debt Collection Practices Act

Passed in 1978, the *Fair Debt Collection Practices Act* protects consumers against unfair methods of collecting debts. According to this law, debt collectors may not

- reveal or publicize a debtor's debt to other people

- contact debtors at inconvenient times (before 8 a.m. or after 9 p.m.) or places (such as work)

- use threats or abusive language

- make annoying, repeated, or anonymous phone calls

- make false or misleading statements about the collector's identity or the consequences of nonpayment

- collect unauthorized fees or charge debtors for calls and telegrams

Preservation of Consumers' Claims and Defenses Ruling

The *Preservation of Consumers' Claims and Defenses Ruling* was issued by the Federal Trade Commission. It protects debtors from being forced to pay for goods and services when they have a legitimate dispute with the seller of those goods or services.

This applies when a retailer sells consumer credit obligations or contracts to a third party creditor. The consumer then owes the third party. If the goods or services purchased with credit are unsatisfactory, the debtor still owes the third party rather than the seller. For this reason, the seller does not feel obligated to correct any problems with the goods or services.

This ruling greatly limits the "holder-in-due-course doctrine." That doctrine says the holder of a consumer contract has a right to collect a debt regardless of any unfair practices on the part of the seller.

Here is an example to show how the rule protects you. Suppose you buy a $500 TV from the Viewing Center. You sign an installment contract calling for 18 monthly payments. The Viewing Center offers credit through a sales finance company. Therefore, you owe the finance company rather than the seller.

After the television is delivered, you find that it does not work. You can get sound but no picture. When you complain, the seller refuses to correct the problem. You threaten nonpayment. The seller says that is not the Viewing Center's problem because you owe the finance company.

You complain to the finance company, but they tell you the television is the seller's responsibility. Legally, you owe the finance company regardless of the seller's performance.

The Preservation of Consumers' Claims and Defenses Ruling protects you in this type of situation. Under the ruling, you have a right to a legal defense in court if you refuse to pay a creditor because you have a dispute with a seller.

Bankruptcy Abuse Prevention and Consumer Protection Act

The main goal of federal law, passed in 2005, was to make the bankruptcy system fairer to both debtors and creditors. However, it has been criticized for disproportionately benefiting the credit card industry.

It made filing for Chapter 7 bankruptcy more difficult. Those who are allowed to file must pass a "means test" that takes into account factors such as income and assets. Those who do not pass the means test must file for Chapter 13 bankruptcy that requires some repayment of debt. Another provision of the law requires debtors to get credit and financial counseling before filing for bankruptcy.

Chapter Summary

Using credit has both advantages and disadvantages. Knowing when to use it and understanding the different types of credit can help consumers enjoy the benefits of using credit and avoid credit problems. Credit use impacts a person's credit rating. Credit reporting agencies use credit scores to summarize a person's payment history, debt owed, and credit account use.

Opening a credit card and using it responsibly is one way to build a good credit rating. When shopping for a credit card, read each contract carefully, know the clauses to avoid, and compare disclosures. Before using credit, consider other alternatives. Some ways to avoid credit problems include tracking spending, checking monthly statements, reviewing credit reports annually, and reporting lost or stolen cards.

Consumers can resolve credit problems by informing creditors when serious financial problems arise and seeking credit counseling. Federal laws protect consumers in many ways, including requiring creditors to disclose the cost of credit, preventing unfair billing practices, and regulating debt collection methods.

Review

1. How does a credit transaction differ from a cash transaction?

2. List three advantages and three disadvantages of using credit.

3. What three factors determine the amount you pay in finance charges?

4. Explain the difference between closed-end and open-end credit. Give an example of each.

5. What steps can you take to build a sound credit rating?

6. What is the function of a credit reporting agency?

7. What factors influence a person's credit score?

8. What contract clauses should be avoided when applying for a credit card? Explain each clause.

9. Explain the difference between variable interest rates and fixed interest rates.

10. What are subprime credit cards?

11. What are some alternatives to using credit?

12. How can consumers obtain free copies of credit reports? How often are free copies available?

13. What are the advantages of filing bankruptcy under Chapter 13 instead of Chapter 7?

14. How can credit-counseling services help debt-troubled individuals and families?

15. What is the purpose of the Equal Credit Opportunity Act?

Critical Thinking

16. How can the use of credit have a positive influence on the economy?

17. How can the use of too much credit contribute to inflation?

18. Suppose you buy a 10-speed bike using credit. After two weeks, the bike only runs on five speeds. Although the bike has a two-year warranty, the seller refuses to do anything about the problem. Your credit contract has been sold to a finance company and the seller has been paid. Describe your rights if you refuse to pay the creditor.

19. How can your financial personality help you decide when and if you can use credit safely? How would you describe your financial personality?

20. Why do you think so many students and young people today are incurring so much

insurance and other resources are basic steps in any financial plan.

The type and amount of insurance needed varies from person to person. It depends on the risks being covered, the amount available to pay for losses, and the financial obligations of the insured persons. For example, a childless unmarried person generally needs less coverage than a head of a family with several children. Protection needs increase with each new dependent and with increased assets. A **dependent** is an individual who relies on someone else for financial support, such as a child, a spouse, or an elderly parent.

When you buy an insurance policy, you become a **policyholder**. You pay a set amount of money, called a **premium**, to the insurance company on a regular basis. The premiums you and other policyholders pay are invested by the company to earn money. Both premiums and earnings are used to pay insurance claims. A *claim* is a bill submitted to the insurance company for payment.

Types of insurance that protect against financial risks include health, disability, life, home, and auto. These are discussed in different sections of this chapter.

10-1

Insurance can help you cover unexpected expenses, such as rebuilding a home after a flood.

Private Health Insurance

Health insurance offers protection by covering specific medical expenses created by illness, injury, and disability. Today, approximately 35 percent of health care costs are paid by private plans offered by insurance companies. Many of these plans are available through employers.

Participants in private insurance plans usually pay a monthly premium plus a deductible. A **deductible** is the amount you must pay before insurance begins to pay. For example, if your deductible is $500 annually, you must pay for health care services until you reach a total of $500, at which time the insurance company begins paying.

Most private insurance programs are group plans sponsored by employers, unions, and other organizations. Individuals may also purchase private health insurance, but it usually costs more and provides less coverage than group plans.

Fee-for-Service Plans

Fee-for-service plans pay for covered medical services after treatment is provided. You can usually go to any licensed health care provider or accredited hospital of your choice, 10-2.

You are responsible for a deductible and coinsurance. **Coinsurance** is a percentage of the service cost that patients pay. For example, if a medical service costs $100 and the coinsurance is 20 percent, your cost would be

$20. In a fee-for-service plan, you pay the $100 at the time of the medical service. Either you or the doctor's office submits a claim to the insurance company. You then receive a reimbursement, or repayment, of $80.

If you have fee-for-service coverage, learn how to file claims and file them promptly. Keep the name and phone number of your plan handy, with membership numbers and other information you may need to receive services and file claims.

Fee-for-service plans generally offer basic and major medical coverage. Basic coverage includes prescriptions, hospital stays, and inpatient tests. An **inpatient** is a person whose care requires a stay in a hospital. Basic coverage also pays for some doctor's visits, outpatient procedures and certain other medical services.

Major medical coverage typically covers the costs of serious illnesses and high-cost procedures and injuries. Often fee-for-service plans combine basic and major medical protection in one policy called a *comprehensive plan*.

10-2

In a fee-for-service health insurance plan, you have the freedom to go to any licensed health care provider you like.

Managed Care Plans

Managed care plans contract with specific doctors, hospitals, and other health care providers to deliver medical services and preventive care to members at reduced cost. Your choice of service providers is limited to those who participate in the plan, except for necessary referrals to specialists outside the plan.

You and/or your employer pay a set amount in monthly premiums. You also pay any required deductibles, coinsurance, or co-payments. A **co-payment** is a flat fee the patient must pay for medical services. Co-payments are due at the time of service. For example, when you have a doctor's appointment or a prescription filled, you pay the co-payment at that time. Co-payment amounts are determined by your health care plan.

Three forms of managed care are health maintenance organizations (HMOs), preferred provider organizations (PPOs), and point-of-service (POS) plans.

Health Maintenance Organizations (HMOs)

These organizations provide a list of participating physicians from which you choose a primary care doctor. This doctor coordinates your health care and carries out routine exams and treatments. The plan normally covers only treatment provided by doctors who participate in the plan. If you go outside the plan for care, you pay part or the entire bill.

Normally, you must go through your primary care doctor for a referral to a specialist if you require specialized treatments, consultations, or from the plan before receiving certain procedures and treatments. A *utilization review* is an insurance company's examination of requests for medical treatments and procedures to make sure they are covered and the patient truly needs them.

Be sure to find out if preauthorizations and utilization reviews are required. Look for coverage of the services that are most important to you. These may include the following:

- inpatient hospital services
- outpatient surgery
- office visits
- preventive care and screenings
- maternity care and well-baby care
- medical tests
- emergency room care
- physical therapy
- x-rays
- mental health services
- drug and alcohol abuse treatment
- prescription drugs
- home health care

Claims Investigators

Claims investigators handle insurance claims when a company suspects fraudulent or criminal activity, such as arson, falsified claims, staged accidents, or unnecessary medical treatments. They often perform surveillance work.

Choice

Some plans allow you to choose your doctors, regardless of where they practice or their hospital affiliation. Other plans limit you to participating health care providers. Consider the following questions:

- How important is it to choose your own doctor and hospital or continue with the providers you already use?
- What health care providers, including doctors, hospitals, and labs, participate in the plan? Where are they located?
- What are the provisions for seeing a specialist if you believe you need one?
- Can you change doctors without prior approval if you are dissatisfied with your primary care physician?

Cost

Make sure you know the answers to the following questions before choosing a plan:

- What premiums must you pay?
- Is there a deductible? If so, how much is it? Which services are subject to the deductible?

- What are the costs of using non-participating providers and facilities?

- What health costs should you be prepared to pay? Check any exclusions, service limitations, or restrictions on preexisting conditions that may apply to you.

- What portion of charges must you co-pay? Do co-payments apply to every medical service you receive or only to specific items such as office visits and prescription drugs?

- In a managed care program, find out whether co-payments are higher if you go outside your health care plan for treatment.

Figure the total cost of the premiums you would pay together with the deductible. Certain plans have lower premiums, but higher co-payments or deductibles. Others may have the reverse. Very often you can reduce monthly premiums by choosing a plan with a higher deductible. This can save you money if you typically require only routine health care services.

You can control your health care costs by developing habits that make the most of your health care dollars. See 10-4.

Government-Sponsored Health Insurance

The government offers health insurance to certain eligible people, including older adults, people with disabilities, low-income families, and children. What each person pays, if anything, depends on various factors.

Ways to Lower Health Care Costs

- Make good health a priority. Follow a balanced approach to diet, exercise, sleep, stress control, and accident prevention.
- Find out what free or low-cost health services and programs are available through your school, employer, community, and government.
- Know exactly what expenses your health insurance covers, keep accurate records, and file claims promptly for covered expenses.
- Discuss fees and prices with health care providers. Cost-conscious patients can often avoid unnecessary expenses.
- Lower hospital costs by asking for outpatient care, if possible, and minimum hospital stays.
- Get a second opinion before agreeing to non-emergency surgery or costly procedures.
- Obtain necessary authorizations before receiving treatments to be sure they are covered by your insurance.
- Keep track of out-of-pocket spending on health care expenses. If these are more than a certain percentage of your income, they may be tax deductible.

10-4

Individuals can lower the cost of health care by following these recommendations.

Filing a Home Insurance Claim

Follow these steps to file a claim on your home insurance.

1. Report any burglary or theft to the police immediately.

2. Notify your insurance agent or company promptly by phone with a written follow-up report. Determine exact coverage your policy provides and find out whether the loss exceeds the deductible. Ask about details of filing a claim and about records and estimates you may need to file a claim for repairs or replacements.

3. Make temporary repairs and take necessary steps to prevent further damage. Keep receipts and records of expenses involved for reimbursement.

4. Make a list of lost or damaged articles with estimated replacement costs and confirming records of purchase and replacement prices.

5. Keep records and receipts for living expenses if damage to your property requires you to find a place to live while repairs are being made.

6. Provide your insurance agent or company with the necessary receipts, records, and information required to handle and settle your claim.

7. Check your policy to find out what steps are involved in settling a claim. If you are dissatisfied or have questions concerning the final settlement, discuss matters with your agent or the claims adjuster.

8. If you find a settlement unsatisfactory or are not satisfied with your insurance company's handling of your complaint, you can contact your state insurance department or call the National Insurance Consumer Helpline for assistance.

Insurance Information Institute

10-7

These guidelines can help you file a home insurance claim.

company such as home and auto coverage. Also, check if discounts are available for devices such as a smoke detector or burglar alarm, for nonsmoker policyholders, or for long-term policyholders. These discounts can reduce your homeowner premiums considerably.

When you are ready to buy home insurance, take time to study the types and amounts of coverage available. Then find an informed, reputable insurance agent or broker who can advise you on the type and amount of coverage you need. Ask friends and business associates about their experience with insurance agents and companies.

A.M. Best & Company rates insurers for financial stability. The ratings are published in *Best's Insurance Reports: Property-Casualty*. This publication is available in the reference section of most public libraries and online at www.ambest.com. Your state insurance department may also help you evaluate a company's service and complaint record. In addition, you can find information online about home insurance coverage, companies, and rates.

Renter's Insurance

Renter's insurance covers losses due to damage or loss of personal property and possessions. These include jewelry, electronics, furniture, bedding, and so forth. The landlord carries coverage on the dwelling itself.

Renters should look for a policy with liability insurance. If guests were harmed in a rental home, liability insurance would cover any expenses incurred by the resident.

College students living in a dorm or renting an apartment may need renter's insurance, a floater, or an endorsement to protect their possessions. A *floater* is a form of insurance that covers specific items wherever you take them. It "floats" with possessions such as a musical instrument or a laptop computer.

An *endorsement* is an attachment to existing insurance coverage, such as a family policy to protect a computer, a television, and other expensive items taken to college.

Auto Insurance

Auto insurance gives policyholders coverage for liability and property damage under specified conditions. When you own or lease a car, you take certain personal and financial risks. If you are involved in a car accident, you may be required to pay thousands of dollars for injuries and property damage, 10-8. If you are in an accident where you are at fault or claims are filed against you, it can cost thousands of dollars in legal fees as well as damages. Practically no one can afford the financial risks of extensive property damage, serious injury, or death without insurance coverage.

All 50 states have *financial responsibility laws* that require drivers to show proof of their ability to pay stated minimum amounts in damages

10-8

Having adequate auto insurance is important. Car accidents can cost thousands of dollars for repairs, medical expenses, and legal fees.

after an accident. Most states also have *compulsory auto insurance laws* that require car owners to buy a minimum amount of bodily injury and property damage liability insurance in order to legally drive their cars.

When you are ready to buy auto insurance, shop carefully to get the coverage you need at the best price. An auto insurance policy may include several types of coverage for the insured individual or family.

Types of Auto Insurance

Of the six basic types of auto insurance coverage, two are liability coverage. They pay other parties for losses you cause. The other auto policies pay you, the insured, for losses outlined in the policy.

Bodily injury liability is coverage that protects you when you are responsible for an auto accident that results in the injury or death of other parties. **Property damage liability** protects you when you are responsible for an auto accident in which the property of others is damaged.

These policies cover the policyholder, family members, and any person driving the car with the owner's permission. They pay damages to the other parties involved in an accident you cause. Both types of liability coverage pay the legal fees for settling claims. They also pay for damages assessed against you, up to limits stated in the policy. These damages include injuries to other parties or damage to the property of others.

Medical payments or *personal injury protection (PIP)* pays you, the insured, for medical expenses resulting from an accident in your car, regardless of who is at fault. It covers you and any person injured in or by your car.

Collision insurance pays you for damage to your car due to an auto accident or collision with another car or object.

Comprehensive physical damage insurance pays you for loss or damage to your car resulting from fire, theft, falling objects, explosion, earthquake, flood, riot, civil commotion, and collision with a bird or animal.

Uninsured and underinsured motorist insurance pays you for injuries caused by an uninsured or hit-and-run driver. It covers insured persons driving, riding, or walking. It covers you if injured as a pedestrian. It also covers passengers in the insured person's car.

Auto Insurance Costs

Auto insurance is a costly service. Coverage for young drivers is particularly high because statistically they have more accidents. Adding a teenage driver to a family policy may increase the insurance premium by as much as 75 percent.

The guidelines in 10-9 can help you select the automobile insurance you need. The cost of auto insurance depends on the following factors.

Driver Classification

Driver classification is determined by the age, sex, and marital status of the driver. Driving record and habits are also considered.

Suggestions for Buying Automobile Insurance

1. Decide on the types and amounts of coverage you need. If you now have a policy, review your coverage and its cost before renewal time.
2. Check with several reputable insurers. Keep in mind the least expensive coverage is not necessarily the best for you. Consider such things as the company's reliability and its reputation for service, including claims handling. If you're in doubt about a company, check with your state insurance department.
3. Consider the amount you would save by paying a higher deductible. You may find it pays in the long run to take care of small losses yourself.
4. Check with your agent regarding your eligibility for premium discounts.
5. Consider special coverages or higher policy limits if you frequently drive other commuters to work or groups of children to school or special events.
6. Consider reducing or dropping collision coverage as cars get older.

10-9

These guidelines can help you select auto insurance.

Statistically, young, single males are involved in more serious accidents than other classes of drivers. Therefore, they tend to pay the highest insurance premiums. If a young man marries, his insurance costs may decrease because, statistically, married men have fewer serious accidents than single men. Rates for women, single and married, are lower than for males.

A poor driving record tends to increase premiums as does a record of previous claims and costly settlements. When your driver classification changes, so might your insurance rates.

Rating Territory

The number and amount of claims an insurance company processes in your area determines rates for auto insurance. Premiums are higher in frequent claim areas such as big cities and high traffic districts.

Premium Discount Eligibility

Some companies offer discounts to drivers who

- have a safe driving record
- get good grades (if still in school)
- are nonsmokers
- install antitheft devices and air bags
- are over a certain age
- have two or more cars on a policy
- have a positive credit report

Check with your insurance company about possible discounts.

Insured Car's Year, Make, and Model

Cars that are costly to repair or that are favorite targets of thieves cost more to insure. Premiums are higher for luxury, sports, and new cars than for standard models and older cars. For older cars, collision insurance may not be cost effective.

Cars that require expensive repairs and parts generally cost more to insure. Very popular models cost more to insure than more ordinary cars. Check the insurance costs for different models before buying a car.

Deductible Amount

Increasing the deductible amount can reduce premiums for collision and comprehensive damage coverage. Increasing your deductible from $250 to $500 could save you 15 to 30 percent on your premium. The higher the deductible is, the lower the premium will be.

Coverage Amount

The more protection you buy, the higher the premium will be. However, the cost per dollar of coverage is usually less for more coverage. For example, a $100,000 policy costs less per dollar of coverage than a $50,000 policy. Just remember to buy the amount of coverage you need. A reliable agent can help you decide.

Insurance Company

Premium rates and service for the same coverage may vary greatly from company to company. It pays to shop carefully. You may be able to save by combining different coverages into one policy rather than buying each separately.

To compare insurance costs, check the cost of coverage you need with several reliable insurance companies. Once you buy auto insurance, read your policy carefully and know what coverage you carry.

It also is a good idea to keep the policy and records of premium payments and claims together in one place so you can find them as needed. You also must carry proof of your insurance coverage in your vehicle in most states. See 10-10 for procedures to follow at the scene of an accident and in filing an insurance claim.

No-Fault Auto Insurance

No-fault auto insurance eliminates the faultfinding process in settling claims. When an accident occurs, each policyholder makes a claim to his or her own insurance company. Each company pays its own policyholder regardless of who is at fault. No-fault insurance is designed to simplify and speed up payments to accident victims. It also acts to lower insurance rates by reducing costly court trials to determine fault.

Auto Accidents and Insurance Claims

At the Scene of an Accident

- Stop your car safely beyond the accident and out of traffic. Turn on flasher or warning light.
- Assist the injured, but do not move anyone unless absolutely necessary.
- Administer any first aid you are qualified and trained to provide.
- Stay calm and help others to do the same.
- Get help as fast as possible. Call or have someone call the police and an ambulance if needed.
- Provide police with information they request.
- Ask for a copy of the police report.
- Write down 1) names, addresses, and phone numbers of those involved in the accident and of any witnesses, 2) license number, make, and model of cars involved, 3) driver's license number of drivers involved, 4) insurance company and identification number of each driver involved, and 5) names and badge numbers of police officers and other emergency assistants.
- For a collision with an unattended or parked auto, try to find the owner. If unsuccessful, leave a note with your name, number, and address. Damages over a certain amount must be reported to the police in most states.

Filing an Insurance Claim

If your car is involved in an auto accident; if it is damaged by fire, flood, or vandalism; or if it is stolen, follow these steps in filing a claim for your losses.

- Phone your insurance agent or a local company representative as soon as possible to report the incident.
- Ask the agent how to proceed and what forms or documents are needed to support your claim. These may include medical and auto repair bills and a copy of the police report.
- Obtain and provide the information the insurer requires. Cooperate fully with your insurance company in the investigation and settlement of claims.
- Turn over copies of any legal papers you receive in connection with the accident and losses you are claiming. If you are sued or claims are brought against you, the insurance company will provide legal representation for you.
- Keep copies of any paperwork and documents you submit with your insurance claim.
- Keep records of any expenses you incur as a result of an automobile accident. They may be reimbursed under the terms of your policy.

Note: If involved in an accident, it is unlawful to leave the scene without proper notification if there is injury, death, or property damage over a certain amount. Check the laws on reporting accidents in your state.

10-10

Follow these steps if you are involved in an auto accident and must file an insurance claim.

State legislators decide whether their state adopts a no-fault insurance plan and what form it takes. Most states with a no-fault plan have a combination no-fault and liability insurance. The no-fault pays for claims up to a set amount called a *threshold*. However, in most states individuals can sue for additional damages when an accident involves severe injuries, death, or major medical bills. Liability insurance pays for damages over and above the threshold amount.

High-Risk Drivers

It can be difficult for individuals with poor driving records to buy insurance. Insurers consider these drivers too great a risk. In such cases, it may be possible to obtain coverage through an assigned risk plan. This is a state-supervised program in which high-risk drivers are assigned to insurance companies. The companies are required to provide coverage, but premiums are considerably higher than for those with better driving records.

Chapter Summary

The types of insurance protection consumers typically buy cover health, disability, life, home, and auto. Protection needs in these areas vary with every individual and family. It pays to shop carefully for the best coverage at the best price.

The high cost of medical care makes it important to investigate all options for obtaining health insurance. Older citizens and certain groups may be eligible for government insurance programs such as Medicare and Medicaid. Disability insurance protects against financial loss if the policyholder becomes disabled and can no longer work.

Adequate life insurance coverage guarantees income for the policyholder's survivors. It is particularly important for those who are financially responsible for a spouse, children, or others. Term life, whole life, and endowment insurance are three main types of protection against the loss of income as a result of the death of a wage earner. Life insurance may also offer investment features.

Once you own a home, you need insurance to protect it. A reliable insurance agent can help you select the type and amount of coverage you need. Costs depend on the type and amount of coverage you buy, the deductible amount, the risk factors where you live, and the opportunity for discounts.

Carrying adequate auto insurance is a major responsibility of car owners. Different types of coverage protect against the different risks individuals assume as a car owner. The cost of insurance depends on many factors, including your driving record, where you live, and the type of car you drive.

Review

1. Give two examples of financial risks that insurance can protect against.

2. Explain how HMO, PPO, and POS health insurance plans differ.

3. How can a health savings account (HSA) save you money?

4. List three disadvantages of individual private health insurance plans.

5. What factors should be considered before enrolling in a health insurance plan?

6. What are the differences between Medicare and Medicaid?

7. What is disability insurance and how does it work?

8. What are the differences between term life, whole life, and endowment insurance?

9. What are two key factors that determine the amount of life insurance to buy?

10. What four major factors determine the cost of home insurance?

11. Which type of insurance coverage pays for damage your car causes someone else's property if you are responsible for the accident?

12. List five factors that determine auto insurance costs.

Critical Thinking

13. Outline the health care costs typically covered by health insurance.

14. Explain and give examples of the following terms as they apply to health insurance.
    A. preexisting
    B. exclusions
    C. co-payments
    D. deductibles

15. What are the advantages of long-term care insurance and who needs it?

16. Name and describe the different types of whole life insurance.

17. List four factors you should consider when selecting a life insurance company and agent.

18. Explain the types of coverage home insurance policies provide.

Create an Emergency Fund

The first savings goal is to build an emergency fund. An emergency fund is savings you can easily access in case of a job layoff, illness, or unexpected expense. Since most emergencies are unplanned, the money should be available to use right away.

The amount of money in this fund varies depending on your needs. However, a common guideline is that you keep enough money in the emergency fund to cover living expenses for six to eight months. This would include rent or mortgage payments, car and other loan payments, taxes, utilities, food, and all other expenses.

Set Goals for Saving

Once you have an emergency fund, you can save for other things. It is easier to save if you have clearly defined goals, 11-1. Begin with a list of what you want to achieve with your money. What would persuade you to give up spending now so you can save enough for the future? Your savings goals need to be

Planning ahead can help you achieve long-term goals, such as paying for a college education.

- *realistic.* Consider your income and expenses, your life situation, and any likely changes. Set up financial goals that you can achieve based on these realities. For example, suppose you can save $300 monthly and you want to buy a car within two years without getting a loan. A used car is realistic while a new luxury car is not. What are your goals? Are they objectives you can achieve?

- *specific and measurable.* Outline your goals in exact terms. "Putting together $1,200 for a ski trip next winter" is more specific than "saving money to travel sometime in the future." Likewise, "saving $50 per month to buy a computer next summer" is more specific than "putting money aside in case you need it next year." What specific goals do you and your family want to reach in the near or distant future?

- *time related.* Put your goals and objectives into a time frame. When will you need your savings? This will vary for different goals.

It is never too soon to start saving for the goods and services you want for your future. Once you know what you want your money to do for you, you can take realistic steps to reach your financial goals.

Maximizing Savings

There are many different places to save your money. Saving money in a financial institution, such as a bank or credit union, provides a safe place

Financial Managers

Financial managers at financial institutions are responsible for directing bank operations and overseeing the management of the products and services offered to customers. They may also resolve customer problems, oversee investments, and manage employees and departments.

to keep money and a way to earn interest. You can maximize your savings by considering the following:

- *Total amount deposited.* Obviously, the more you deposit, the more interest you earn.
- *Interest rate.* The higher the interest rate, the more you stand to gain.
- *Time span of deposit.* The longer money remains in savings without withdrawals, the more you accumulate.
- *Interest type.* There are two types of interest. **Simple interest** is computed only on the *principal* or the amount of money originally deposited. The principal does not include interest earned. **Compound interest** is figured on the money deposited plus the interest it earns. The interest previously earned is included in the total before new interest earnings are computed. Earning interest on the interest makes money grow faster.
- *Frequency of compounding.* The more often interest is compounded, the faster savings grows. Compounding may be done on a daily, quarterly, monthly, or semi-annual basis. Over time, compound interest increases the value of your savings. This concept is known as the *time value of money.* See 11-2.

11-2

The dual effects of time and compound interest add value to savings.

Watch Your Savings Grow			
Weekly Savings at Different Interest Rates, Compounded Monthly			
Weekly Amount:	**Number of Years**		
	10	**20**	**30**
$10 4.5%	$ 6,550	$ 16,814	$ 32,897
25	16,375	42,035	82,243
50	32,750	84,069	164,486
$10 5.5%	$ 6,910	$ 18,871	$ 39,576
25	17,274	47,176	98,940
50	34,548	94,353	197,880
$10 6.6%	$ 7,294	$ 21,243	$ 47,914
25	18,236	53,107	119,786
50	36,472	106,214	239,572
$10 7.7%	$ 7,707	$ 23,984	$ 58,361
25	19,267	59,959	145,903
50	38,533	119,918	291,807
$10 8.8%	$ 8,148	$ 27,155	$ 71,491
25	20,371	67,888	178,729
50	40,741	135,776	357,459
Original Amounts Saved:			
$10	$ 5,200	$ 10,400	$ 15,600
25	13,000	26,000	39,000
50	26,000	52,000	78,000

Bonds

A **bond** is a certificate of debt issued by a corporation or government. When you buy a bond, you are lending money to the issuer of the bond. Until the bond matures, you, the bondholder, are a creditor. The issuer owes you the amount of the loan plus interest on the bond's face value.

Information stated on a bond includes the following:

- *Maturity date* is the date a bond or other obligation is due to be paid.

- *Face value* is the amount for which a bond is issued and on which interest payments are figured. At maturity, the bondholder receives the face value.

- *Yield* is the percentage of a return on an investment.
  Other important terms relating to bonds include the following:

- *Coupon rate* is the annual interest the issuer promises to pay on the face value.

- *Market value* is the amount for which a bond sells. It may be more, less, or the same as the face value.

- *Current yield* is the annual interest or coupon rate divided by the market price of a bond.

Types of Bonds

The three major issuers of bonds are corporations, municipalities, and the federal government.

Corporate bonds are issued by businesses that need money to operate and expand. The quality, coupon rates, and yields of these bonds vary with the financial soundness of the issuing corporation. Yields and market prices move up and down as market interest rates change.

Most corporate bonds are bought and sold by brokers. Some bonds are bought and sold on securities exchanges and are listed in newspapers and online. High-grade corporate bonds are considered safer investments than stocks because they are debt instruments. If a company goes bankrupt, it must pay its debts first.

Municipal bonds are issued by state, county, and city governments. Coupon rates and yields depend on market rates and the financial soundness of the issuing municipality. Interest on these bonds is exempt from federal income tax and in some cases state and local taxes as well. This makes municipal bonds attractive to upper income investors in high tax brackets.

Most municipal bonds are bought and sold by brokers. Some municipalities may allow investors to purchase bonds directly from the local government. Corporate and municipal bond listings are in the financial section of major newspapers and online. Look for certain key information when reviewing bond quotations, 12-3.

Bond Quote							
Issuer Name	**Symbol**	**Coupon**	**Maturity**	**Rating**	**Close**	**Change**	**Yield %**
Bank ABC	B. ABC	2.250%	Mar 20XX	Aaa	100.985	−0.073	1.861
Corp. Y	COR.Y	8.500%	May 20XX	A	106.695	2.375	7.520
Z Corp.	Z.CO	2.250%	Mar 20XX	Aaa	101.042	−0.041	1.839

Symbol: Abbreviated name of the issuing corporation.

Coupon: The annual interest paid on the bond. Coupon rates generally are higher on lower quality bonds to reward buyers for taking greater risks.

Maturity: The date the bond is due.

Rating: The quality/risk rating of the bond. As the risk increases, the ratings decline from the highest quality or safest rated, Aaa or AAA, to the lowest quality rated, C or D.

Close: The closing price of the bond at the end of the day. Prices are usually shown as a percentage of the face value.

Change: Compares the closing price with the price paid the previous day. Some quotes show the change in increments of ⅟₃₂.

Yield: The actual return on investment. Calculations are based on the coupon rate and the current market value of the bond.

12-3

Corporate bond quotations provide the information you need to track bond yields and prices in the marketplace.

Corporate and municipal bonds are rated for quality and risk. The first four rating categories—AAA, AA, A, and BBB—are recommended for conservative investors. The other four categories—BB, B, C, and D—are considered too risky for average investors.

U.S. government bonds are issued by the U.S. Treasury and are the safest bonds you can buy. When you buy one, you lend money to the federal government. Treasury bills, notes, and bonds sell in increments of $100.

- *Treasury bills (T-bills)* are short-term debts with maturities ranging from a few days to 52 weeks. They are the most actively traded government debt. Treasury bills sell for less than the face value. They do not pay interest before maturity. You pay less than $100 for a T-bill and receive the full $100 at maturity. The difference between the price you pay and the amount you receive at maturity is the interest.

- *Treasury notes and Treasury bonds* are sold at auction and carry a stated interest rate. Buyers receive semiannual interest payments. Treasury notes are short-term securities with maturities of two, three, five, seven, or 10 years. Bonds are long-term investments with maturities of 30 years. Both notes and bonds are sold in increments of $100. The actual price you will pay for these securities depends on the interest coupon and the yield at auction. These may be paper

ECONOMICS in ACTION

Credit Ratings Agencies

Credit ratings organizations evaluate debt securities, such as bonds, and rate them according to risk. Investors use the ratings to help guide investment choices.

The U.S. Securities and Exchange Commission designates certain agencies as Nationally Recognized Statistical Ratings Organizations (NRSOs). To be considered an NRSO, the agency must reveal its method used to determine ratings. Some of the most well-known NRSOs are Standard and Poor's Ratings Services, Moody's Investor Services, and Fitch, Inc.

Critics question the objectiveness of ratings organizations. NRSOs have been accused of giving high ratings to risky securities to please issuers who pay for the rating services. When agencies receive payment from the corporations whose securities they are rating, critics cite a conflict of interest.

In the future, the SEC may establish stricter rules and regulations for NRSOs to prevent conflicts of interest.

certificates or entered into an electronic account. Today most are sold electronically.

- *U.S. savings bonds* were discussed in Chapter 11.

Mutual Funds

A **mutual fund** is created by pooling the money of many people and investing it in a collection of securities. Professional managers at investment firms select the securities that make up a mutual fund.

Inexperienced investors often start with mutual funds because of three key advantages:

- *Professional management.* Mutual funds are managed by professional investors who follow the markets carefully and are assisted by a team of researchers.

- *Diversification.* Mutual funds offer diversification in a single investment. As mentioned earlier, when you invest in several securities, you spread your risks.

- *Liquidity.* Mutual fund shares are easy to buy and sell.
  Mutual funds also have some drawbacks:

- *Management fees.* Mutual fund managers charge fees to pay for research, administration, sales, and other expenses. Usually the fees are near industry averages. However, some management fees are extremely high and cut into your earnings significantly. These costs must be paid even if the fund performs poorly.

- *Lack of control.* You give up control over the selection and timing of your investments. The fund managers make these decisions.

- *Minimum investment.* Many mutual funds require a minimum investment of $1,000 or more.

Types of Mutual Funds

The two basic types of mutual funds are closed-end or open-end. A *closed-end fund* offers a fixed number of shares. These shares are traded like stocks on securities exchanges and secondary markets. You buy and sell shares in these funds through investment brokers, not through an investment company.

The *open-end fund* has an unlimited number of shares. It sells and redeems shares at their net asset value. Current market value or **net asset value (NAV)** is the fund's assets minus its liabilities. The *value per share* is the NAV of the fund divided by the number of shares outstanding.

Most mutual funds are open-end funds. Open-end mutual funds may be load or no-load funds. *Load funds* charge a commission or "load" of up to eight percent of the amount you invest when you buy shares. The average commission is three to five percent. *No-load funds* do not charge fees when you buy shares. However, you may be charged fees when you sell or redeem your shares.

Several different types of mutual funds are available.

- *Income funds* buy conservative bonds and stocks that pay regular dividends. Their primary goal is to provide current income.

- *Balanced funds* invest in common stock, preferred stock, and bonds. Their goal is to provide a low-risk investment opportunity with moderate growth and dividend income.

- *Growth funds* invest in securities that are expected to increase in value. They emphasize growth over income, but involve more risk.

- *Specialized funds* invest in securities of certain industries or sectors, such as all technology or all health care companies. They may also invest in certain types of securities, such as all municipal bonds or common stock. Some concentrate on foreign securities.

Mutual funds are often divided into families. Each fund has its own name and investment objectives. Mutual fund quotations display the names of individual funds listed within each family group, 12-4.

A **money market fund** is a type of mutual fund that deals only in high interest, short-term investments, such as U. S. Treasury securities, certificates of deposit, and commercial paper. *Commercial paper* is a short-term note issued by a major corporation. The funds are managed and sold by investment companies, brokerage firms, and other financial institutions.

The interest earned, minus management fees for operating the fund, is passed along to the depositors. Interest rates on money market funds go up and down with money market rates.

Investing in money market funds has many advantages. These funds provide small savers with high yields when interest rates are high. They

Mutual Fund Quote				
Fund	**NAV**	**Chg**	**YTD % return**	**3-yr % chg**
Fund Company 123				
BalFundA	9.89	0.01	28.1	−4.7
SpecFundB	31.72	0.02	28.6	1.2

Fund: Name of the fund company that sells the funds, followed by the names of individual funds offered.

NAV: The dollar value of one share of the mutual fund.

Chg: Difference between the day's NAV and the previous day's NAV.

YTD (Year to Date) %: The percentage gain or loss since the first trading day of the year.

3-yr % chg: The fund's total gain or loss over the past three years, indicated as a percentage.

12-4
Mutual funds quotes appear in the financial pages of major newspapers and online.

can be liquidated at any time since they have no term or maturity date. No interest penalties apply for early withdrawals. They can be used as collateral for loans.

Money market funds have some disadvantages, too. The rate paid on money market funds changes daily. If money market rates drop, so does the rate of return. A minimum investment of $1,000 or more may be required. Unlike money market deposit accounts, the savings instrument discussed in Chapter 11, money market funds are not FDIC-insured.

Factors Affecting Returns

In a market economy, the laws of supply and demand determine the price of stocks and many other investments. *Supply* is the amount of a product or service producers are willing to provide. *Demand* is the quantity of a product or service consumers are willing to buy. Both supply and demand are closely connected to price.

Certain information can help predict investment returns, including economic indicators, current events and trends, and data about particular economic sectors, industries, and companies.

Business Cycle Fluctuations

When the economy is growing, most businesses and investors do well. However, when economic growth slows, many businesses and investors lose money as sales decline. Cyclical industries are more sensitive to the ups and downs of the business cycle. The performance of these companies is often tied to interest rates, fuel costs, and products that are not immediately essential to the consumer. The stock issued by companies within these industries is categorized as cyclical.

Being aware of the ups and downs of the economy can help investors make wise choices. The Chapters in Unit 1 discussed some economic indicators that help economists assess the health of the economy. These include the unemployment rate, GDP, consumer price index, and consumer confidence. These statistics are released by government economists and other groups on a regular basis.

Interest Rate Fluctuations

Fluctuations in interest rates affect the value of securities and other investments. Bonds and real estate are directly affected by interest rate ups and downs. For example, as interest rates rise, bond prices fall. This is because investors can receive higher returns by investing in bonds with the new higher rates. Conversely, as interest rates fall, bond prices rise. Real estate sales increase as interest rates fall and suffer when they rise. Business growth generally is more robust when interests rates are low and suffers when rates increase.

Stock Market Fluctuations

Bull and *bear* are terms used to describe the strength or weakness of the stock market. **Bull market** is an extended period of consumer confidence and optimism when stock prices rise. The sense of optimism often encourages the exploration of other investment opportunities, including real estate and valuable goods.

Bear market is an extended period of uncertainty and pessimism when stock prices fall. It occurs when investors feel insecure and uncertain about the economy. Fearing further drops in the value of their investments, they often sell them. However, this is often a buying opportunity because prices are low.

Product Innovation

Historically, investors who financed winning products in their infancy, such as the automobile, microwave oven, and cell phone, made handsome profits. Those who invested in products that did not succeed lost their money. Most investors fall somewhere between high profits and big losses.

Business failure is caused by many factors ranging from poor management to new competition and government regulations. Technological advancement can cause new companies and industries to spring up, while making outdated companies obsolete.

Government Actions

Actions by government can impact the value of an investment positively or negatively. Product recalls, new regulations, and increased taxes often have a negative impact on company stock. Trade barriers protecting companies from foreign competition often improve the outlook of stock in protected industries.

Exchange-Rate Risk

For investors who trade securities of companies in other countries, the currency exchange rate needs to be considered. It may be necessary to exchange dollars for another currency. Dividends and gains or losses may be presented in foreign currency. The ups and downs of the exchange rate, whether buying or selling, become a potential risk for the investor.

Real Estate

Buying *real estate* (land or buildings) is another way to invest for future profit. This type of investment usually requires enough money for a down payment plus a long-term loan.

For most people, buying a home is their first experience in real estate. When the real estate market is strong, owning your home can increase your net worth and protect against inflation. Property usually increases in value over time. Still, most financial experts advise thinking of a home first in terms of a place to live and second as an investment.

Buying land or buildings for investment purposes is not for amateurs. Before investing in real estate for profit, buyers need to know about property values and property management. They also need to learn about mortgages, down payments, taxes, titles, insurance, and the legal aspects of leases and property ownership. These considerations are described in Chapter 18.

REITs and Real Estate Mutual Funds

Purchasing stock in a *Real Estate Investment Trust (REIT)* is a way to invest in real estate without the complications and financial commitment of owning property. A REIT is a company that owns profit-earning real estate, such as apartments, shopping malls, office buildings, or hotels. Mortgage REITs specialize in buying and selling mortgage-backed securities.

The government requires that REITs distribute most of their profits to shareholders through dividends. Shares of many REITs are traded on securities exchanges.

Real estate mutual funds are another way to indirectly invest in real estate. Funds may include a mixture of securities from REITs, commercial developers, and other types of real estate companies.

Investing in REITs and real estate mutual funds requires less capital and offers more liquidity than purchasing property. Changes in interest rates, housing prices, and demand for housing can affect the rate of return. As with other securities, investors should research before investing and carefully review prospectuses and annual reports.

Valuable Goods

People have collected precious goods and objects for thousands of years and continue to do so today. These items can be attractive investments because their value is not eroded by inflation as paper money can be. Valuable goods include the following:

Real Estate Appraisers

Real estate appraisers estimate the value of land and buildings, ranging from residential homes to major shopping centers. They write detailed reports on their research observations and explain reasons for arriving at their estimates.

- *Collectibles* are objects purchased for the pleasure of ownership and because they are expected to increase in value. Common collectibles include rare coins, books, stamps, art, antiques, sports memorabilia, and vintage automobiles.

- *Precious metals* include gold, silver, platinum, and other metals. People buy them in the form of pieces of jewelry, coins, bars, or ingots from banks and dealers. An *ingot* is a bar of metal that is sized and shaped for easy transportation and storage.

- *Precious gemstones* include diamonds, emeralds, sapphires, and others. They are collected as stones or as pieces of jewelry.

Consider the risks before you choose these investments. They are less liquid than stocks, bonds, and mutual funds. Like real estate, valuable goods can be difficult to sell quickly. When collectors are ready or forced to sell these assets, they sometimes must accept less than what they originally paid. These valuable goods can also be hard to store and protect from damage and theft.

Judging the worth of valuable items is often difficult unless you have expert knowledge and considerable experience. Only then are you safe in purchasing these items from dealers and online auction sites. Before buying valuable goods for investments, consult a reputable professional with experience in estimating value. Ask for a formal appraisal before making a significant investment in collectibles.

Prices for precious metals, particularly gold, silver, platinum, and copper, are posted on business Web sites. Prices for these goods are often volatile.

Keep in mind there is no guaranteed return on investment in valuable goods. Putting money into a savings account generates interest. Over time, investing in securities usually pays off. Historically, real estate goes up in value. The rate of return on collectibles and precious metals and gems is less predictable.

Choosing Investments

An **investment portfolio** is a collection of securities and other assets a person owns. Successful investors diversify their portfolios. **Diversification** refers to spreading risk by putting money in a variety of investments. Building a diversified portfolio involves gathering information, considering strategies, and selecting investment methods.

Sources of Information

Check the following sources before choosing an investment. Consult a professional for advice on complex investments. Financial experts can help in areas where you do not feel confident and competent on your own, 12-5.

Financial Experts		
Job Title	**Description**	**Credentials**
Accountant	• Keep, audit, and inspect financial records of individuals and businesses • Prepare financial reports and tax returns	**CPA (Certified Public Accountant)** indicates an accountant is certified by the American Institute of Certified Public Accountants.
Financial Planner	• Assist consumers in forming a financial program • Give advice on insurance, savings, investments, taxes, retirement, and estate planning	**CFP (Certified Financial Planner)** indicates completion of training and certification administered by The Certified Financial Planner Board of Standards, Inc. **ChFC (Chartered Financial Consultant)** may be used by those who have completed additional education and training with the CFP Board. Financial planners are not required by law to be certified or licensed.
Investment Broker-Buyer	• Buy and sell securities and other investment products	Must be registered with the Securities and Exchange Commission (SEC) and the Financial Industry Regulatory Authority (FINRA).
Registered Representative	• Salespeople who work for broker-buyers, commonly known as brokers	Must be registered with FINRA and licensed by the appropriate state securities regulator.
Investment Adviser	• Provide information and advice on different types of securities	Advisors managing over $25 million in client accounts must be registered with the SEC. Advisors managing less must be registered with the state securities regulator.

For more information, visit www.finra.org/investors.

12-5

Consulting an experienced professional can help in managing financial and legal matters.

Online Resources

Today's technology allows you to use the Internet to view important investment information. In the recent past, this type of information was only available to brokerage firms and investment analysts. Investment-related Web sites provide useful information about individual securities and market movements. On company Web sites, look at investor information or press releases to evaluate the company's investment potential.

The U.S. Securities and Exchange Commission (SEC) is the government agency that regulates the securities industry. Its mission is to combat fraud as well as ensure the securities markets operate efficiently and fairly. All publicly traded companies are required to file financial statements and documents with the SEC. The SEC manages the EDGAR database and keeps it up-to-date as a guide for investors. Visit www.sec.gov to explore this database.

Annual Reports

Most corporate Web sites offer access to annual and quarterly reports. These sources give a good picture of current and predicted market performance.

One piece of information in annual reports—earnings per share (EPS)—is especially important. When earnings per share increase from year to year it is an indication the company is doing well. *Earnings per share* is the total corporate earnings, after taxes, divided by the total number of shares.

Prospectuses

A **prospectus** is a legal document that gives a detailed description of a security. When an investor buys a security, the issuer must provide a prospectus. You may also get a copy mailed to you if you are considering buying a security. A prospectus can usually be found on a company's Web site or the SEC's EDGAR database.

A prospectus lists company officers, describes business history and operations, and outlines plans for the future. It also includes the following financial information:

- *Risks.* This section spells out the ways an investor can lose money by investing in the security.

- *Performance summary.* This indicates how the investment has performed and how its performance compares with that of similar investments. Past performance does not necessarily indicate future results.

- *Fees and expenses.* This section outlines any fees or commissions you must pay when buying, selling, or redeeming shares.

- *Management.* This section identifies the qualifications and experience of the directors and officers of the company or fund.

Market Quotations

Stock, bond, and mutual fund quotations, or listings, contain important financial information, including records of past and current performance. Market information on securities appears in the financial section of *The Wall Street Journal* and other major newspapers. For up-to-the-minute information, review listings on the Internet.

Investment Strategies

Smart investing is a balancing act. It requires balancing risks against returns, 12-6. Younger investors can usually take more risks than older investors. A young investor has many wage-earning years ahead. However, as people get closer to retirement, they need to choose more conservative investments to preserve principal and provide income.

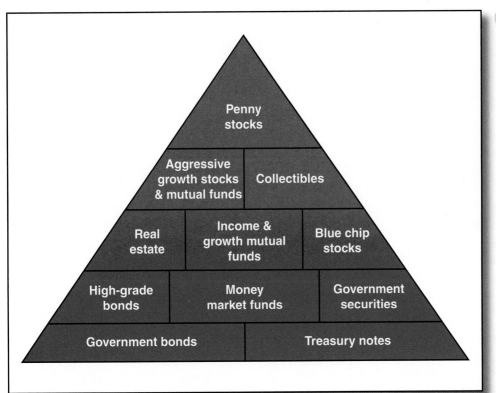

12-6
High-risk investments, at the top of the pyramid, have a greater chance of earning high returns. Low-risk investments, at the base of the pyramid, usually have low returns.

Investing at an early age allows you to benefit from two common investment strategies: *buy and hold* and *dollar-cost averaging*.

Buy and Hold

Buy and hold is the strategy of buying securities and holding them for long term gains as opposed to frequent trading. An investor using this strategy stays invested during market fluctuations. Investors who sell stocks when they drop in value lose money. Investors who hold onto stocks usually gain in the long run.

If your stock earns dividends, you will earn money over the years you own the stock. Also, if you hold a stock for a period of time, the company may split its stock, thus increasing your holdings.

Buy and hold does not mean buy and forget. You need to check your investments periodically to know how well they are performing. When an investment is not performing well it may be time to sell and reinvest in a more promising company. Consult an accountant or tax professional to evaluate the tax implications of selling.

Dollar-Cost Averaging

Dollar-cost averaging is a strategy of investing a fixed dollar amount at regular intervals, such as monthly, without regard to the price of the investment at the time you buy it. You end up buying more shares when the price is low and fewer when it is high. This buying strategy eliminates the risk of investing a lump sum when it may not be the best time to buy.

Linking to... Math

How Dollar-Cost Averaging Works

The following example illustrates dollar cost averaging. Investor A buys $1,000 worth of Stock X. At $25 a share, the chart shows that Investor A bought 40 shares. Using dollar-cost averaging, Investor B buys $250 worth of Stock X every month.

The stock's price drops over the next three months. By the fourth month, the 40 shares of Stock X purchased by Investor A would sell for $800—a loss of $200. However, after four months, Investor B owns 51.7 shares of stock. Investor B's shares would sell for $1,034—a gain of $34.

Month	Price/Share	Investor A		Investor B	
		Investment	# Shares	Investment	# Shares
1	$25	$1,000	40	$250	10
2	$20			$250	12.5
3	$15			$250	16.7
4	$20			$250	12.5
Total		$1,000	40	$1,000	51.7

Brokerage Clerks

Brokerage clerks compute and record data pertaining to securities transactions. They may also take customer calls, create order tickets, record a client's purchases and sales, and inform clients of changes to their accounts.

Dollar-cost averaging offers the added advantage of convenience. You can set up an automatic payment and make it a part of your overall budget. It helps you make a habit of investing amounts of money you can afford. You can invest as little as $25 monthly. Brokerage firms, mutual funds, and retirement accounts all offer opportunities for dollar-cost averaging.

Buying Securities

Once you have decided on a few specific securities you wish to buy, there are several ways to acquire them.

Brokerage Firms

To buy stocks, bonds, and other securities, you may open an account with a brokerage or securities firm. The main mission of a brokerage firm is to buy and sell for its customers. The fee you pay for these services is called a commission.

You make an application to open an account with a firm. Once your application is accepted, you call your broker with your orders to buy and sell. Most firms also offer online services.

Full-service brokerage firms maintain research departments to follow market trends and individual securities. In addition, they provide investment advice, portfolio management, and other services. The commission you pay covers the cost of trading and support services provided by the firm. Both experienced and beginning investors can benefit from the expertise of full-service brokerage firms.

Discount brokerage firms execute orders to buy and sell securities, but offer few other services. For instance, a discount brokerage does not offer investment advice. The commission is considerably lower than that of a full-service broker. However, you will need to do your own research and investment planning when you buy from a discount broker. Some experienced investors may prefer to use discount brokers to save money on commissions.

Online brokerage firms have hundreds of online brokers available to help consumers buy and sell securities. Use the following guidelines when investing through an online brokerage firm:

- *Check online brokers carefully before becoming involved.* Make sure the people you deal with are reputable and legitimate. You can check out brokers and securities firms with your state securities regulator or the nearest SEC office.

- *Print information on any investment you are considering.* You also may want to obtain other written material, such as a prospectus, an annual report, and recent company news. Study this information carefully. Before placing an order, know exactly what you are buying and what risks are involved.

- *Obtain and keep written confirmations of your buy-and-sell orders and their completion.* File all your investment records and information in a safe place where you can locate them easily. You will need these records to file your tax returns.

- *Follow your investments' performance.* Prices can rise and fall swiftly in active markets. When you invest directly online, no one will be supervising your account. This makes it essential to follow market trends and prices of securities you own. You want to buy and sell at the most advantageous times.

When you buy and sell securities online or by phone, you will need to use certain types of orders to conduct your trades.

- A *market order* instructs your broker to buy or sell a stock at the best price available. The price may be higher or lower than when you placed the order. Stock prices can change between the time you place an order and the time it is executed.

- A *limit order* instructs your broker to buy or sell a certain stock at a set price or better. If the broker cannot buy or sell at the price you request, the order will not be executed.

- A *stop order* instructs your broker to buy or sell a stock when and if it reaches a specific price. It will be carried out only when stock reaches the target price. This type of order helps you protect your gains and limit losses.

The brokerage firm keeps a record of your transactions. You should receive a statement outlining your account activity periodically, usually every month. You will also receive year-end statements and forms for filing income tax returns.

What Wills Should Include

Generally, it is wise to ask a lawyer for advice on what to include in a will and to draw up the document. A will should do the following:

- *Name beneficiaries,* the people or groups who will receive assets. Assets include personal property and real estate, money, securities, jewelry, and family heirlooms. It should clearly outline a person's wishes for the transfer of his or her property.

- *Name an executor,* the person who will manage the affairs of the estate. He or she pays off funeral expenses, medical bills, taxes, and other liabilities. The executor also performs other duties outlined in the will.

12-7

A copy of your will should be easily available when needed. Another copy may be kept in a safe-deposit box.

- *Name a guardian,* the person responsible for the care of any beneficiaries who are young children. A guardian may also manage an estate on behalf of the dependents, or a trustee may be named to do this. A **trustee** is a person or institution named to manage assets on behalf of the beneficiaries.

A will must be signed in the presence of witnesses. If you change your will after it has been signed, an amendment called a *codicil* is added. The codicil must also be signed in the presence of witnesses. If you need to make major changes in an existing will, you may wish to write a new will. In this case it is important to add a clause that cancels all previous wills and codicils.

The cost of a will varies. The more complex the estate, the more expensive the will may be. You can write your own will. A do-it-yourself kit that contains basic information and sample formats may cost less than $20. However, this is unwise for large estates, situations with many tax issues, or when there are complicated instructions for distributing assets.

Since legal requirements for wills vary from state to state and may change with new laws, consulting an attorney is a wise choice. This is especially true for people who own their own businesses or have estates that total more than $1 million. Attorney fees vary and consumers can usually arrange a free consultation with a lawyer. Your local American Bar Association can refer you to an attorney who can help.

When people die without a will, it is called dying *intestate.* When there is no will, property is divided according to state laws. This is not ideal because it can take a lot of time and the government decides how to distribute assets.

The Living Will or Healthcare Proxy

The **living will**, or *healthcare directive*, is a statement of instructions for specific medical treatment if a person becomes unable to make medical decisions. The primary purpose is to make known what medical treatments you do or do not wish to receive in the face of terminal injury or illness. It outlines your desires about medically prolonging your life. This is a serious and very personal step to take. It needs to be discussed with family members, loved ones, and your physician.

Trusts

In addition to a will, you may need one or more trust agreements, particularly if your estate is complicated or if you wish to make special arrangements for its settlement. A **trust** is a legal document that gives a named trustee the authority to manage the assets in an estate on behalf of the beneficiaries.

When you create a trust, you become the *grantor*. As grantor, you transfer assets to the trust. You name a trustee to manage the assets according to terms outlined in the trust. You also name the beneficiaries who are to receive the assets.

You can establish either a living trust or a testamentary trust. A *living trust*, set up during your lifetime, can provide for the management of your assets before your death and for the distribution of assets as directed after your death. Prior to death you may serve as grantor, trustee, and beneficiary of the trust.

A *testamentary trust* is set up under the terms of your will and becomes effective when you die. Normally, drawing up a trust agreement calls for the services of a competent lawyer who is familiar with estate planning.

Purposes of Trusts

Trusts are used to achieve different goals. People can use a trust to

- provide income and asset management for beneficiaries

- set forth specific provisions for the support and education of minor children or dependents with disabilities

- have a plan in place for managing financial affairs if they should become incapacitated or unable to manage for themselves

- minimize estate and gift taxes

- protect their privacy and avoid probate court

Probate court is the government institution that processes a deceased individual's will and estate. The probate procedure requires

- proof the will is valid

- an inventory and identification of the deceased person's assets and property

- property appraisals

- settlement of debts and taxes

- distribution of property according to terms of the will

Probate can be a costly and time-consuming process that involves paperwork, court appearances, and lawyers. Probate fees are paid out of the estate before assets are distributed. The process can take several months, a year, or longer. The executor of the estate must manage the assets during this period. These proceedings are a matter of public record. You can establish a trust to avoid this lengthy and costly process.

Case Study: Making Plans

Final Decisions

Kelly and Jerome owned a very successful office supply business. Over the years, they made enough money to buy a house, raise two children, travel, and retire in comfort.

Sadly, Jerome died just a few years after they retired. Not only had Kelly lost her husband, she also faced a sea of financial confusion. Neither Kelly nor Jerome could face the thought that one of them would die, so they had not planned accordingly.

Since there was no will, Jerome's estate was divided according to state law. Half of his property went to their children. The amount Kelly received did not allow her to live comfortably for long. She had no legal right to the money the children inherited. Since Kelly and Jerome also did no tax planning, Kelly had to pay taxes that could have been avoided.

Case Review

1. When does it become important to draw a will and look to estate planning?
2. Why is a will important even to those who do not have large amounts of money or property?
3. What are some estate planning steps that can ease financial burdens following the death of a loved one?
4. What are some consequences of dying without a will when one leaves young children behind?
5. What advice would you have given to Jerome and Kelly before they reached retirement age?

Chapter Summary

Investing money offers the opportunity to accumulate more money to meet future needs and goals. Investment choices include stocks, bonds, and mutual funds. Higher risk investments frequently offer the possibility of greater gains—and greater losses than less risky choices. No matter where you put your money, it is smart to investigate before you invest.

Real estate is another way to invest. It can bring handsome profits but also involves considerable risks. Investing in real estate is not for amateurs. You need to do your homework and seek the advice of reliable professionals.

Building an investment portfolio begins with defining objectives and gathering information. Choosing where to invest is an important step. Finally, consulting a reputable financial advisor can help you make sound decisions.

Early planning for retirement is the key to living comfortably in the later years. Today, people are living longer and retiring sooner, which makes early retirement planning even more important.

Estate planning is a part of financial planning that requires careful consideration. This includes drawing up a will and possibly a trust to direct the distribution of assets upon one's death.

Review

1. Define *investing*.

2. List three reasons people choose to invest.

3. What are the key characteristics to consider when choosing an investment?

4. Where are stocks bought and sold?

5. What information on a stock quotation helps investors determine the value of the investment?

6. What is the main difference between a bond and a stock?

7. What are the three main types of bonds?

8. Why do mutual funds offer more diversity than buying individual stocks and bonds?

9. Name and describe one factor affecting investment returns.

10. Name and describe two ways to indirectly invest in real estate.

11. What is a prospectus and what should it tell you?

12. Explain the purpose of brokerage firms and describe three types.

13. Name two sources of retirement income.

14. What retirement plans are designed for self-employed persons?

15. Name the primary objectives of estate planning.

Critical Thinking

16. If you were going to invest in stocks, would you buy common or preferred stock? Which is more likely to increase in value? Which do you think is the better investment? What are the advantages and disadvantages of each?

17. Research and discuss the pros and cons of international securities exchanges.

18. Compare the three types of bonds. Which type of bond would you prefer to buy? Why?

19. What are the advantages and disadvantages of investing in a mutual fund?

20. What should you consider before buying shares in a mutual fund?

21. Name five reliable sources of information on stocks, bonds, and mutual funds.

22. Compare the advantages and disadvantages of buying and selling investments through brokerage firms, investment clubs, and DRIPs.

23. Describe employer sponsored and personal retirement plans, their characteristics, and their tax advantages.

24. Describe the possible consequences of dying without a valid will.

25. If you were to write a will today, what would it contain? How might it change if you were 30 years old, single, and earning $60,000 annually? if you were 30, earning the same amount, and married? with children?

Consumer Cooperatives

Consumer cooperatives are nonretail associations owned and operated by a group of members for their own benefit rather than for profit. Members contribute services and dues to participate in the association. Goods and services usually sell at lower prices than in retail stores. However, the selection of merchandise and customer services are limited to what the membership can provide.

Vending Machines

Vending machines started primarily as places to buy snacks and soft drinks. Today, a large variety of merchandise is available through vending machines, including food, cosmetics, clothing items, grooming supplies, and jewelry.

Vending machines offer the advantages of easy, fast purchases and often are available 24 hours, seven days a week. However, since the actual vendor or seller is not present, dissatisfaction with items purchased from a vending machine can be difficult to resolve.

Consumer Information Sources

There is no substitute for reliable information when you go shopping. As goods, services, and markets become more varied and complex, knowledge is ever more important. Common sources of consumer information on specific goods and services include other consumers, advertisements, labels and hangtags, product rating and testing organizations, salespeople, and the Internet. Knowing how to find, evaluate, and use available information can help you become a smarter shopper.

Other Consumers

Most people get information about products and services from friends, relatives, neighbors, and other people they know. When was the last time you bought something because a friend had it? Friends often provide information about everything from new trendy fashions and exciting movies to computer games and electronic products. Friends can provide valuable information about their experiences with a product, a service, or a seller.

Consumer reviews of products and services have become a prominent feature on the Internet. Many consumers rely on reviews to guide their buying decisions. Products and services frequently reviewed include hotels, restaurants, and autos. Bookseller sites often allow readers to post book reviews. Consumer reviews have expanded to include all types of services, including those of doctors and other professionals.

Reviews are available on company Web sites, independent rating service Web sites, and government or consumer advocacy Web sites. Many of these sites are free. Others charge a fee or require membership to access evaluations.

Emotional Triggers for Spending

For many people, shopping is a fun social pastime. For some it is an unwelcome necessity. For others, shopping is a way to cope with stress, sadness, or low self-esteem. Sometimes, shopping to meet emotional needs causes people to spend more than they can afford. Routine overspending leads to financial problems.

Sometimes people overspend because they seek approval from others. For example, you probably know someone who bought an overpriced pair of sneakers or jeans because everyone else was wearing them. *Peer pressure* is the power a social group has over someone who seeks the group's approval and acceptance.

Another type of pressure to buy is exerted by *role models*, or the people you admire and strive to imitate. A role model can be a parent or other relative, a teacher, a coach, or even a politician. It can be a celebrity, such as a famous athlete or model. Many fads start when famous people adopt them.

When people follow the spending decisions of others, they often make spending mistakes, especially the mistake of overspending. They also buy things they do not need.

Advertising messages often suggest that acquiring possessions brings success, happiness, and satisfaction. However, for most people, being involved and participating in meaningful activities offers a more reliable path to happiness and fulfillment. Hobbies, volunteer work, and sports can relieve stress, build self-esteem, and provide joy and contentment.

Advertisements

Advertising is probably the most readily available source of information about goods, services, and sellers. **Advertising** is a paid message touting the attributes of something in order to convince consumers to buy it. Advertising comes in many formats including ads in magazines, commercials on television, pop-ups on the Internet, and billboard images. Most ads contain some useful information. You can usually count on advertising to

- introduce new products and services

- keep you up-to-date on existing products

- give changing price information

- tell where to find advertised items

To make the best use of ads and commercials, concentrate on the facts. Look and listen for specifics on brands, features, and prices. Keep in mind when looking for the "facts" that advertising is intended to promote and sell goods and services.

Labels and Hangtags

Information on labels and hangtags tells you about the content, quality, performance, care, and maintenance of various products. This information

Copywriters

Copywriters work with artists to conceive, develop, and produce effective advertisements. They create the written message in print ads, posters, brochures, and Web pages as well as the scripts of radio and television spots.

(Your Address)
(Your City, State, Zip Code)
(Date)

(Name of Contact Person)
(Title)
(Company Name)
(Street Address)
(City, State, Zip Code)

Dear (Contact Person):

On (date), I purchased (or had repaired) a (name of product with serial or model number or service performed). I made this purchase at (location and other important details of the transaction.)

Unfortunately, your product (or service) has not performed well (or the service was inadequate) because (state the problem).

Therefore, to resolve the problem I would appreciate your (state what you want—repair, replacement, refund, apology, etc.). Enclosed are copies (copies, NOT originals) of my records (receipts, guarantees, warranties, canceled checks, contracts, model and serial numbers, and any other documents).

I look forward to your reply and a resolution to my problem, and will wait (set a time limit) before seeking third-party assistance. Please contact me at the above address or by phone at (home or office numbers with area codes).

Sincerely,

(Your Name)
(Your Account Number)

14-6

This sample complaint letter shows what information to include when writing about a consumer problem with a product or service.

- *Be prompt.* Do not wait weeks or months to act. Put your case in writing right away and send the letter using registered mail. The receiver must sign for a registered letter, and the sender receives a record of its delivery.

- *Address the right source.* Direct your complaint to the right person and place. If an adjustment requires approval from higher up, the department or store manager is the person to see. Contact the credit department for billing errors and other credit problems. Complain to the top management of a company if a problem is serious or is not solved at lower levels. For names and addresses of local businesses and organizations, check the business's Web site or your local phone book. To find the names of officers of large business firms, use *Standard and Poor's Register of Corporations* available online or in most public libraries.

- *Be specific and factual.* Clearly identify the product or service in question and describe the problem. Include the date and place of purchase, the product name and model number, and the purchase price. Include your account number or the last four digits of your credit card number if the purchase was charged.

- *Be reasonable.* You are more likely to get a satisfactory response if you state your problem reasonably and sympathize with the reader. For example, you might write, "I realize it takes time to correct a computer error, but…" or, "I know it must be difficult to give one-day service on appliances, but…" Threatening or sarcastic letters rarely lead to satisfactory solutions.

- *Suggest a solution.* You may not always get your way, but it helps to outline the solution you are seeking. Do you expect a repair, a replacement, a refund, or an apology?

- *Be businesslike.* Put your grievances and transactions with business firms in writing. Keep a written record of phone conversations with the date, the name of the other party, and promises made or action to be taken. Keep important receipts and records together. You may need to furnish papers or documents such as sales slips, bills, receipts, warranties, and previous correspondence. Send copies of these papers and keep the originals.

- *Be persistent.* Most problems can be solved with one letter directed to the right person. However, if you do not get the desired results, write a follow-up letter. Enclose a copy of earlier correspondence and indicate a date by which you expect some action. If a third letter is necessary, include copies of the previous letters and outline the action you will take if the matter is not settled by a certain date.

Consumer Advocates

If you cannot settle differences directly with sellers, it is often helpful to contact an outside party or organization, such as a consumer advocate. Government agencies that offer consumer assistance and services were listed and described in Chapter 2. Figure 14-7 is a listing of Web sites for key government agencies that assist consumers in different areas.

When dealing with dishonest and fraudulent business practices, contact the appropriate government regulatory agency. Most federal agencies will have local or regional offices. In addition, local and state governments provide regulatory and law enforcement functions to deal with fraud in the marketplace. Check your telephone book for names and numbers of consumer advocacy agencies that assist consumers in your area. Most major city phone books provide a separate listing of government services.

Nongovernment consumer advocacy comes from a variety of sources and offers a range of services to consumers. The advocacy groups fall primarily into the following categories:

- United States Department of Agriculture: www.usda.gov
- Consumer Product Safety Commission: www.cpsc.gov
- Environmental Protection Agency: www.epa.gov
- Federal Trade Commission: www.ftc.gov
- Food and Drug Administration: www.fda.gov
- Health and Human Services: www.hhs.gov
- Housing and Urban Development: www.hud.gov
- National Institutes of Health: www.nih.gov
- United States Postal Service: www.usps.gov
- United States Department of Transportation: www.dot.gov
- United States Department of Justice: www.usdoj.gov
- Securities and Exchange Commission: www.sec.gov
- Social Security Administration: www.ssa.gov

14-7
These Web sites will connect you to key government agencies that serve and protect consumers.

- *Better Business Bureaus (BBBs).* These are nonprofit organizations supported largely by local businesses. They promote ethical business practices, and in some cases, offer dispute resolution programs. Call a local BBB to learn what assistance and services it offers consumers.

- *National Consumer Organizations.* Consumer interest groups offer a variety of services. They advocate for consumer causes, and provide educational materials and information on products and services. Many of these groups work actively for better consumer protection and services, 14-8.

- *Trade Associations and Dispute Resolution Programs.* Companies that produce or sell the same types of goods and services may belong to an industry association. These associations often act as go-betweens for the companies they represent and consumers. They provide consumer

- American Association of Retired Persons (AARP): www.aarp.org
- Consumer Federation of America (CFA): www.consumerfed.org
- Consumers Union: www.consumersunion.org
- Consumer World: www.consumerworld.org
- Federal Reserve Education: www.federalreserveeducation.org
- Identity Theft Resource Center: www.idtheftcenter.org
- Internet Scam Busters: www.scambusters.org
- National Consumers League: www.nclnet.org
- National Foundation for Credit Counseling: www.nfcc.org
- National Consumer League's Fraud Center: www.fraud.org

14-8
This chart lists some of the better known nongovernment organizations that serve and protect consumers.

information on products and services and may offer dispute settlement programs. Most of these associations have Web sites.

- *Corporate Consumer Departments.* Many companies operate consumer affairs departments that deal with consumer concerns and resolve disputes. When you cannot get satisfaction with a seller, you can contact the consumer affairs department at the company headquarters. Very often these departments have toll-free numbers and Web sites.

Difficult Cases

Some problems require some form of legal action. However, legal action is costly and time consuming, and a favorable outcome is not guaranteed. For these reasons, most consumers consider it only as a last resort. Options depend on the nature of the problem and the amount of money involved. These options include binding arbitration, small claims court, a class action lawsuit, or an individual lawsuit.

Binding arbitration is a method of settling disagreements through an objective third party. Once both parties agree to arbitrate, each presents his or her case to the arbitrator to resolve. The arbitrator's decision is final and legally binding. Arbitrators are chosen from a pool of volunteers or professionals depending on the program. Binding arbitration is quick, low cost, and relatively simple and informal.

Small claims court offers a simple, prompt, and inexpensive way to settle minor differences involving small amounts of money. Procedures are relaxed with consumers normally representing themselves without a lawyer. They collect and bring documentation and evidence to support their cases. Claim amounts are limited to a maximum of $1,200 in some states and up to $5,000 in others. Since procedures vary from state to state, contact your local courthouse for more information.

Class action lawsuits are legal actions in courts of law brought by a group of individuals who have been similarly wronged. In these cases, the courts permit members of a common class to pool their grievances. They can then sue for damages on behalf of the entire class or group. One example is a group of consumers who have been similarly harmed or defrauded. Laws governing this type of lawsuit vary from state to state.

Individual **lawsuits** are civil actions brought by a person (a plaintiff) against another party (the defendant). The plaintiff claims to be damaged, or negatively impacted, from actions by the defendant. He or she seeks a legal remedy to be determined by the court. If the plaintiff is successful, a judgment will be entered in his or her favor. The judgment may involve court orders to enforce the plaintiff's rights or award damages to the plaintiff. The court may also issue an order to prevent or compel specific action by the defendant.

The Informed Consumer

Unfortunately, the information you need to be an informed consumer includes constantly changing facts and figures. Products, services, laws, and economic conditions can change a great deal from year to year. It is to

Mediators

Mediators listen to two parties involved in a dispute, sort through differences between them, and find a compromise. Mediators must be neutral and have excellent listening and communication skills.

your advantage to stay up-to-date. Following are some pointers on where to look for consumer information and how to evaluate and use it.

Community Resources

To be an informed consumer, you need to know what data sources are available to you. Figure 14-9 lists some of the resources available in most communities. The people, places, and organizations listed can provide valuable information to help you make wise economic decisions in the marketplace.

A valuable resource that is sometimes overlooked is the newspaper. Almost every daily and weekly newspaper offers articles and advertisements related to consumer issues. Most newspapers are also available online.

The Internet

The Internet opens a whole world of consumer information and resources. You can find product information, the latest on consumer laws and protection, and comparison shopping data. Credit and financial information, health and medical news, and other helpful data are also available. You can research and buy almost anything online.

When using the Internet for information, shopping, or personal business, take care to check the reliability of sources and sites. It is important to follow a few basic guidelines for dealing with distant merchants whether they are selling online or by telephone, mail order catalogs, or television.

14-9
Knowing and using the resources available in your community will help you make intelligent consumer decisions.

Community Resources*

People
Bankers
Business people
Credit managers
Customer service managers
Financial advisers and planners
Insurance agents
Stockbrokers

Places
Brokerage houses
Courthouses
Financial institutions
Insurance companies
Libraries
Real estate firms
Small claims court

Organizations
Bankers associations
Better Business Bureau
Chambers of commerce
Consumer organizations
Trade associations

Government Agencies
Consumer Information Center
Consumer protection agencies
Extension Service
Federal Communications Commission
Federal Trade Commission
Food and Drug Administration
Internal Revenue Service
Social Security Administration

*Most of these resources can be accessed online.

Dealing with Distance Sellers

To make the most of shopping with a seller who does not have a local store, follow these guidelines:

- *Understand what you are buying, from whom you are buying, and all the details of the sale.* Find out the name and physical location of the company. Before you buy, ask questions about the company and its products and services. If you have doubts about the quality of the company or its products, check with the organizations listed in 14-7 and 14-8. Use the checklist in 14-10 to mark off what you need to know before completing a telephone, Internet, television, or catalog purchase.

- *Maintain your security when shopping online.* Buy only from secure sites. Secure site addresses show an icon such as a lock at the bottom right corner of the browser window. If you pay by credit card, you may want to have one card with a low credit limit that you use only for online and other distance purchases.

- *Check the seller's privacy policy before giving your credit card number or other information.* Find out what information about you the site collects, how it is used, and how it is protected. Most reliable sites have an easily accessible "privacy statement" explaining their policies. *Caution: When buying online, provide only the information required to complete transactions. This should not include passwords, Social*

14-10

Use a checklist/form similar to this one before you make a major purchase.

Consumer Checklist
___ Date _____
___ Name of the salesperson _____
___ Name, address, and phone number of the company _____
___ Description of the product or service _____
___ Identifying model and order numbers _____
___ Purchase price _____ Sales tax _____
___ Cost of handling and shipping _____
___ Total cost _____
___ Delivery date _____ Delivery method _____
___ Seller's policies regarding returns, exchanges, refunds _____
___ Terms of any warranties _____
___ Terms of any credit agreement _____
___ Customer service contract _____ Phone number _____

Security numbers, birth dates, bank account numbers, or other personal and financial information.

- *Keep a complete record of each transaction.* Get any information in writing so you have a record of the transaction if you need it. Ask to have a copy of your orders e-mailed to you with confirmation numbers and details of the order. Save and print information on your order—date, delivery promises, merchandise descriptions, prices, guarantees, model numbers, and shipping charges.

- *Pay by credit card.* Credit cards offer the advantages of easier returns and exchanges, convenience in resolving problems, and the protection of consumer credit laws.

- *Know your rights.* Consumer protection laws apply to online transactions. Contact the appropriate law enforcement agency if you have problems. See 14-7 and 14-8 for a listing of agencies and organizations that offer consumer protection and assistance.

- *Take your time.* Do not let sellers rush you into a buying decision, particularly for costly items. Study the offer. Discuss it with a person you trust if you have any doubts or questions. Compare similar offers from other sellers.

- *Do not fall for the unbelievable.* If an offer sounds too good to be true, it probably is not true. Check out "good deals" before you buy.

Regardless of what you are buying, deal only with reputable sellers who are fair and honest with customers. This is the best way for you to protect your interests. The checklist in 14-11 can help you evaluate the many sellers in the marketplace.

Evaluating Consumer Information

After identifying reliable sources of information, you may want to begin a consumer information file. This will put the latest facts and figures at your fingertips when you need them. You can then use material in your file to make intelligent consumer decisions. You will need to evaluate articles and booklets to see what is worth keeping. The following guidelines will help you evaluate materials.

Evaluating Sellers
1. Are policies concerning returns, exchanges, and refunds reasonable?
2. Is advertising believable? Are goods and services available at advertised prices?
3. Are salespeople helpful without being pushy?
4. Can you get straight answers to questions about products, services, and store policies?
5. Does the seller belong to the local chamber of commerce, Better Business Bureau, or other associations that set standards for fair business practices?
6. Do prices and services compare favorably with those of other sellers?
7. Have people you know had favorable experiences dealing with the seller?
8. Do you get prompt, courteous attention when you have questions, problems, or complaints?
9. Does management accept responsibility for the actions of salespeople and other employees?
10. Does the seller have a good reputation in the community?

14-11

These questions can help you evaluate the reliability and fairness of sellers. Several *no* answers should warn you away from a seller.

Use Reliable and Informed Sources

A reliable source on one subject may not be the best place for facts on other topics. For example, a banker may give sound financial advice, but know nothing about buying furniture. A medical association can tell you how to find a doctor, but not how to buy a car. The Food and Drug Administration can tell you how to read a nutrition label, but not how to judge auto repair services.

Determine the Primary Purpose of the Information

Is it intended to inform the buyer or to sell a product, service, or idea? Both news articles and advertisements can offer helpful information, but advertisements generally present only positive facts.

Evaluate the Usefulness of the Information

Look for material that is up-to-date and easy to understand. Read to see if recent developments on the product or subject are discussed. Consider whether the data is complete. Does it tell what you need to know about products, services, features, quality, performance, warranties, and prices?

Once you begin collecting consumer materials, you will need to organize the information for easy use. Find a drawer or box large enough to hold all the materials you collect. Then sort according to subject matter. As you gather new materials, add them to your file. Periodically review what you have filed and discard information that is no longer current or useful. If you keep information electronically, organize it by folders.

Consumer Rights and Responsibilities

In a message to Congress in 1962, President John F. Kennedy outlined four basic consumer rights. Since 1962, four more rights have been added. The eight rights are

- the right to safety

- the right to be informed

- the right to choose

- the right to be heard

- the right to satisfaction of basic needs

- the right to redress

- the right to education

- the right to a healthful environment

Today, these eight consumer rights have been endorsed by the United Nations and affirmed by Consumers International, a worldwide consumer organization. (See www.consumersinternational.org.) Each of these rights carries responsibilities. Together they form the basis for fairness in meeting consumer needs.

Safety: Rights and Responsibilities

The right to safety means protection against the sale and distribution of dangerous goods and services. The government plays an important role in protecting consumers.

However, responsibilities for safety also rest with consumers. For example, it is up to the consumer to read and follow directions that come with a product, especially those that can present hazards with misuse. These include electric and gas appliances, household chemicals, and yard equipment. Care in the safe use, storage, and disposal of potentially dangerous products is also a key consumer responsibility, 14-12. Consumers have a responsibility to report product-related health and safety problems promptly to the seller and the manufacturer. If the problem is serious, such as a shock from an electric product, consumers should also inform the proper government agency. The agency can take prompt action to prevent an injury or accident for other consumers. The Consumer Products Safety Commission handles problems involving hazardous products. The Food and Drug Administration deals with issues related to food, drug, and cosmetic products.

14-12

These labels are required on products containing hazardous substances.

Truthful Information: Rights and Responsibilities

Consumers are entitled to accurate information on which to base their choices and buying decisions. The most common sources of consumer information include advertising, product labels, warranties, articles in newspapers and magazines, salespeople, and other consumers. Government protects the consumer's right to information through various agencies and laws. For example, it requires labels with specific information on certain products. Contracts and agreements are also required to provide specific information for the consumer. In addition, government prohibits false and misleading advertising.

With this right comes the consumer responsibility to seek, evaluate, and use available information on products, services, and sellers. Before you buy, investigate a seller's policies on sales, returns, and exchanges. It also pays to check a store's reputation for honesty and fair play, to evaluate advertising claims and product performance, and to compare quality and prices.

Choice: Rights and Responsibilities

Consumers have the right to choose the goods and services they buy and the places they shop. To have free choices, the market must provide a number

of sellers offering a variety of goods and services at competitive prices. Laws protect consumers' free choice in the marketplace by prohibiting practices such as monopoly and price fixing.

Consumers are responsible for carefully choosing those products and services that will best meet their needs at prices they can pay. Choosing is not always an easy matter. The average supermarket alone carries over 15,000 items with a wide variety in almost every product category. This calls for informed and careful decisions, 14-13.

The responsibilities of choice go beyond the goods and services you buy. Consumers also have an obligation to deal only with reliable, reputable businesses. This is for their own protection and for the overall good of the marketplace. Every buying choice expresses approval of the purchase and the seller. Consumers need to be aware of the message they send with their choices and their money.

14-13

Consumer choice in a market economy is well illustrated in the modern supermarket. Each department offers an abundance of choices.

A Voice: Rights and Responsibilities

When consumers have legitimate problems or concerns, they have the right to speak up, be heard, and expect results. This requires that both business and government respond.

Consumers are responsible for speaking out and expressing their concerns to appropriate business and government representatives. This means learning and using appropriate and effective means of communication. Consumers need to develop the ability to compliment and complain. Let businesses know what you like and want, as well as what you dislike.

Satisfaction of Basic Needs: Rights and Responsibilities

Consumers have the right to access goods and services that satisfy their basic needs. These include adequate food, shelter, clothing, health care, education, and sanitation. The basics should be available to all consumers. To satisfy basic needs, you need both enough income to purchase essentials and a marketplace that provides them.

Governments play a major role both in defining basic needs and ensuring that all citizens are able to satisfy them. The U.S. government provides public housing and social programs, Medicare and Medicaid, Social Security, tax-supported schools and hospitals, and sewer and sanitation systems. However, providing these for everyone is an ongoing challenge.

Responsibility for satisfying basic needs rests also with consumers themselves. For example, it is up to the consumer to put essential needs

Key Nutrients		
Nutrient	**Functions**	**Sources**
Vitamins Vitamin A	Helps keep skin clear and smooth Helps keep mucous membranes healthy Helps prevent night blindness Helps promote growth	Liver, egg yolk, dark green and yellow fruits and vegetables, butter, whole milk, cream, fortified margarine, ice cream, cheddar-type cheese
Thiamin (Vitamin B-1)	Helps promote normal appetite and digestion Helps keep nervous system healthy Helps body release energy from food	Pork, other meats, poultry, fish, eggs, enriched or whole-grain breads and cereals, dried beans, brewer's yeast
Riboflavin (Vitamin B-2)	Helps cells use oxygen Helps keep skin, tongue, and lips normal Helps prevent scaly, greasy areas around mouth and nose Aids digestion	Milk, all kinds of cheese, ice cream, liver, other meats, fish, poultry, eggs, dark leafy green vegetables
Niacin (a B vitamin)	Helps keep nervous system healthy Helps keep skin, mouth, tongue, and digestive tract healthy Helps cells use other nutrients	Meat, fish, poultry, milk, enriched or whole-grain breads and cereals, peanuts, peanut butter, dried beans and peas
Vitamin C	Helps wounds heal and broken bones mend Helps body fight infection Helps make cementing materials that hold body cells together Promotes healthy gums and tissues	Citrus fruits, strawberries, cantaloupe, broccoli, green peppers, raw cabbage, tomatoes, green leafy vegetables, potatoes and sweet potatoes cooked in the skin
Vitamin D	Helps build strong bones and teeth Helps maintain bone density	Fortified milk, butter and margarine, fish liver oils, liver, sardines, tuna, egg yolk, sunshine
Vitamin E	Acts as an antioxidant although exact functions are not known	Liver and other variety meats, eggs, leafy green vegetables, whole-grain cereals, salad oils, shortenings, and other fats and oils
Vitamin K	Helps blood clot	Organ meats, leafy green vegetables, cauliflower, other vegetables, egg yolk
Protein	Builds and repairs tissues Helps make antibodies, enzymes, hormones, and some vitamins Regulates fluid balance in the cells Regulates many body processes Supplies energy when needed	Complete proteins: Meat, poultry, fish, eggs, milk and other dairy products, peanuts, peanut butter, lentils Incomplete proteins: Cereals, grains, vegetables

(Continued.)

15-1

A well-balanced diet provides the body with the six types of nutrients: vitamins, proteins, fats, carbohydrates, minerals, and water.

Nutrient	Functions	Sources
Fat	Supplies energy Carries fat-soluble vitamins Protects vital organs Insulates the body from shock and temperature changes Adds flavor to foods Provides essential fatty acids	Butter, margarine, cream, cheese, marbling in meats, nuts, whole milk, olives, chocolate, egg yolks, bacon, salad oils, dressings
Carbohydrates	Supplies energy Provides bulk and fiber in the form of cellulose (needed for good digestion) Helps the body digest fats efficiently	Sugar: Honey, jam, jelly, sugar, molasses Fiber: Fresh fruits and vegetables, whole-grain cereals, and breads Starch: breads, cereals, corn, peas, beans, potatoes, pasta
Minerals **Calcium**	Helps build bones and teeth Helps blood clot Helps muscles and nerves function properly Helps regulate the use of other minerals in the body	Milk, cheese, other dairy products, leafy green vegetables, and fish eaten with the bones
Phosphorous	Helps build strong bones and teeth Helps regulate many body processes Aids metabolism	Protein and calcium food sources
Iron	Combines with protein to make hemoglobin Helps cells use oxygen Aids metabolism	Liver, lean meats, egg yolk, dried beans and peas, leafy green vegetables, dried fruits, enriched and whole-grain breads and cereals
Water	Is a basic part of blood and tissue fluid Helps carry nutrients to cells Helps carry waste products from cells Helps control body temperature	Water, beverages, soups, and most foods

Key Nutrients *(continued)*

15-1

(Continued.)

state lines. Products that carry government inspection and grade markings include raw meat, raw poultry, processed meat and poultry products, eggs, and dairy products.

Organic Foods

Most food stores today feature organic foods, particularly in the produce, meat, and dairy sections. **Organic foods** are produced without manufactured fertilizers, pesticides, growth stimulants, genetic engineering, and other banned processes. Organic meats and poultry must come from animals raised without the use of growth hormones, antibiotics, or feed made from animal parts. The only drugs that may be used are those that treat sick animals.

Organic foods are always more expensive than non-organic counterparts. They are more costly to produce and bring to the market. The USDA Organic stamp may be used only on foods that are certified at least 95% organic, 15-11. Organic foods are generally no more nutritious than other foods. However, they are often purchased by consumers who are concerned about the effects of pesticides, growth stimulants, and genetic engineering.

Buying Food Online

In some areas, you can do your food marketing on the Internet. Buying food online offers the advantages of shopping at any time of day or night and having groceries delivered to your door. Some large supermarkets

USDA

15-11

Foods that are certified as organic by the USDA may carry this stamp.

offer online and telephone shopping. In some urban and suburban areas, independent non-store marketers sell food and groceries only online.

Though online services vary, the basic operation is similar for all. The seller maintains a warehouse of food and grocery products. The customer selects staples and products listed in the online menu, which usually has categories similar to those in the supermarket. These will include dairy products, produce, meats and poultry, canned goods, frozen foods, and general grocery supplies. Most sites also offer weekly specials.

Customers click items they want, filling their online shopping carts, and pay with a credit card. The seller delivers the order within a specified time period. While delivery and other fees may be involved, many consumers claim they save money because they do less impulse buying and more planning. People with disabilities, parents with infants, and those who dislike grocery shopping appreciate this convenience.

Buying Specific Foods

Knowing how to judge the quality and nutritional value of specific foods is essential to getting your money's worth in the supermarket. Following are some general guides to follow when shopping in different departments within the food store.

Dairy Products

Dairy products are one of the best sources of calcium and are excellent sources of other essential nutrients including protein, phosphorus, and vitamins A, B-2, and D. You can choose from a wide variety of dairy foods, such as milk, cheese, ice cream, and yogurt.

Milk and Milk Products

Fresh milk is popular for drinking and many other uses. You can buy it fat-free or with three different levels of fat content: low-fat 1%, low-fat 2%, or whole, which is over 3% fat. All forms of milk contribute the same nutrients except for fat. Flavored milk drinks are also available. Cultured buttermilk and yogurt are other milk products found in the dairy section of food stores.

Concentrated milk products include canned evaporated milk and sweetened condensed milk plus nonfat dry milk. These are usually used in recipes and are not interchangeable.

Cream is available with fat content ranging from a small amount to 40%. Cream products include half-and-half, light cream or coffee cream, light whipping cream, and heavy whipping cream. Also available are sour half-and-half and sour cream.

Ice cream is a frozen dessert with high fat and sugar content. Lower-fat varieties are also available.

Cheese

Cheese is a dairy food that is made from a concentrated form of milk or cream. Nutrients, color, texture, aroma, flavor, and cost vary with each of the many varieties of cheese. When buying cheese, compare the prices of various forms of the same type of cheese. Sliced, cubed, shredded, or grated cheese usually costs more than the same quantity of cheese sold in a solid piece.

Butter

Butter is a dairy product made from the fat or cream of milk. Commonly sold in sticks, butter is available salted or unsalted. Whipped butter costs more than regular butter. National brands and higher grades cost more than house brands and lower grades. Butter is usually more expensive than margarine, which is a widely used butter substitute. Margarine is made from vegetable oils and is not a dairy product.

Eggs

Eggs are high in protein and can be served as a less-expensive substitute for meat. They also provide B vitamins, iron, phosphorus, and vitamins A and D. Since egg yolks are high in cholesterol, many health experts recommend using whole eggs or yolks in moderation.

A variety of egg products are available at most food stores. They are similar to whole eggs in the nutrients they provide. These can be found in the dairy section near whole eggs.

The price of eggs depends on their grade and size. Higher grades and larger sizes are more expensive. Government grades are based on the appearance of the egg yolk, white, and shell. The three grades are U.S. Grade AA, U.S. Grade A, and U.S. Grade B. Most stores sell only Grade AA or A eggs.

When shopping, select eggs with clean, uncracked shells, 15-12. Shell color has nothing to do with quality, nutritive value, or flavor.

Meats

Beef, veal, pork, and lamb are the most commonly chosen meats. All are high in protein as well as phosphorus, iron, copper, and B vitamins. Different cuts vary in tenderness, size, and amount of fat and bone. The

15-12

When buying eggs, check to make sure no shells are cracked.

amount of meat you need to buy depends on the cut and the number of people you plan to serve. Between two and three ounces of cooked lean meat is considered one serving. Boneless, fat-trimmed cuts yield more servings than cuts containing bones and fat. Ask in the meat department for advice on the amount to buy for the number of servings you need. When shopping for meats, use the following tips:

- *Look for government inspection and grading.* The "U.S. Inspected and Passed" stamp indicates that meat is wholesome and produced under sanitary conditions. Meat grades indicate quality characteristics such as flavor, juiciness, and tenderness. *Prime, Choice,* and *Select* are the grades most commonly found in retail stores for beef, veal, and lamb. All grades are comparable nutritionally. Prime, the top grade, is sold primarily to fine restaurants. Choice meats are the better-quality cuts available in supermarkets. Select meats are less-flavorful and tender.

- *Choose firm, moist, fine-grained, and well-marbled meat.* Marbling refers to the small flecks of fat throughout the lean that help make meat tender. Veal has little fat and little marbling. High-quality beef is bright red in color; veal is light pink; pork is grayish-pink; and lamb is pinkish-red.

- *Compare meat cuts and prices.* Although one pound of meat with bones may cost less than a pound of boneless meat, it yields fewer servings. Compare meat prices on the basis of cost per serving rather than cost per pound.

- *Consider variety meats, such as liver, kidney, heart, and tongue.* These are highly nutritious and are usually priced lower than other meats.

Poultry

Poultry includes chicken, turkey, duck, goose, and Rock Cornish hens. All of these, if sold across state lines, are federally inspected and marked for wholesomeness. Poultry may also be graded for quality. The highest grades go to the meatiest birds with the least pinfeathers and skin defects.

The age of a bird, not its grade, determines how tender it will be. Birds become less tender as they mature. Young chickens are labeled *broiler, fryer, capon, roaster,* or *Rock Cornish hens.* Young turkeys and ducks are labeled *young.* Mature chickens are stewed, steamed, or pressure-cooked. They are labeled *hen, fowl,* and *stewing chicken.*

When shopping for poultry, choose clean, moist, plump birds with meaty breasts, legs, and thighs. You can buy poultry whole, halved, or cut up. Larger birds usually cost less per pound than smaller birds. Whole chicken is less expensive than chicken cut into pieces. Chicken with the bone in is less expensive than boneless.

Fish

The two types of fish available are those with fins and backbones versus shellfish varieties with no backbones. Fresh fish is usually sold by the pound. Allow about two ounces of cooked boneless fish per serving. Check the labels on packaged, canned, and frozen seafood products for the amount to buy for the number of servings you need.

Inspection and grading of fish is not mandatory, but there is a voluntary inspection program for the fish industry. Since not all fish are inspected or graded, careful selection is especially important. Look for firm flesh; tight, shiny scales; and bright, bulging eyes. The fish should have no smell. Fresh fish and shellfish should always be refrigerated or kept on ice in the marketplace and transferred promptly to the refrigerator at home.

Whole fish is sold as it comes from the water. Dressed fish has head, fins, scales, and tail removed. Fish fillets are the sides of the fish cut lengthwise. Fillets have few or no bones and are ready to cook. Fish steaks are cross-sectional slices of a dressed fish with one large central bone. Steaks are also ready to cook.

Fruits and Vegetables

Fruits and vegetables are available in a variety of forms—fresh, canned, frozen, and dried. Fresh fruits and vegetables are called **produce**, 15-13. Price depends on the quality, time of year, growing conditions, and transportation costs.

The best time to buy various types of fresh fruits and vegetables is when they are "in season." Supplies are plentiful and lower in price then. When you shop for produce, consider size, weight, freshness, ripeness, and appearance. The way you use fruits and vegetables can influence your

15-13

A supermarket usually has a large produce department with many choices.

choice. For example, there is no need to buy top-quality produce if you plan to mix it into a salad or casserole.

Compare prices of fresh, frozen, and canned fruits and vegetables. Usually frozen fruits and vegetables cost less than fresh produce. Canned foods cost less than frozen or fresh. You may also want to compare prices of different forms and brands of fruits and vegetables. Canned or frozen fruits and vegetables that are chopped, sliced, or cut cost less than whole pieces. Different brands of the same food also vary in cost, and the most expensive is not necessarily the best or more nutritious.

Grain Products

Grain products include breads, cereals, rice, and pastas. Whole-grain products provide fiber and more nutrients than products made from refined grains. For these reasons, half of your daily intake should be from whole-grain sources. Compared to many other foods, most grain products are inexpensive, well liked, and easy to include in meal plans.

Baked Goods

Wheat, barley, corn, oats, rice, and rye are the grains from which most baked goods are made. Flour is the basic grain product that is used to make breads and bakery products. Most flour is made from wheat, but you can also buy rye, potato, rice, and buckwheat flours.

Baked goods include rolls, cakes, and pastries. Ready-to-serve products generally cost more than home baked or those requiring some preparation. Fresh bakery goods usually cost more than refrigerated or frozen goods. Because of their sugar and fat content, you may want to limit your intake of these foods.

Breakfast Cereal

Cereals made from grains come in a variety of forms, flavors, and nutritive values. Many have added sugar plus other ingredients, such as nuts and dried fruit. Ready-to-eat and instant cereals are more convenient and more costly than cereals that require cooking. Small boxes and individual serving-size boxes of cereal cost more per serving than larger boxes. More breakfast cereals are including whole grains.

Pasta

Pasta comes in different shapes and sizes. Although pasta is a relatively inexpensive food, it is a favorite in a variety of recipes among consumers of all income levels. Look for whole-grain pastas for greater nutritive value.

Rice

Special rice products, such as wild rice, seasoned rice, and the instant rice varieties, tend to cost more than white rice that requires cooking.

Chinese fried rice and other seasoned and flavored rices are available canned or frozen, ready to heat and serve. These forms of rice cost more because of the additional processing required. Brown rice contains more nutrients than the more highly processed white rice products.

After You Shop

What you do with food at home is the key to enjoying all that you have carefully purchased. Proper storage is necessary to maintain food quality, flavor, and nutritive value. Proper handling is important to ensure food safety.

Food Safety

Guaranteeing food safety and avoiding foodborne illnesses begins in the grocery store and ends when you sit down to eat. The following guidelines can help you keep your food safe.

- Separate raw and cooked foods during shopping, storage, and preparation.

- Be sure hands and food-contact surfaces are clean.

- Wash fruits and vegetables, but do not rinse meats and poultry prior to cooking.

- Refrigerate perishables and leftovers promptly and defrost frozen items according to directions.

- Cook foods to high-enough temperatures to kill microorganisms. Use a food thermometer and follow temperature recommendations.

- Avoid unpasteurized milk, milk products, and juices.

- Do not eat raw sprouts or raw or partially cooked eggs, meats, or poultry.

For more detailed information, go to www.fsis.usda.gov, the USDA Food Safety and Inspection Service Web site.

Food Storage

There are three places to store foods—on a shelf, in the refrigerator, and in the freezer. Packaged foods usually have storage suggestions on their labels, 15-14. Bread and fruit that are used in a couple days usually stay fresh at room temperature. However, they keep for longer

15-14
Nonperishable food items can be stored in cabinets.

periods of time in the refrigerator. Other items, such as meat or casserole dishes, keep one to three days in the refrigerator. They should be stored in the freezer for longer periods.

Food Preparation

Planning and preparing food in an attractive, appetizing way increases mealtime pleasure. Preparation also can affect the nutritive value, appearance, and taste of different foods. You can get more satisfaction from food dollars if you learn how to prepare foods that appeal to the people you are feeding.

Consider food contrasts. Try to combine foods that complement each other in flavor and appearance. Serve a colorful combination of hot and cold foods, sweet and tart flavors, and crisp and soft textures. Try to preserve natural colors and textures of food.

Include one or two known favorites in each meal, but try new foods and combinations. Fresh recipes and menus add interest and variety to mealtime.

Use recipes from a respected cookbook, magazine, or Internet site to guide you in planning meals. A pinch of this and a handful of that may work for experienced cooks. However, written, tested recipes are always more reliable.

Eating Out

Americans spend a considerable amount of money eating out. Whether eating away from home is a necessity or a pleasure, you will want to get a good food value for your money.

Choosing a Restaurant

When you eat out, you are paying for more than just the food. You are paying for someone to buy, prepare, cook, and serve the food. Even at inexpensive fast-food operations, meals usually cost more than similar foods you prepare at home. Consider how much and how often you are willing to pay someone else to shop and cook for you.

Before choosing a restaurant for a leisurely meal, find out about the types of foods served and the prices. A phone call before you leave home or a few questions before you are seated may save you time, money, and embarrassment. By calling ahead of time, you can find out if reservations are required or accepted; if a certain type of clothing is required or not allowed; and if credit cards are accepted. Much of this information can also be found on a restaurant's Web site. If you go to a restaurant and find it is not what you want, it is a good idea to leave quietly and find a place you can enjoy.

Case Study: Dining Out

Leroy and His Date

Leroy plans to take Patty to dinner and a movie on Saturday night. For this occasion, he wants to find a nice restaurant with a little atmosphere. He has heard commercials for a new place called Le Chateau.

Leroy doesn't realize they will need reservations. After waiting almost 45 minutes, Leroy and Patty are seated at a small table in a noisy, cramped spot. A waiter brings them a menu that is printed in French, which neither Leroy nor Patty understands. They both order the least expensive item on the menu. Even that is more than Leroy can easily afford.

The food they ordered is a baked egg dish with finely ground goose liver. It is not a dish either of them ever wants to try again. They both eat quickly with very little conversation and not much appetite.

When the check comes, it is twice the amount Leroy had planned to spend. Luckily, he has enough money with him to pay. All he has to do now is figure out what to do with the rest of the evening. He has no money left for a movie.

Case Review

1. How could Leroy have avoided this unforgettable evening at Le Chateau?
2. What might Leroy have done once they arrived at Le Chateau and he realized that it was not what he expected? How would you plan a dinner at a restaurant you have never tried before?

Restaurant reviews in local papers and magazines and online can be very helpful. They describe the types of food served, house specialties, atmosphere, and service. They tell the price range and the hours the restaurant is open. Sometimes you can find bargains as well as atmosphere at ethnic restaurants. In metropolitan areas you can find a wide variety of choices. Italian, Greek, Asian, Mexican, and German are among the popular ethnic restaurants. They usually serve foods and dishes you may not normally prepare at home. Prices are often reasonable, too.

If you are eating out with friends, decide ahead of time how you want to pay. Ask for separate checks when each person is paying his or her own way. Separate checks save figuring and hassling when the bill comes.

Case Study: Dining Out

An Even Split

Haajid has $10 to stretch over three more days until he gets paid again. He and four friends are eating at the Macho Taco. Haajid orders very carefully, trying to keep his tab under $5. He manages to get two tacos and a lemonade for $4.75. He is congratulating himself on his cheap meal while the other guys order big dinners.

The waitress puts all the orders on the same bill. When they are ready to leave, Haajid's friend Sam takes the check. He divides the total by five instead of trying to figure out who had what. He tells the guys that each share is $7.25. Haajid doesn't have the nerve to speak up and say his share is really only $4.75. He is afraid of looking cheap.

Case Review

1. How could Haajid have avoided this problem?
2. What would you have done if you were Haajid? How can you prevent similar experiences from happening to you?

Selecting Healthful Choices

It can be a challenge to follow a healthful diet when eating out. Restaurants frequently offer large portions, high-calorie meals, and tempting dishes that are high in sugar, fat, and salt. Here are some suggestions to help you stay healthy even if you eat out frequently.

- Choose baked, broiled, or grilled foods over fried foods.
- Limit or stay away from foods that are high in sugar, fat, and salt. Look for "heart healthy" and low-calorie selections.
- Order whole-wheat breads, pastas, and cereals.
- Look for fresh fruits and vegetables.
- Take part of a super-size portion home for tomorrow's meal.
- Split orders or ask for a junior size where serving sizes tend to be too large.

Tipping

Include tips when you figure the cost of eating out. Fast-food, self-serve places do not usually call for tips. In most other restaurants, tipping is expected.

Be prepared to leave 15 to 20 percent of the bill for a tip. For a total food bill of $30.00, a 15 percent tip is $4.50 and a 20 percent tip is $6.00. A 20 percent or slightly higher tip is appropriate in expensive restaurants and for exceptionally good service.

Chapter Summary

Food is an important item both in your budget and in your overall health and well-being. You will spend a sizable share of income in grocery stores and restaurants. The food you eat will affect the way you look, feel, and function.

Smart eating begins with nutritious meals and snacks. Two reliable guides to nutrition and good health are the Dietary Guidelines for Americans and MyPyramid. They offer suggestions for healthful eating.

To get the most for your dollars when shopping for food, you need to understand how supply and demand affect food prices. Establishing a food budget will help you control spending and get more for your money. Consider who eats in your household, any special dietary needs, and your family's food preferences. Your budget will also depend on how much you entertain and eat out, where you shop, and how skilled you are as a food shopper.

Planning purchases is one key to smart shopping. Food pages of local papers can give you ideas for menus. Using a list helps you remember all the items you need and gives direction to your shopping. Certain shopping aids in grocery stores can help you find the best buys. The labels on food products will be one of your most reliable guides.

Storing foods properly is a key factor in preserving flavor, freshness, and quality. The type of storage will depend on the food and how soon you intend to use it. Preparation of foods is a vital part to enjoying meals and snacks.

There are several factors to consider when eating in restaurants. Call ahead or check online when trying a new place to eat so you will know what to expect. Look for healthful choices on the menu. Be prepared to leave a tip in most restaurants.

Review

1. List the six types of nutrients.

2. List the five food groups represented in MyPyramid.

3. List five questions that can help you establish a food budget.

4. How can planning food purchases make consumers better food shoppers?

5. Name two reasons for shopping in the same one or two stores for groceries.

6. List three ways the UPC system can affect food shopping.

7. What information is required on nutrition facts panels?

8. How can you use unit pricing to save money?

9. What is the last day a product should be sold called?

10. What type of chicken should you select for frying, roasting, and broiling?

11. Why is it a good idea to call a restaurant ahead of time if you have never eaten there before?

Critical Thinking

12. Name three good food sources for each of the six types of nutrients the body needs.

13. How can MyPyramid help you plan meals and shop for foods?

14. How would you decide where to shop for food?

15. Why is proper food storage and food preparation important to successful food budgeting? For two weeks, keep track of the food that becomes waste in your home. Report to the class what foods were wasted, why, and how much money was lost.

16. Prepare a guide to healthful eating in restaurants.

If you can afford everything you want, you are ready to start shopping. If you cannot buy all you need, prioritize your needs and focus on your highest priorities. For example, if you have enough casual clothing, do not buy another casual shirt just because it is on sale. Look for the clothes that will fill the gaps in your wardrobe.

There are several ways to save money on your wardrobe purchases. Here are a few ideas:

- Compare the prices and quality of merchandise between different sellers. Comparison shopping can help you save money if you know how to judge quality and style.

- Try bargain-hunter sources such as clothing warehouses, factory outlets, surplus stores, resale shops, and discount stores.

- Watch store ads for specials and preseason sales. End-of-season sales offer some of the best savings. For example, in mid-July, swimwear and summer clothing is often reduced by 30 to 50 percent. By August, summer items will be marked down even more.

- If you or someone in your family sews, some of your clothes can be made at home. Sewing skills can cut wardrobe costs substantially.

Sometimes a low price signals a real bargain. Other times it signals poor quality or outdated fashions. It is important to know the difference.

Shopping for Clothes

You need to know how to judge quality and what quality level will best serve different purposes. You also need to know how much you can spend. It can be helpful to shop with a trusted friend who can help you make choices.

As you shop consider fit, style and color, fabrics, and construction features. Try garments on in front of a full-length mirror to check fit, appearance, and comfort. Hands-on inspection is the best way to check construction details and fabric characteristics. Labels and tags will give you the best care information. These tips apply to in-store shopping.

Catalog and online outlets often have values and variety that may be hard to find in local stores. Many clothing manufacturers sell clothing online or through catalogs. Once you know and like particular brands, you usually can trust their online and catalog offerings.

If you buy from these and other distance sellers, it is important to follow the suggestions in Chapter 14 under "dealing with distance sellers." Wherever you buy, be sure to

- check garment construction
- know what fibers, fabrics, and finishes have been used
- check fit, comfort, and appearance
- read labels and tags for use and care information

Clothing Construction

The way garments are put together can affect appearance, fit, and durability. Poorly made garments look worn and unattractive quickly.

Human Services

Buyers
Buyers determine which fashions their establishments will sell. They must have the ability to predict what will appeal to consumers. They must constantly stay informed of the latest trends, to maximize the profits and reputation of their company. They keep track of inventories and sales levels through computer software.

Better-quality clothes are usually more expensive, but they may be better buys. With proper care, they look attractive much longer.

To judge the quality of construction, check sewing and finishing details on the seams, linings, hems, collars, lapels, buttonholes, zippers, and pockets. Construction features to look for in well-made clothing include

- smooth seams, hems, zippers, and lapels
- reinforcement at points of strain
- firmly attached buttons, hooks and eyes, snaps, and trim
- generous allowances for seams, hems, pleats, slits, and lapels
- appropriate trim and decoration for the garment
- smooth and firmly stitched buttonholes

Fibers, Fabrics, and Finishes

Fiber content, construction methods, and finishes affect the way a fabric looks and feels, its performance and care, and its price. Knowing how fabrics are made can help you make informed clothing choices.

Fiber Content

Most fabrics are made from *natural* or *manufactured fibers*. **Natural fibers** come from plants and animals. They include cotton, linen, silk, wool, and

Arts, A/V Technology & Communications

Fashion Designers

Fashion designers study fashion trends and sketch designs of clothing and accessories. They then select colors and fabrics and oversee the final production of their designs.

Organic Fabrics

Interest in clothing labeled *organic* is growing. Items ranging from diapers to T-shirts to jeans, for example, are using organic cotton. Such items often cost more based on how much organic fiber is used.

Only raw natural fibers such as cotton and wool are eligible to be called *organic.* They come from crops and livestock, so are considered agricultural products. The U.S. Department of Agriculture (USDA) sets rules to assure consumers that agricultural products marketed as organic meet consistent, uniform standards. The rules are part of USDA's National Organic Program (NOP) regulations.

Only textiles that meet strict NOP production and processing standards are eligible for the

- *"100 Percent Organic" label*, which requires all fibers to be organic
- *"Organic" label*, which requires at least 95 percent of fibers to be organic

In both cases, the USDA Organic seal may be displayed. The claim "Made with Organic Fibers," however, has no use restrictions. This means consumers need to contact clothing manufacturers or retailers who use the claim to find out what percent of fibers are truly organic.

A USDA-licensed agent monitors production and processing steps to certify that producers and handlers comply with the standards. Organic crops are raised without most common pesticides, petroleum-based fertilizers, or sewage sludge-based fertilizers. Animals raised organically must have organic feed and access to the outdoors. They are given no antibiotics or growth hormones.

other hair fibers, such as camel's hair and cashmere. Following are some of the key characteristics of natural fibers commonly used for clothing.

- *Cotton* is absorbent, comfortable, easy to dye, and easy to combine with other fibers. If untreated it tends to wrinkle easily, shrink in hot water, and be highly flammable. It is reasonably durable and suited to many uses.

- *Linen* is absorbent, comfortable, durable, and lustrous in appearance. If untreated it wrinkles and creases easily and has poor resistance to mildew. It will be expensive if it is good quality.

- *Silk* looks and feels luxurious, combines well with other fibers, resists wrinkling, and is strong but lightweight. It also is expensive, requires dry cleaning unless labeled *washable*, and tends to water spot unless treated.

- *Wool* is the warmest of natural fibers. It is wrinkle resistant, easy to dye, durable, and absorbent. It also retains its shape and combines well with other fibers. Wool shrinks when moisture and heat are applied. It requires dry cleaning unless labeled *washable* and it burns easily. It is attractive to moths and carpet beetles.

Most **manufactured fibers** are made from chemicals. They include polyester, nylon, rayon, acrylic, acetate, and a host of others. Following are some of the key characteristics of manufactured fibers commonly used for clothing.

- *Polyester* is strong and durable, easy to dye, and colorfast. It retains its shape well and resists wrinkles, stretching, shrinking, moths, and mildew. It generally is easy to launder, but is subject to oily stains, soil, and pilling.

- *Nylon* is lightweight, stretchable, strong, and durable. It drapes well and dyes well. It dries quickly, cleans easily, and resists abrasion. It is nonabsorbent and can be uncomfortable in hot weather.

- *Rayon* is a soft, durable, comfortable, and absorbent fabric. It drapes and dyes well and is resistant to insect damage. If not treated, it wrinkles easily, is highly flammable, and shrinks in hot water.

- *Acrylic* is a soft luxurious fabric that resembles wool. It drapes well, dyes well, and gives warmth without weight. It is an absorbent, comfortable, easy care fabric that is resistant to wrinkles, moths, oil, and sunlight.

- *Acetate* is a soft, luxurious fabric that dyes and drapes well. It is resistant to shrinkage, moths, and mildew. It is nonabsorbent and usually requires dry cleaning.

A **blend** is made by combining two or more fibers. Blends usually have the best characteristics of the different fibers used. For example, cotton/polyester is a very common and popular blend. It combines the absorbency and comfort of cotton with the wrinkle-resistance and easy-care property of polyester.

16-2

Knit sweaters and hats are comfortable because they stretch to fit the body.

Fabric Construction

The way fibers are made into fabric affects appearance and performance. Weaving and knitting are the two most common methods of fabric construction.

Woven fabrics are made by interlacing two or more sets of yarns at right angles. A number of weaving variations are used to achieve special effects. Generally, weaving produces durable fabrics that hold their shape well. Fabrics that are tightly woven or knitted tend to hold their shape better than those loosely woven or knitted.

Knit fabrics are made by looping yarns together. Depending on the knitting methods and fibers used, fabrics can vary greatly in appearance and texture. Most knit fabrics offer natural stretch that makes them wrinkle-resistant and comfortable to wear, 16-2.

Some types of cloth are made from construction methods other than weaving or knitting. These include **nonwoven fabrics**, such as felt and artificial suede, bonded fabrics, quilted fabrics, lace, and net.

Finishes

A **fabric finish** is a treatment applied to a fabric to achieve certain characteristics. Finishes affect the appearance, comfort, feel, durability, performance, and care of fabrics.

Finishes can change the appearance of fabric by improving its color, luster, texture, and versatility. Certain finishes make clothing more comfortable to wear because they provide greater insulation, reduce static cling, resist water, or soften fabrics.

Before buying a garment, be sure you know how to care for the garment. Read labels and tags to know just what you are buying. Find out if it has a finish that requires special care when being cleaned. Also check the durability of the finish. Will it last for the life of the garment? Will it have to be renewed after laundering or dry cleaning? Following are some of the finishes commonly applied to fabrics along with their functions.

- *Antistatic* finish prevents the buildup of static electricity so garments will not cling.

- *Durable-press* or *permanent press* helps fabric retain its original shape and resist wrinkling after laundering.

- *Flame-resistance* makes fabrics resist flame. It is required on flammable fabrics used in children's sleepwear and other clothing and household items.

Science, Technology, Engineering & Mathematics

Textile Engineers
Textile engineers specialize in the design of textile machinery, new textile production methods, or the study of fibers. They do research and development as well as initiate projects and plan and schedule production.

Case Study: The Shopping Scene

Tina Buys a Mistake

Tina is going to a school party and wants to look her best. Nothing in her closet is right. Tina takes $95 she earned from babysitting and goes shopping for a new outfit.

Tina tries on several outfits at her favorite store, but none appeal to her. She goes into an unfamiliar store and sees some beautiful things. The clothes in this store cost more than she normally spends. A salesperson asks Tina what type of outfit she wants. Tina is not sure. The salesperson brings out several dresses, all of which cost more than Tina can afford. Since the salesperson is so persistent, Tina feels obliged to try on at least one or two of the dresses.

One dress looks great on Tina. The salesperson insists that she must have it. Not knowing how to say no, Tina buys the $125 dress, and must use a credit card instead of cash.

When Tina arrives home, she realizes her only coat is too casual to wear with the dress. None of her shoes look right either. To make matters worse, she learns that everyone else is wearing casual clothes to the party.

Case Review

1. Have you ever let a salesperson talk you into buying something you really did not want?
2. How might Tina have avoided her expensive mistake?
3. What information would you want to know about a store before buying something from that store?
4. Where could Tina have found information and ideas that might have helped her make a better choice?

- *Mercerization* increases luster and strength of cotton, linen, and rayon fabrics.
- *Mildew-resistance* helps prevent mildew from forming on fabrics.
- *Moth-resistance* is added to wool fibers to repel moths and carpet beetles.

- *Sanforized®* guarantees that a fabric will not shrink more than one percent.

- *Scotchguard®* creates resistance to water and oil stains.

- *Soil-release* makes it possible to remove oily stains from durable-press fabrics. It makes water-resistant fibers more absorbent so detergents can release soil.

- *Waterproof* makes fabric completely resistant to water and air passage.

- *Water-repellent* makes fabric resist wetting, but does not make it waterproof or resistant to heavy rain. This finish must be renewed after several launderings.

Fit and Appearance

A dress or suit that is just right on one person may be all wrong for another. The only way to know which garments do the most for you is to try them on. As you evaluate the fit and appearance, ask yourself the following questions:

- Where will I wear these clothes? For what occasions are they suited?

- Can I use these clothes to look taller, thinner, shorter, or rounder?

- How can I combine these purchases with clothes in my wardrobe?

When possible, try on clothes with the shoes, accessories, and other garments you plan to wear with them. It is particularly important to check skirt lengths and pant cuffs with the shoes you will wear. You also may want to check skirt lengths with coats you will wear over them.

Stand, sit, move, and stretch to check comfort and fit of new garments. Inspect your overall appearance in a full-length mirror from the front, side, and back. If clothing fits well, it will not bind, wrinkle, or pucker. Select colors, lines, styles, and textures that flatter your figure type and coloring, 16-3. These elements can also call attention to your positive features and take attention away from negative features. You can use color, line, and texture to look thinner or heavier and shorter or taller. You can mix and match separates to stretch your wardrobe and create different looks.

Labels and Legislation

The labels and tags on clothes provide important information. Most labels will identify the manufacturer, designer, or seller; the name of the country where the garment was made; and the fiber content. If a special finish has been applied to the fabric, it is usually listed. Labels also give care instructions and size information.

Much of the data listed on clothing labels and other textile products is required by law. Four of the most important laws and regulations that govern the labeling, marketing, and safety of clothing and textile products are described in 16-4.

Create the Look You Want Through Color, Line, and Texture

Look thinner with

- cool colors (colors related to blue and green)
- dark, subtle colors
- vertical lines
- smooth, nonlustrous, medium weight textures
- subtle prints, checks, and plaids
- clothes that skim the body and are not tight
- simple, uncluttered styles
- thin shapes and narrow widths in coats, sleeves, collars, trousers, and belts

Look heavier with

- warm colors (colors related to red, orange, and yellow)
- bright, light colors
- horizontal lines
- nubby, bulky, or stiff textures with surface interest
- bold prints, checks, and plaids
- full sleeves, wide-leg trousers, large pleats, and gathers
- wide contrasting belts

Look taller with

- one color or related color tones head to foot
- vertical lines
- designs, lines, and trims that lead the eye up instead of down
- narrow, uncuffed trousers
- emphasis at or above the neckline

Look shorter with

- bright, contrasting colors
- horizontal lines
- designs, lines, or trims that lead the eye down instead of up
- wide-cuffed trousers
- emphasis below the waist or at the feet

Accentuate positive features with

- warm, bright, light colors
- lines and designs that lead the eye to your best features
- fabrics and textures that emphasize your best features

De-emphasize negative features with

- cool, dark, subtle colors
- lines that lead the eye away from poor features
- styles, fabrics, and textures that hide or cover poor features

16-3

Color, line, and texture in clothing can help you highlight attractive features and de-emphasize negative features.

Regulations Governing Clothing and Textile Products

Wool Products Labeling Act	Requires products containing wool to be labeled with the percentage and type of fibers used—new or virgin wool, reprocessed or reused wool. This act is enforced by the Federal Trade Commission.
Textiles Fiber Products Identification Act	Requires textile products to be labeled with the generic name, fibers used, and the percentage of each fiber present by weight. The name or identification of the manufacturer and the country of origin, if the item is imported, must also be listed. This is required for wearing apparel, accessories, and textile products used in the home such as draperies, upholstered furniture, linens, and bedding. This act is enforced by the Federal Trade Commission.
Permanent Care Labeling Rule	Requires manufacturers to attach permanent care labels to apparel explaining the best way to clean a garment including methods and temperatures for laundering, drying, ironing, and dry cleaning. Fabrics, draperies, curtains, slipcovers, upholstered furniture, carpets, and rugs must also be labeled with care instructions. This rule is enforced by the Federal Trade Commission.
Flammable Fabrics Act	Sets flammability standards for children's sleepwear, general wearing apparel, carpets, rugs, and mattresses to protect consumers from unreasonable fire risks. This act is enforced by the Consumer Product Safety Commission.

16-4

These laws regulate the labeling, marketing, and safety of clothing and textile products.

Career and Work Clothes

Performance will be the most important factor in advancing on the job. However, your manner and appearance help you get from an interview to a job, and they contribute to your success at work.

When you are interviewed, you may want to ask what type of dress is expected in the workplace. A careful look at what other employees are wearing can guide you at a new job. If you already have a job, ask your employer if you are unsure about what is and is not acceptable.

There are some legal protections for employees whose dress or appearance relates to their religious practices. However, for the most part, employers have the right to set standards for dress and appearance in the workplace. These standards are important because they can lose business if employees' clothing offends customers.

It is a good idea to begin your career wardrobe with a few basic items and fill in as you become familiar with the dress codes and customs of your workplace. Workplace dress codes are often classified as *business* or *business casual*, 16-5.

Law firms, accounting firms, banks, insurance companies, and some government agencies often follow a business dress code. People in these fields usually work in office settings and frequently meet with clients. Employees are expected to present a professional image. This usually means suits and tailored clothing.

16-5

Follow the dress code established by your workplace.

Guide to Career Clothing	Women	Men
Business	• Suits with pants or skirt (stylish but not trendy) • Leather shoes, no sandals • Conservative, neutral colors • Hose in neutral colors • Simple jewelry and accessories • Smart handbag, not too bulky	• Suits of good quality • Dress shirt with tie • Dress shoes, polished • Dark or neutral colors • Socks in color to go with suit • Jewelry limited to watch and wedding band
Business Casual	• Khakis or other semitailored pants or skirts • Cotton shirts, polo or knit shirts with sleeves • Sweaters or turtlenecks • Blazers • Flats, loafers—no flip-flops, sandals, or sneakers • Neat, crisp, simple look	• Khakis or semitailored pants • Long sleeved cotton shirts, polo shirts with sleeves • Shirts tucked into trousers • Loafers—no sneakers or sandals • No T-shirts • No hats

Business casual varies from workplace to workplace. Even conservative offices may relax the dress code for "casual Fridays." Knowing what to wear in more casual settings can be tricky. Even if the dress code is relaxed, the following are not acceptable in the workplace:

- sloppy, baggy, soiled, tight, revealing, transparent, or simply inappropriate clothing

- clothing with a social message, particularly if the message is controversial

- workout clothes and flip-flops. Sneakers may be okay in a very casual workplace

Case Study: Clothing Speaks

The Scene Changes

Until Natesh graduated from high school, he never thought much about the clothes he wore. Everyone in school dressed pretty much alike. It was simple to wear the "right" clothes.

Now Natesh is more concerned about his appearance. He is wondering what clothes he will need for a summer office job and for college in the fall. He wants to make the right choices so he won't have to worry about the way he looks. He also has a limited budget so he wants to select useful and appropriate clothes.

Case Review

1. What do you think Natesh should wear for job interviews? How do you think the way he looks might influence possible employers?

2. What do you think Natesh should wear if he worked at the following jobs?
- stock clerk at a supermarket
- salesperson in a clothing store
- aide at a hospital
- Little League coach
- door-to-door salesperson
- file clerk in an office

3. What type of wardrobe do you think Natesh will need at college? How can he find out what he needs before buying?

For almost any job, clothes need to fit well and be clean, pressed, and in good condition. There should be no missing buttons, lint, or sagging hems.

Some jobs require uniforms that take the guesswork out of dressing. Simply make sure the uniform is clean, pressed, and properly fitted.

Shoes at work need to be suited to what you are doing. For example, if you are on your feet and moving around, shoes need to offer more comfort and support than if you sit at a desk. Keep shoes polished and in good condition.

Shopping for Footwear

As a rule, buy the best-quality footwear you can afford. In addition to comfort and quality, consider the style. Choose colors and designs that look well on your feet and fit into your wardrobe. The best-looking, well-made shoes are worthless if they do not fit.

Fit

The right fit adds to your comfort and helps you avoid aching feet and serious foot problems. Do not plan to "break in" a pair of shoes. If they do not fit in the store, they will not be comfortable later. Do not rely on size only when buying footwear. Sizes often vary with different styles or brands. Try on both shoes to check fit. Following are more tips to help you find a good fit:

- The entire shoe should fit snugly without being tight.
- Shoes should not slip or pinch your feet when you stand or walk.
- If you cannot move your toes freely, try a different size, width, or style.
- Check fit with the socks or hosiery you plan to wear with footwear.

Construction

Before buying shoes or boots, examine the construction.
- Are they stitched well and lined smoothly?
- Are the shoes made of soft, durable, flexible materials?
- Are they adequately cushioned for comfort?
- Do they provide adequate support?
- Are they easy to clean and maintain?

The materials used to make shoes can affect comfort. Feet need to "breathe" inside a shoe to stay dry and comfortable. Sandals and footwear made of leather allow air to circulate around the foot. Plastic, vinyl, and rubber materials do not allow feet to breathe well.

Athletic Shoes

Athletic shoes come in a variety of styles, materials, and weights. Specific types of athletic shoes provide support and protection against the

Health Care Specialties	
Medical	**Area of Treatment**
Cardiology	Diseases of the heart
Dermatology	Diseases of the skin, hair, and nails
Gynecology	Women's reproductive system
Internal medicine	Wide range of physical illnesses and health issues
Neurology	Disorders of the brain, spinal cord, and nervous system
Obstetrics	Medical care of pregnant women
Oncology	Diagnosis and treatment of tumors and cancer
Ophthalmology	Care of the eyes
Orthopedics	Fractures, deformities, and diseases of the skeletal system
Otolaryngology	Diseases and disorders of the ear, nose, and throat
Pediatrics	Development and care of children
Psychiatry	Mental and emotional issues and disorders
Surgery	Operations to diagnose or treat a variety of diseases or physical conditions
Urology	Urinary tract and male reproductive system
Dental	
Oral surgery	Operations to extract teeth or to treat injuries and defects of the jaw and mouth
Orthodontics	Irregularities and deformities of the teeth—often with braces

17-2
This chart lists some of the medical specialties in the health care field.

Chiropractors, optometrists, podiatrists, and psychologists provide limited medical services. (Coverage of these services varies with insurance and managed care plans.) A *chiropractor* treats problems of the musculoskeletal system and their impact on the nervous system. Treatments may include manipulating parts of the body, particularly the spinal column.

An *optometrist* tests eyes for vision defects and prescribes corrective glasses and contact lenses. A *podiatrist* diagnoses and treats minor foot ailments. A *psychologist* diagnoses and treats mental and emotional problems and learning difficulties. Licensing requirements for these fields vary from state to state. Do not rely on these health care providers for medical advice beyond their limited fields.

If you do not have a primary care physician, use the following qualifications as a guide. When choosing health care professionals, select well-qualified persons who are

- graduates of approved medical or dental schools
- licensed to practice in your state
- board certified in their area of practice

members in one or more local, state, and national professional societies and associations

Look for doctors who are well established in their practice with a good reputation among both patients and fellow professionals. One way to find qualified health care providers is to ask friends, relatives, employers, and coworkers for advice, 17-3. The following are also sources of recommendations for medical professionals:

- If you move to a new area, your former doctor may be able to refer you to a new physician.

- If medical or dental schools are located in the area, administrators there can provide a list of faculty doctors and graduates who practice in the area.

- National and state medical associations operate referral services.

17-3

Friends and family members can recommend health care providers they are happy with.

- Local hospitals can also be good sources of information.

- If you receive care through a managed care program, you may be required to choose a physician or hospital or other care provider that participates in the plan.

Before you make a final decision about a doctor, find out what services are performed in the office. Some doctors' offices are equipped to take X-rays and perform other tests that require special equipment. Tests performed in the office can save you a trip to the lab, hospital, or clinic. Ask in advance about charges and fees for routine office visits, a complete physical, and other services you may need.

You may also want to consider the location of the office, the office hours, and the backup staff available in the doctor's absence. If you have any special medical needs, make sure the doctor or group practice you choose can meet them.

Evaluating Hospitals and Medical Facilities

Doctors normally arrange for the hospitalization of their patients who need hospital care. The hospital or clinic where patients go for treatment may be determined by their choice of a primary care physician or their health care plan. Managed care plans often require that members use specific doctors or medical facilities.

Nevertheless, patients are wise to evaluate the facilities that provide care as well as the health care professionals who supervise their hospital stays. If the patient is unable to do this, a family member or a friend, acting as his or her advocate, may be able to help. The following questions are helpful in assessing health care facilities:

- *Is the hospital accredited?* A hospital should be accredited by the Joint Commission on Accreditation of Health Care Organizations or by the American Osteopathic Association. An accredited hospital must meet certain quality standards in providing health care.

- *Who owns or finances the hospital?* A nonprofit hospital is supported by patient fees, contributions, and endowments. A proprietary hospital is owned by individuals or stockholders and operated for profit. A government-supported hospital is operated with local, state, or federal funds. Ownership can make a difference in the eligibility for treatment, the services offered, and the charges.

- *Is it a teaching hospital?* Hospitals and clinics affiliated with a medical or nursing school generally provide a high level of training for students. As a result, they are likely to provide high-quality medical services.

- *Who staffs the hospital?* Does the hospital employ an adequate, qualified staff of physicians, specialists, nurses, therapists, and technicians? If a hospital is under staffed or if the staff is under qualified, patients may not receive the quality of medical care they need.

- *What types of facilities are located at the hospital or clinic?* Is there an intensive care unit? Is the emergency room well equipped and staffed? Look for the up-to-date equipment and facilities required to provide quality care.

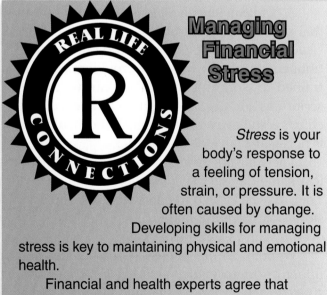

Managing Financial Stress

Stress is your body's response to a feeling of tension, strain, or pressure. It is often caused by change. Developing skills for managing stress is key to maintaining physical and emotional health.

Financial and health experts agree that finances are one of the leading causes of stress. Circumstances beyond consumer control can trigger stress, such as an economic downturn, rising health care costs, or layoffs. Poor financial habits, such as overspending or carrying large credit card debt, may also lead to stress.

Taking action to improve financial habits is the first step in reducing finance-related stress. The U.S. Department of Health and Human Services offers the following coping techniques for managing stress:

- ***Keep things in perspective.*** Recognize and focus on the positive aspects of life.

- ***Strengthen relationships with family and friends.*** They can provide emotional support through tough times.

- ***Engage in physical exercise, sports, hobbies, or other activities.*** Doing things you enjoy reduces stress and anxiety.

- ***Develop new skills.*** Learning new skills is a practical way to increase employment opportunities and earnings, leading to greater financial stability.

www.samhsa.gov/economy

- *What type of care and services are provided?* An acute care facility diagnoses and treats a broad range of illnesses and emergencies. A special disease facility diagnoses and treats a specific illness or group of diseases. A chronic disease facility provides continuing care for ongoing illnesses. People need to choose a hospital according to their specific medical needs.

- *Does the hospital enjoy a good reputation in the area?* If both medical professionals and patients speak highly of a hospital, that is a sign of quality health care.

- *How sensitive is the staff to patients' private and special needs?* Patients and their families are concerned with privacy. They want complete and honest information on diagnosis and treatment. They are also concerned with the attitude of nurses and others who deal directly with patients. Look for sensitivity to patients' comfort and special needs.

It pays to check out emergency room and ambulance services in the area before you are in an emergency situation. Knowing you are being treated in a facility that provides quality medical care can have a positive effect on your mental and physical health.

Walk-in Clinics

A **walk-in clinic** is a health care facility that provides certain routine medical attention. Usually these clinics are staffed by nurse practitioners or other health care providers who are trained to work in clinics. They can write prescriptions and give vaccinations as needed. The clinics also have a doctor on call if consultation is necessary.

These clinics generally offer quick, economical, same-day service with short waiting times. They may be located in pharmacies, workplaces, stores, or shopping malls. Often they are open evenings and weekends.

Walk-in clinics typically treat sinus and upper respiratory infections, bladder infections, strep throat, minor injuries, and other relatively minor illnesses. They may provide routine physicals and tests along with vaccinations, 17-4.

17-4

Staff at walk-in clinics provide routine care, such as conducting school physicals, and can diagnose and treat minor illness.

The costs of services at a walk-in clinic will normally be less than services of hospital emergency rooms. Generally you pay by cash, check, or credit card. Some clinics take insurance but not all insurance companies pay for treatments at a walk-in clinic.

Ideally these clinics cut down on emergency room visits and unnecessary trips to the doctor. However, under some conditions you need to go directly to an urgent care clinic or emergency room. Following is a partial list of these conditions:

- a fever over 103 degrees in connection with strep throat or other infections

- deep tissue damage or blistered burns

- stiff neck or severe pain along with ear or respiratory infections or strep throat

- life-threatening illness, such as a severe asthma attack, or injury

- heart attack symptoms, including chest discomfort, shortness of breath, and/or nausea, lightheadedness, and cold sweats

- complicated health problems

Emergency Health Care

You should go to a hospital emergency room or an emergency care center if you have an injury or sudden illness that requires immediate attention. When you go for emergency care, be ready to give

- your name, address, and phone number

- information on your injury or illness

- your managed care or insurance card or identifying data

- information on any current medication you take or allergies you have

If you call an ambulance, emergency medical technicians (EMTs) may provide preliminary health care. EMTs are trained to make an immediate, accurate diagnosis and give temporary treatment.

Alternative Medicine

Alternative medicine includes a group of health care practices and products that are not presently a part of conventional medicine. Alternative health care treatments include

- mind-body interventions such as patient education, cognitive-behavioral counseling, hypnosis, meditation, music and art therapy

- biological-based approaches such as herbal products, diet supplements and natural therapies

- manipulative and body-based methods such as manipulation and/or movement of the body as done by chiropractors, some osteopaths, and massage therapists

- energy therapies such as acupuncture, therapeutic touch, and magnetic field therapies

Some conventional health care providers combine alternative treatments with conventional methods. It is advisable to check with your health care provider before relying on alternative treatments.

Keeping Health and Medical Records

Up-to-date health and medical records are valuable for many reasons. If you switch doctors or health care plans, you will need to give your new care providers a thorough knowledge of your medical background.

Some medical background also will be required if you are admitted to a hospital. Health and medical records can help doctors with the diagnosis and treatment of illnesses as well as with the prevention of certain diseases. Having health facts readily available is very important for anyone with health conditions that would require special treatment in an emergency.

Data from health histories is also helpful when filling out school records and insurance forms. Organized receipts for paid medical bills and the purchase of medications are needed for filing insurance claims and tax forms.

Chart 17-5 lists types of information to keep in personal and family medical records. You may want to write some of this information on a card to carry with you. You may receive a medical identification card to carry with you as well. This card will identify the insurance company or managed care plan that covers your medical services and gives the necessary information to confirm your coverage.

17-5

Record this type of medical information for each family member.

Personal Medical Records

- Name, address, date and place of birth, height, weight, occupation, and blood type.
- Persons to notify in an emergency with addresses, phone numbers, and relationship.
- Personal physicians and health care providers with names, addresses, and phone numbers.
- Allergies.
- Medications with dosages, prescription numbers, prescribing physician, and pharmacies.
- Chronic illnesses with important details on history, medication, and treatment.
- Visual or hearing defects and other disabilities.
- Immunizations, screening tests and results, and dates for follow-up.
- Infections and childhood diseases with important details.
- Hospitalizations, injuries, and surgeries with dates and details.
- Physical checkups and laboratory tests with dates and details.
- Social security, Medicare, and Medicaid numbers.
- Details of employer-sponsored or individual health insurance or managed care plans including names, addresses, and phone numbers of plan managers or claims officers, medical services covered, policy and membership numbers, premium amounts and due dates, claims records, agent or contact person, and related membership data.
- Dental treatment records.
- A copy of advance directives, if any. This is a legal document describing what kind of care you want if unable to make medical decisions (such as going into a coma).

of the country. Business and world almanacs also give cost of living and other economic information on different places. Cost of living comparisons are available from a number of sites online.

It pays to find out the costs of food, housing, health care, transportation, and utilities for places where you would like to live. What are the rates for home and car insurance? What are the sales, income, and real estate tax rates? The cost of maintaining similar lifestyles in different areas can vary greatly.

Climate

What type of weather do you like—warm, dry, wet, cold, or mild? Is a change of seasons important to you? Would you rather live near the desert, the mountains, or the ocean? A world almanac or the National Climatic Center of the U.S. Department of Commerce can provide weather statistics for different cities. These statistics include average high and low temperatures, rainfall and snowfall, humidity, and wind speed.

Lifestyle

Will you be living alone or with a roommate or spouse? Do you expect to have children? Young, single persons or childless couples may prefer living in the heart of a city. Families with young children may want to live in a suburb or small town where there is more space and a stronger sense of community.

Try to decide what is most important to you. Do you want to live close to your family or friends? Do you want to live near a college or university to further your education? Do you want to be close to the mountains so you can ski in the winter? Would you rather be near water so you can enjoy water sports? Your answers to these and similar questions will help guide your choice of location.

Neighborhood

Once you have narrowed your choices to a specific region or city, you can begin evaluating different neighborhoods. Appearance is one of the most obvious factors to consider in a neighborhood. Are the buildings attractive? Do the architectural styles offer both variety and harmony? Are both private and public areas well kept? Are the yards attractively landscaped with trees, bushes, and flowers? Is the street layout attractive and functional?

What is the overall character of the neighborhood? Does it appear residential, commercial, industrial, or mixed? What zoning laws and building codes apply to the neighborhood? Is the area relatively free of heavy traffic, noise, and air pollution? How would you assess property values now and in the future? Does the neighborhood seem safe and crime-free? Local newspapers and law enforcement agencies may have information about crime rates.

You may want to consider the ages, interests, occupations, and educational backgrounds of the people in the area. Is the overall income level

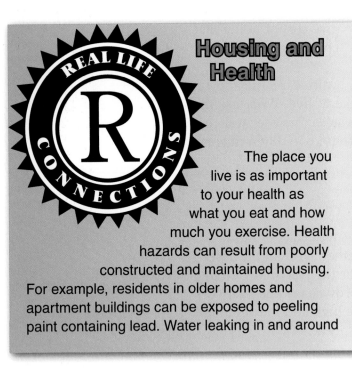

Housing and Health

The place you live is as important to your health as what you eat and how much you exercise. Health hazards can result from poorly constructed and maintained housing. For example, residents in older homes and apartment buildings can be exposed to peeling paint containing lead. Water leaking in and around a home can trigger the growth of black mold that causes and aggravates health problems.

Neighborhoods near industrial areas, factories, and highways are more exposed to airborne pollutants. Breathing these pollutants has been linked to respiratory problems, such as asthma, and other illnesses.

Crime impacts health in some communities. In high crime areas, parents may not let their children outdoors to play. Even if parks and recreational facilities exist, people are afraid to use them. As a result, residents do not get the exercise they need.

Individuals and families can take action to improve their health. However, urban planners, health experts, law enforcement personnel, and others also play a role in creating healthful living environments.

18-2

Families with young children will probably prefer to live near a park or playground.

similar to your own? Are most people living in the area single or married? Are there children in the neighborhood? Are there enough similarities to make life comfortable and enough differences to make it interesting?

Community Facilities

Check out the community services and facilities. Are services convenient to use and reasonable in cost? Is fire and police protection adequate? What is the cost of utilities? Does the community provide trash pickup, recycling, and snow removal? Are streets and other public areas well maintained? Learn what you can about health care in the area. Is public transportation convenient and reliable?

Look for services and activities that are important to you, 18-2. For example, does the community sponsor athletic programs and cultural events? Are citizens actively involved in local government? Will you have access to a public library, churches, parks, and athletic facilities? Are there a variety of shops and stores?

Schools

The education system is important because its quality affects local property values. It is also important if you have children. Find out whether the schools in the area are noted for quality education. What are teacher qualifications and pay scales? What is the average class size? Are textbooks and lab equipment up-to-date? Are special education programs offered? What extracurricular activities are offered?

Sources of Information

Be sure to check out a location carefully before you settle. Moving into a place that does not suit you can be costly in terms of happiness, time, and money. The following sources can provide helpful information about specific regions and communities:

- chambers of commerce
- local newspapers and magazines
- classified ad pages and local government listings in phone books
- long-time and new residents of an area
- travel books and almanacs
- community organizations in the area
- real estate brokers
- the Internet

Types of Housing

At different times in your life, you will most likely choose different types and styles of housing. Your choices will be based on what you need and want, what you can afford, and what is available.

Apartments, Condominiums, and Cooperatives

Most rental apartments, condominiums, and cooperatives are multi-family dwellings. They are in buildings with more than one living unit. Each unit has private living quarters. Residents share common areas, such as lobby, grounds, laundry facilities, and other building facilities.

Apartment buildings vary in the types of services and facilities they offer. They may or may not have laundry equipment, parking space, recreational facilities, and other extras. If you are considering apartment living, the checklist in 18-3 can help you choose.

The main difference that separates rental apartments from condominiums and cooperatives is ownership. A person who lives in a rental apartment leases the apartment from the owner. A person who lives in a condominium or cooperative generally owns it. Condominium and cooperative ownership are somewhat similar. Buyers share common areas and have some voice in the management of the property. However, there are some distinct differences.

18-3

This checklist can help you compare available apartments, condominiums, and cooperatives.

Checklist for Apartments, Condominiums, and Cooperatives

Building and Grounds

- ❑ Attractive, well-constructed building
- ❑ Good maintenance and upkeep
- ❑ Clean, well-lighted halls, entrances, stairs
- ❑ Reliable building management
- ❑ Locked entrances, protected from outsiders

Services and Facilities

- ❑ Laundry equipment
- ❑ Parking space (indoor or outdoor)
- ❑ Swimming pool or tennis courts
- ❑ Convenient trash disposal
- ❑ Adequate fire escapes
- ❑ Storage lockers
- ❑ Locked mailboxes
- ❑ Elevators
- ❑ Engineer on call for emergency repairs

Inside Living Space

- ❑ Adequate room sizes
- ❑ Windows located to provide enough air, light, and ventilation
- ❑ Windows have screens and storm windows
- ❑ Attractive, easy-to-clean floors
- ❑ Furnished appliances in good condition
- ❑ Clean, effective heating, thermostatically controlled
- ❑ Up-to-date wiring
- ❑ Conveniently placed electric outlets
- ❑ Well-fitted doors, casings, cabinets, and built-ins
- ❑ Extras—air conditioning, dishwasher, fireplace, patio

A **condominium** is a form of home ownership where a person owns the unit he or she occupies. The ownership of the surrounding building and grounds is shared. The owner pays a monthly *assessment* or maintenance fee to cover the costs of operating, maintaining, and repairing the shared property. The owners generally elect a board of managers to make policy and management decisions for the shared property.

In some ways, owning a condo is like owning a single-family house. Most people obtain a mortgage when buying a condo. They make mortgage payments and pay property taxes. Condo owners have the same tax and equity benefits as the house owner. Another similarity is both condo and house owners can make their own decisions about redecorating, refinancing, or selling their homes.

A **cooperative** is a form of home ownership in which a person buys shares in a corporation that owns the property. In return, the buyer lives in a designated unit and becomes a member of the cooperative. Owners pay a monthly fee that covers their share of maintenance and service costs. The fee also covers the building mortgage and taxes. Usually it is necessary to obtain approval from an elected board of directors before selling or remodeling a unit.

When buying a condominium or a cooperative, it is important to do some thorough homework. The soundness of this type of investment depends greatly on the management, restrictions, operating policies, and types of people involved in both ownership and management. Here are a few questions to answer before buying.

- How is the property managed, and by whom? What voice do owners have in management decisions?

- Are current residents generally satisfied with the management and the building?

- What is the financial status of the building? Is there a mortgage on the property? Are any major repairs or renovations anticipated? If so, are funds available to cover the cost? Does the appraised value compare favorably with the selling price?

- How much is the monthly maintenance fee or assessment? What does it cover? When and how can it be increased?

- What control do occupants have over their units? Are there restrictions on selling, remodeling, renting, or refinancing? Are pets permitted?

- How does the condominium or cooperative unit compare with similar units in other buildings and with other forms of available housing in the area?

Single-Family Houses

The single-family house is still the most popular type of housing. If you decide to live in a house, you will face many decisions. A few people choose to build a house of their own. Most people rent or buy an existing house. If you decide to buy or build a home, there are many professionals who can help, 18-4. Become familiar with the various experts, what they do, and how they can help you make housing decisions.

If you are planning to move into a single-family house, there are a number of factors to consider, 18-5. If you are buying, solid construction is of great importance. Be sure to check both outside and inside construction features. It pays to carefully evaluate the outside of the house, the yard, and the neighborhood as well as the inside living space.

Choose a house that is conveniently designed for your lifestyle and housing needs. Looking at different types of houses can help you decide what you like best. If you are buying, it generally pays to hire an independent contractor to inspect the house and evaluate construction details you cannot judge.

If you decide to build a home you will have a host of decisions to make in the process. Single-family houses are built in a variety of ways.

- *Custom-built houses* are usually designed by architects to meet the specific needs and wishes of their clients. A contractor is hired to build the house according to an architect's plan. This can be a costly and lengthy project.

- *Tract houses* are neighborhoods of new homes built by developers who erect many houses at once within a given area. These houses are built from similar plans in order to keep costs down. Most tract

The Experts		
Title	**Description of Services**	**When To Use Them**
Real Estate Agents	Bring buyer/tenant and seller/landlord together and negotiate a deal acceptable to both. Provide helpful information on community tax rates, schools, services, shopping, property values, etc. Recommend lenders and help arrange financing for home purchase. Represent the seller in a sale and receive a commission for services—usually a percentage of the price.	When you need help finding the housing you want in an area you like at a price you can pay. When you are unfamiliar with an area and need facts to decide exactly where and what to buy or rent. When you need help finding professional services and home financing. When you want to sell a home at a fair price in a reasonable length of time.
Lawyers	Represent either buyer or seller in transferring real estate. Protect client's interests when selling, buying, building, or leasing a home. Draw up agreements for client and check agreements drawn by others before the client signs. Represent client at the closing of a real estate transaction.	When you buy or sell a home. When you have questions about a housing contract or lease. When you become involved in a dispute with a landlord, seller, builder, or buyer in a real estate transaction. Before you sign any contract or agreement involving more money or time than you can afford to sacrifice.
Architects	Draw up plans for building or remodeling. Choose suitable building materials. Help find a lot suited to the house design, or design a house suited to the lot. Hire and work with the contractor and supervise building.	When you want to build a house or do extensive remodeling. When you want a custom-designed home.
Contractors	Accept responsibility for building or remodeling a home. Order building materials. Hire and supervise workers. See that work is done according to specifications and terms in the contract.	When you want to build a home or make home improvements.

18-4

These experts can help you buy, sell, lease, build, or remodel a home.

houses look alike and lack the individuality of custom-built houses. They are less expensive, however, and builders often make minor alterations to meet individual buyers' needs.

- *Modular and kit houses* are partially built in factories. They are then moved in sections to the home site for completion. These houses are relatively inexpensive. Quality depends on the manufacturer as well as the builder who puts the house together.

Checklist for Single-Family Houses

Outside House and Yard

- ❏ Attractive, well-designed house
- ❏ Lot of the right size and shape for house and garage
- ❏ Good drainage of rain and moisture
- ❏ Mature, healthy trees—placed to give shade in summer
- ❏ Well-kept driveway, walks, patio, and porch
- ❏ Parking convenience—garage, carport, or street
- ❏ Well lighted and sheltered entry

Outside Construction

- ❏ Durable siding materials—in good condition
- ❏ Solid brick and masonry—free of cracks
- ❏ Solid foundation walls
- ❏ Weather-stripped windows and doors
- ❏ Noncorrosive gutters and downspouts, connected to storm sewer or splash block to carry water away from house
- ❏ Copper or aluminum flashing used over doors, windows, and joints on the roof
- ❏ Screens and storm windows

Inside Construction

- ❏ Sound, smooth walls with invisible nails and taping on dry wall surfaces
- ❏ Well-done carpentry work with properly fitted joints and moldings
- ❏ Properly fitted, easy-to-operate windows

- ❏ Level wood floors with smooth finish and no high edges, wide gaps, or squeaks
- ❏ Well-fitted tile floors—no cracked or damaged tiles—no visible adhesive
- ❏ Good possibilities for improvements, remodeling, expanding
- ❏ Dry basement floor with hard, smooth surface
- ❏ Adequate basement drain
- ❏ Sturdy stairways with railings, adequate head room—not too steep
- ❏ Leakproof roof—in good condition
- ❏ Adequate insulation for warmth and soundproofing

Living Space

- ❏ Convenient work areas (kitchen, laundry, workshop) with adequate drawers, cabinets, lighting, workspace, electric power
- ❏ Bedrooms located far enough from other parts of the house for privacy and quiet
- ❏ Social areas (living and dining room, play space, yard, porch, or patio) convenient, comfortable, large enough for family and guests
- ❏ Adequate storage—closets, cabinets, shelves, attic, basement, garage
- ❏ Windows located to provide enough air, light, and ventilation
- ❏ Usable attic and/or basement space
- ❏ Extras—fireplace, air conditioning, porches, new kitchen and baths

18-5

This checklist can help you evaluate the appearance, construction, and living space of single-family homes.

- *Town houses* are single-family units that share one or both sidewalls with other town houses. The units are usually built at the same time from similar blueprints.

Manufactured Homes

A manufactured home is a single-family house built in a factory and shipped to the home site where it is erected. These homes are constructed in compliance with the *Manufactured Housing Construction and Safety Standards Code,* called the *HUD Code.*

Manufactured homes generally cost considerably less than other types of housing with comparable living space and equipment. Maintenance

Building Code Officials

Building code officials examine buildings, highways and streets, sewer and water systems, bridges, and other structures. They ensure that their construction, alteration, or repair complies with building codes and ordinances, zoning regulations, and contract specifications.

costs are usually low, too. However, over time they may decrease rather than increase in value.

They often are located in manufactured home communities but may be built on private lots. The home owner may purchase the lot that the manufactured home rests on. It may also be owned by a business that charges the home owner a monthly rent. Look to the following guidelines if you wish to consider a manufactured home:

- **Choose a dealer carefully.** Check dealer reputation with local banks, businesses, the Better Business Bureau, chamber of commerce, and previous customers. Also find out if the dealer is a member of the state manufactured housing association.

- **Figure and compare total costs.** Find out what the purchase price does and does not include. Compare the costs of finance charges and insurance. Check the prices of a home lot, delivery to the lot, and installation.

- **Check warranty terms.** Study the warranties on the manufactured home and on the appliances and equipment that come with it. Find out what is warranted, for how long, what the owner must do to receive warranty benefits, and who is responsible for carrying out warranty terms.

- **Check features and extras.** Find out how the home is heated, cooled, insulated, and furnished. Also check the capacity of the hot water heater. Make sure the model you choose will provide basic comfort, convenience, and safety.

- **Investigate the manufactured home community.** Look at the design and management. Find out what services and facilities are available free or for a fee. Ask about the rules and regulations. Talk to people who live there.

Monthly Housing Costs

Most financial advisers suggest that total monthly housing costs come to no more than one-third of monthly take-home pay. Take-home pay is the amount of money you receive after taxes and other deductions are subtracted from your paycheck.

Housing costs include not only rent or mortgage payments, but also utilities, maintenance, property taxes, and home owner's or renter's insurance. You can use the budgeting exercise in Chapter 6 to determine your monthly housing allowance. In summary, a budget takes you through the following steps.

1. Total the amount you have to spend each month. Include all income and earnings.

2. Total monthly non-housing expenses. Include food, clothing, transportation, recreation, loans, insurance, taxes, and any other ongoing obligations.

3. Subtract total monthly non-housing expenses from total monthly income to arrive at the amount you can afford for housing each month.

4. Adjust earnings, spending, and housing costs as needed.

If you do not have enough money for the home you want, you have three choices. You can try to increase your income, spend less on non-housing expenses, or choose a less expensive home. Before choosing a place to live, determine how much money you can spend on housing. The amount you can afford will depend on several factors. These include your income, other expenses and obligations, housing needs, and your expected future income.

Since housing is generally a monthly expenditure, begin by figuring a reasonable monthly housing allowance. If you plan to buy a home, you will need to determine a purchase price, a down payment, closing costs, and a mortgage you can handle over a long period of time. The cost of moving and furnishing your home should also be considered. Home buying expenses are covered later in this chapter.

Renting Versus Buying

The primary financial responsibility of renting a place to live is to pay the stated rent each month. The renter is also responsible for taking reasonable care of the rental unit and paying any utility bills that are not included in the rent.

Renting a home offers certain advantages. They include the following.

- *Fewer financial responsibilities.* You do not need a large sum of money for a down payment. Rents are generally lower than mortgage payments. You do not have to pay property taxes. Renters do not pay for major repairs and maintenance, such as a new roof or purchase of major appliances.

- *More free time.* Since renters are often not responsible for home maintenance, such as landscaping, and home repairs and improvements, they have more free time, 18-6.

- *Less financial risk.* Renters do not need to worry about property values or the inability to pay a mortgage.

- *Greater mobility.* Renters can usually move at the end of their lease if they give a month's notice.

For many people, owning a home gives a sense of permanence and financial security. It is a source of pride and satisfaction. Buying a home is a smart move for the following reasons.

18-6
Some people prefer to rent because they do not want to spend time on exterior maintenance tasks, such as landscaping and lawn care.

- *Can increase wealth.* When you buy real estate, you build up equity or ownership in property. You are buying something you often can resell for a profit.

- *Tax benefits.* In addition, home mortgage interest and property taxes paid on a home are deductible expenses when figuring federal income tax. Renters do not enjoy these financial advantages.

- *Greater control.* When you buy a home, you generally have the freedom to make most of the decisions concerning your property: what color to paint it, where to hang pictures, whether or not to put in a swimming pool, etc. Condominiums and some housing subdivisions have rules that limit home owner freedoms.

The advantages of both buying and renting must be weighed against the disadvantages. The disadvantages of renting include

- *No buildup of equity.* Buying a home can be an investment and renting is not. Over time, homes generally increase in value. The mortgage payments that home owners make are payments on an asset that they eventually own. Rent payments do not benefit renters, but go into the pockets of landlords.

- *Little control.* Renters have less control over their living space. At the end of a lease period, landlords can raise their rent or ask them to mo ve out. They may not be allowed to own pets, hang pictures on the walls, or paint and decorate. Some renters have irresponsible landlords who do not maintain properties or make needed repairs. Inadequate heat, hot water, and pest control are just a few of the problems these renters endure.

- *No tax benefits.* There are no tax benefits from renting.

The disadvantages of buying a home include the following.

- *Greater costs and financial responsibilities.* When they purchase a home, most home owners make a down payment. This is often a large sum of money. Monthly costs include mortgage payments, home owners' insurance, and property taxes. Owners are also responsible for repair and maintenance costs, 18-7.

- *Less mobility.* Moving usually involves selling a home, which is often complicated and time consuming. In a slow real estate market, it can take many months to sell a house or condominium.

- *Complicated relationships.* When friends or roommates buy a home together, they usually plan on living together for a while. However, if they decide to go their separate ways, it can be difficult to agree on what to do with the home.

- *Greater financial risk.* Although property values generally rise over time, home owners risk losing money if property values drop or if they cannot keep up with mortgage payments. People who do not pay their mortgage can lose their home.

Your Offer

Buying a home is not like going to a department store to buy a jacket. Home buyers usually do not pay the asking price. There is some back-and-forth haggling involved. For example, if a home is selling for $300,000, you may offer 5 percent or $15,000 less. The buyer can accept or reject the offer. He or she may not accept your offer, but drop the price nevertheless. Now you must decide whether or not to accept the new reduced price.

Before making an offer, a buyer needs to research the sale price of comparable homes in the area. For example, if the home you are interested in is a 3-bedroom, 2-bath home with a 2-car garage, look for other homes of that description that have sold in the previous months in that neighborhood. What were the asking prices and the prices paid? A real estate broker can do this research for you. Use the prices paid as a guide to formulate your bid.

If the property is an exceptional value and others are also submitting offers, you will want to submit the asking price or near the asking price. However, there are many reasons to offer less than the asking price. A buyer may offer less if

- the property needs repairs

- the home has not sold despite being on the market a long time

- other comparable homes nearby sold for much less

- the seller is desperate to sell

- the buyer is flexible about the move-in date

- the market for selling homes is bad and there are many homes on the market

When you have an offer price, then an agent or real estate attorney can draw up a purchase agreement.

Purchase Agreements

When the buyer agrees to buy and the seller agrees to sell, they both sign a contract called a **purchase agreement**. Sometimes this contract is called a sales agreement. It should include a description of the real estate, its location, the purchase price, and the possession date.

The agreement should state all of the conditions and terms of the sale. For example, if the seller agrees to make any home repairs, these should be stated in the agreement. If the owner promises to leave the draperies, dishwasher, range, and refrigerator, these should also be listed and described.

When you sign a purchase agreement, you must also give the seller an **earnest money** check. This shows that your purchase offer is serious and prohibits the seller from selling the home to someone else. This is usually a percentage of the home price. It is applied toward the down payment at the closing of the sale. Buyers can lose the earnest money if they fail to go through with the agreement. A home purchase agreement may contain a **contingency clause** that calls for certain requirements to be met before the contract is binding. For example, the validity of the agreement may depend upon obtaining a mortgage within a certain period of time or at a certain rate. It may be made contingent upon the sale of the buyer's current home.

Home Inspection

A common contingency is that the home must pass an inspection by a home inspector hired by the buyer. For a fee, home inspectors examine the home for problems that may affect the value of the home or require costly repair. These include cracks in the foundation, a leaky roof, and plumbing and electrical problems. Inspectors also check to make sure appliances work.

Buyers who live in areas where termites thrive or where mold is common may also have the home inspected for these problems by specialists. Specialized inspectors can also be hired to find problems with lead or asbestos exposure. If problems are found, buyers can ask sellers to fix them before they purchase the home. Buyers can use the inspection findings to negotiate a reduction in the sales price.

Obtaining a Home Mortgage

Most home buyers get loans to finance home purchases, 18-11. A home loan, called a **mortgage**, is a contract between a borrower and a lender. The lender is usually a bank or a mortgage company. The borrower promises to repay the lender the loan amount plus interest. The mortgage is paid in monthly installments over a set number of years. If the borrower fails to pay according to the terms of the mortgage contract, the lender can repossess the home.

18-11

Homes are one of the most expensive purchases people make. Most home buyers must secure a mortgage to finance their purchase.

Rent-to-Own Plans

Do not confuse furniture rental agreements with aggressive rent-to-own (RTO) plans. RTO plans are not regulated under the *Truth in Lending Act* or state credit laws. Fees typically add up to much more than rented items are worth and more than the cost of buying on credit. For example, a $500 television might be offered at $60 per month for 18 months. That comes to a total cost of $1,080.

Protect yourself if you consider renting furniture or appliances. Determine the total cost by multiplying the amount of each rental payment by the number of payments required in the contract. Compare this total with the cash price and the credit price of similar merchandise at reputable stores. Find out what will happen if you miss a payment. Check out provisions for servicing or repairs on rented appliances, insurance requirements and fees, and penalties for late payment or default. Read the fine print carefully.

Help with Problems and Complaints

The vast majority of manufacturers, retailers, and service people want to satisfy you, the consumer. Even so, there may be times when you have problems with appliances, furniture, electronics, and other home products. When you do, the first places to seek help include the manufacturer and the dealer or retailer where you bought the product.

Most manufacturers operate toll-free numbers and Web sites to deal promptly with consumer inquiries and problems. The operator's manual or other printed material that comes with products will usually list these consumer contacts along with troubleshooting information.

If you fail to obtain satisfaction from the retailer or the manufacturer, you may want to contact one of the following associations for assistance:

- National Home Furnishings Association, www.nhfa.org
- Association of Home Appliance Manufacturers (AHAM), www.aham.org
- Consumer Electronics Association (CEA), www.cnet.com and www.myceknowhow.com
- Carpet and Rug Institute, www.carpet-rug.com

These organizations also provide very helpful consumer information about the selection, use, and care of their products.

Home Care and Maintenance

When you move into your first home, whether it is a one-room apartment or a house, you will face home care and maintenance responsibilities. In a rental apartment this is largely a matter of keeping the space clean and caring for the appliances. If problems arise with the heating, air conditioning, plumbing, or major appliances, the landlord is usually responsible. When you buy a home, you become your own landlord and responsibilities increase dramatically.

Home Owner Responsibilities

Maintaining a home is both costly and time-consuming. When you buy a home, housing experts recommend setting aside one to three percent of the purchase price each year to cover maintenance and repairs.

Maintenance involves routine chores you can often perform yourself. These include keeping drains running freely, faucets drip free, toilets flushing, floors and carpets clean and in good condition. You also need to periodically clean gutters, windows, garage, and basement.

Yards and plantings need seasonal attention, too. To maintain home appliances and equipment, follow instruction manuals and owners guides. Many manufactures operate interactive Web sites to address your questions and problems with their products.

Home repairs can become more involved. They include attention to roof leaks, broken windows, fallen trees, plumbing problems, and foundation damage. The electric and the heating and cooling systems also need routine maintenance as well as occasional repairs and replacement.

Regular inspection and maintenance is the best way to keep a home in good condition. It also helps you catch small problems before they become major and costly repair jobs. The checklist in 18-15 can help you identify areas that may need attention.

Hiring Workers for Your Home

Use care when selecting people to repair or work on your home. The bigger the job the more thoroughly you need to investigate them. Here are some tips:

- Contact your local government. Find out if permits must be obtained before the work is started. Ask about any guidelines you should follow in hiring people to work on your property.

Inspection Checklist	
Interior	**Exterior**
<li>Walls</li><li>Ceilings</li><li>Doors</li><li>Windows</li><li>Stairs</li><li>Plumbing</li><li>Heating and cooling system</li><li>Hot water heater</li><li>Electrical</li><li>Basement</li><li>Attic</li>	<li>Foundation</li><li>Brick/siding</li><li>Windows/screens</li><li>Storm windows/doors</li><li>Steps</li><li>Porch(es)</li><li>Garage</li><li>Roof</li><li>Chimney</li><li>Gutters</li>

18-15

This chart lists items to inspect for maintenance and repair both inside and outside the home.

- Find reputable workers by asking acquaintances for the names of people they have used with satisfaction. Check for memberships in trade or professional organizations and the local better business bureau. These offer some assurance of a worker's qualifications and reliability. Investigate carefully before hiring someone who comes to your door unsolicited.

- Interview the worker before you hire him or her. Ask for work experience and references from other customers. Follow up and check references. Ask workers about licensing and insurance. They should be insured and bonded. Ask to see the insurance certificate. Look for coverage that protects you from property damage workers may cause and any other financial risks associated with the work being done.

- Interview several candidates and get several written estimates for the work to be done. After you select someone, you will probably be asked to sign a contract. Read it carefully and ask any questions you might have before you sign. If a job is lengthy and expensive, you should refuse to pay the entire cost before work is begun. You will probably be asked to pay for a portion upfront, and the rest upon completion of the job.

Chapter Summary

Types of housing include apartments and houses. Multifamily buildings may be apartments, condominiums, or cooperatives. Single-family housing includes custom-built homes, tract houses, town houses, and manufactured houses. Choices will depend on the amount you can spend and on housing needs. These needs change with different stages of the life cycle.

Before making any decisions, set up a budget for housing costs. This involves determining how much you can spend on home and related costs, such as utilities, insurance, and taxes.

Renting a home usually involves signing a lease. It will state the rights and obligations of both landlord and tenant. Since this is a legal document that can be enforced in a court of law, it is important to fully understand all of the terms before signing.

When buying a home, a number of legal documents must be signed. To protect your interests, study these carefully. The mortgage is one of the most important commitments. Shop carefully for the best mortgage terms to fit your situation. Compare interest rates and other terms of different mortgages and compare the closing costs charged by different lenders.

When you begin to make furnishing and decorating decisions, consider your resources and your immediate needs. Floor plans can guide furniture choices. When buying furnishings consider quality, durability, style, and price.

Once you move into a place of your own, home care and maintenance become a new responsibility. Regular maintenance and inspection is the best way to keep a home in good condition.

Review

1. Name four factors to consider when deciding where to live.

2. What is the main difference that separates rental apartments from condominiums and cooperatives?

3. If you were considering a manufactured home, name five guidelines to follow in making a choice.

4. List three advantages and disadvantages of renting a home.

5. List three advantages and disadvantages of buying a home.

6. What are some of the questions renters should answer before signing a lease?

7. List three factors that might permit a buyer to offer less than the asking price on a home.

8. What percent of gross monthly income do most lenders allow for a mortgage commitment?

9. Name five factors to consider when shopping for a mortgage and comparing lenders.

10. Why do lenders require a survey of property?

11. Why is it important to take an inventory of your possessions before you move?

12. Name six factors to consider when shopping for furniture.

13. How much money can home owners expect to spend annually on home maintenance and repairs?

14. What is the best way to keep a home in good condition?

Critical Thinking

15. How does a person's lifestyle tend to influence housing location? Give examples.

16. What sources of information can help you find a place to live?

17. How would you prefer to finance a home if you were buying today? Why?

18. What are the advantages of an FHA-insured or a VA-guaranteed loan?

19. What are some ways to save money when decorating and furnishing a home?

For first-time buyers, the used car market can be the best place to satisfy both budget and transportation needs. Used cars cost less to buy and to insure. They also depreciate more slowly. You can choose from a wide selection of makes, models, and sizes. Generally, it is a good idea to look for a two- to three-year-old car with low mileage and in good condition. It is a plus if the manufacturer's warranty is still in force.

What You Can Afford

Buying a car is not a spontaneous purchase. Many people save money for months and even years before they accumulate enough to buy a car. Following the advice about budgeting in Chapter 6 can help you meet the goal of having your own car.

To determine how much you can afford to spend on a car, start with the amount of cash you have on hand for a down payment and initial costs. If you own a car you can sell or trade, add its value to the amount you can spend. You will also need cash up front for licensing, registration, taxes, and insurance.

Next, determine how much you can spend each month to cover ongoing costs of car ownership. These will include fuel, maintenance, payments, insurance, parking, and an allowance for miscellaneous expenses.

Take a look at your overall income and expense picture. Total your monthly income after deductions and subtract your total monthly expenses. You will need to cover monthly car costs out of the amount left. To buy the car you want, it may be necessary to increase your income or cut your spending in other areas.

Linking to... Science

Fuel Efficiency

Fuel economy is a topic on everyone's mind. Gasoline prices continue to rise while resources decrease. Auto manufacturers continue to experiment with other sources of power to reduce dependence on fuel and to reduce carbon dioxide emissions.

Hybrid vehicles are autos that use two or more sources of power. Hybrids frequently combine a gasoline or diesel engine with an electric motor. The cars have a gas tank and small gasoline or diesel engine along with an electric motor powered by battery. An onboard computer balances power between the gasoline engine and the electric motor, using both for high speeds and for heavy acceleration.

Neighborhood electric vehicles (NEVs) are powered by electricity and used for short distances at speeds not exceeding 25 to 30 miles per hour. These vehicles are particularly useful in small communities.

The U.S. government is also helping to promote fuel efficiency. For vehicles manufactured in the 2011 model year, fuel efficiency standards were raised for the first time in over 20 years. In the past, passenger cars were required to meet a standard of 24.1 mpg (miles per gallon). Vehicles in the 2011 model year will need to meet 30.2 mpg. By 2020, passenger cars will be required to meet at least 35 mpg.

The Final Four-Point Check

After answering the many questions about car buying, you may be ready to zero in on the car of your choice. However, before you part with your money, take time to check the car over carefully—in the driver's seat, on the road, under the hood, and on paper.

In the Driver's Seat

Sit in the driver's seat and see if you are within comfortable reach of the steering wheel, foot pedals, and controls. Also check for good visibility. Make sure you can see well out the front, side, and rear windows. Check seat position and adjustments for comfort.

On the Road

Test-drive the car to see how well it handles in traffic, on the open road, and when starting, stopping, turning, and parking. Is it comfortable and easy to drive? Also test all the equipment and controls, such as the emergency brake, turn signals, horn, radio, windshield wipers, and headlights.

Under the Hood

A careful check of the engine and working parts of a car is particularly important when buying a used car. Unless you know all about cars, ask an independent, certified automotive technician to look under the hood with you.

Take an overall look at the engine. Check the levels of all the fluids— oil, water, brake, transmission, and power steering. If fluid levels are low, it could be a sign of leakage or of poor maintenance.

Also check the condition of the tires. Then start the engine. If you hear any strange noises, find out the cause. The car should idle smoothly and should not emit any burning odors.

On Paper

The checklist in 19-7 should help you evaluate the items that are important to you when buying a car. When the car you are considering passes the four-point check, you are ready to buy with confidence.

Wherever you shop, whether you buy or lease, start the process with a low offer. Negotiate the cash price of the car first, then negotiate the trade-in allowance, if any. Do not be afraid to walk away if you are not getting what you want. You always can come back.

If you are looking at a used vehicle, ask to see the service record, which will tell you how the vehicle has been maintained. Check out the VIN history as well.

Car Review Checklist		
Cost Factors	**O.K.**	**Not O.K.**
Total price including:	_____	_____
base price	_____	_____
options	_____	_____
delivery, preparation, and other charges	_____	_____
Down payment requirement or capitalized cost reduction	_____	_____
Amount and number of monthly payments	_____	_____
Finance charge or money factor in a lease	_____	_____
Estimated cost of maintenance and service	_____	_____
Projected fuel economy	_____	_____
Warranty Coverage		
Number of miles and period of time	_____	_____
Parts covered	_____	_____
Labor covered	_____	_____
Owner responsibilities	_____	_____
Safety Features and Considerations		
Visibility	_____	_____
Acceleration speed	_____	_____
Braking speed	_____	_____
Ease of handling	_____	_____
Antilock brakes	_____	_____
Air bags	_____	_____
Automatic restraint system	_____	_____
Other features	_____	_____
Comfort and Convenience		
Smooth riding	_____	_____
Sound insulation	_____	_____
Passenger space and seating comfort	_____	_____
Ease of getting in and out	_____	_____
Luggage space	_____	_____
Air conditioning	_____	_____
Sound system	_____	_____
Other features	_____	_____
Seller		
Reputation of the dealership, superstore, or Web site	_____	_____
Service facilities and competence	_____	_____
Convenient location	_____	_____
Appearance of the Car		
Design	_____	_____
Model	_____	_____
Color	_____	_____
Interior	_____	_____

19-7
This checklist can help you run a final check on what is important to you in a car before buying or leasing.

Be sure the title is in order and get all of the figures and quotes in writing when you are shopping. Take a day or two to think over the deal you are offered before committing.

Financing

Most purchases of new and used cars are financed. This means the buyer takes out a loan and pays for the car with monthly payments. Financing a car costs more than paying cash because you pay interest on the amount borrowed. By understanding the ins and outs of financing a car, you will be able to shop more intelligently for auto loans.

Sources of Financing

Common sources of car loans include auto dealers, banks, credit unions, and finance companies. It is a good idea to shop around for loans before you go to the car dealer.

In general, the minimum age for obtaining a car loan is 18. When you apply for a car loan, the lender will want proof that you have a job and earn income. The lender will also look at your credit report and/or credit score to determine whether or not you are creditworthy.

Dealer financing is a convenient, on-the-spot source of financing. Rates may also be attractive when dealers are overstocked and need to sell cars to reduce their inventories. When asking a dealer about auto financing, be sure to insist on separate quotes for the car and the financing. This is the only way you can accurately compare finance charges and terms with other loan sources. Be wary of a dealer who tries to package the car and the financing together. This can be a costly package.

After looking at the dealer's credit terms, check financing terms from other sources. You can always come back to the dealer. You can also investigate financing sources online and compare rates and terms.

To obtain an auto loan, the borrower pledges the car as security or collateral. This means the creditor will hold the title to the car until the loan is paid in full. If the borrower fails to repay the loan, the lender may legally take back or repossess the car and sell it.

The installment loan is the most common form of auto financing. It is repaid in monthly payments over a period of time. The size of the monthly payments and the length of the repayment period for installment loans vary greatly. Loan periods are usually between 3 and 7 years for new cars and 2 to 5 years for used cars. This makes it relatively easy for car buyers to obtain loans they can afford to repay comfortably.

Cost of Financing

The overall cost of auto financing varies with the principal, or the original amount borrowed; the annual percentage rate (APR); and the length of the repayment period. These concepts were covered in Chapter 9. Consider them carefully if you shop for a loan.

Questions for Service Providers

Whichever system you are considering, here are some questions to pose in your search for an ISP or other service provider that will best meet your needs.

The Provider

Is the provider local, regional, or national? What reputation does the provider have for prompt, responsive customer service and tech support? Is this support available both online and by phone? How long is the typical wait for over-the-phone tech support?

Services

What functions will the company provide? Also ask about any emerging technology. Will the provider be offering these services, and when? Make sure the company offers what you are looking for.

Cost

How much will service cost—both initially and in ongoing monthly costs? Compare service plans and costs for different service packages. Most carriers offer a variety of plans based on usage, geographic area covered, functions used beyond basic service, and contract terms.

For cell phone service, for example, look at both monthly and per minute charges. Also check other charges such as those for roaming, texting, Internet browsing, and other functions your phone may perform. Finally, note how much you are paying for taxes. If you sign a contract for the service, check the penalty for early termination.

Equipment

What are the equipment requirements? Does the provider supply necessary equipment, or must you buy or rent it? Who pays repair costs? Make sure you receive and understand the answers to these questions before choosing equipment.

Reliability

How reliable is performance and connectivity? You want to avoid frequent interruptions in service. For instance, if you are choosing a cell phone carrier, is reception clear without static and dropped calls?

Software and Product Information

Does software come with the service? For Internet service, this may include a firewall and anti-virus, anti-spam, and anti-spyware packages. Is the software user-friendly? Are you given adequate and clear information about the service it provides and the installation and operating packages available to you?

Buying Consumer Electronics

Some of the most popular consumer electronics products are discussed in this section. However, in a few years' time, these products may be obsolete and replaced with upgrades. Many of the tips you will find here will also apply to upgrades. For new products, you will want to do careful research. Find out as much about the product as possible using consumer Web sites and magazines. Make careful comparisons of different brands and features. Speak to friends who have purchased the product. Above all, never make an impulse decision about an expensive electronic product. Become informed before you shop.

Computers

As you shop for a computer, you will find a dizzying selection of features and functions to consider. Knowing how you intend to use the computer can help you make intelligent choices and avoid paying for extras you do not need.

20-6

Laptops make it easy to do computer tasks no matter where you are.

Desktop or Laptop

If you have no need for portability, a desktop computer generally will offer more capabilities for less money than a laptop. It is likely to provide more hard-drive capacity and better sound quality. There will also be more options for expanding and adding functions you may decide you want later. *Upgrade potential* refers to the ease and expense of adding new memory and other features that make the computer faster and more useful. Desktop computers are usually easier to upgrade than laptops.

If portability is important to you, or if space is limited, a laptop or notebook may be a better choice. A laptop can do almost anything a desktop computer can do, but it will generally cost more for comparable capabilities. The key advantage to a laptop is its portability, which permits you to take your computer wherever you wish to use it, 20-6. *Notebooks* are similar to laptops, but with smaller screens and keyboards and less upgrading capabilities. The newer *netbooks* generally offer Internet access and few other features. Notebooks and netbooks are less expensive than laptops because of their more limited functions.

Keep in mind that portability can be a disadvantage because these devices can be lost or stolen. You will need to guard against theft. You will also have to be more cautious with online security if you use wireless connections.

If you are considering a laptop, think about the weight and size that best suits your needs. Powerful laptops that are both thin and lightweight are available, but they are higher priced. A smaller, less expensive notebook or netbook may work for you. However, neither has all the features of the larger and heavier laptops.

A large battery capacity is also a plus. The laptop manufacturer should tell you how many hours you can use the laptop between charges and how long it takes to charge.

Basic Features

Computers are often sold as a system that includes a monitor, printer, keyboard, speakers, and either a mouse or touchpad. Knowing exactly what you are looking for will help you decipher computer advertisements and find the best deal.

The computer's speed depends on the power of the microprocessor and the amount of working memory. However, the faster a computer works, the more it costs. You will want to buy a computer with as much processor power as you can afford. People who play high-end computer games or edit videos and photos usually buy the most powerful CPUs.

Random Access Memory (RAM) is also called working memory. The higher the RAM, the faster the computer runs. RAM is measured in gigabytes (GB). If you need more RAM, it can usually be added fairly easily. More RAM means a higher price.

Software programs are instructions that tell a computer what to do. A computer's *operating system* controls the basic functions of a computer. Adding **software applications**, or programs that perform specific tasks, enable consumers to customize their computers.

Some of the most popular applications software allow users to do word processing, prepare spreadsheets, and create presentations. Other applications include those for gaming, computer security, and education. The number and types of applications are endless. Many programs are tailored to the needs of a particular business or profession.

Software is constantly updated. Software companies usually offer updates to their programs. However, eventually they come out with new versions and stop selling or supporting older versions. People usually buy the most recently released software programs.

Peripheral devices include printers, keyboards, and digital cameras. When a new peripheral device is added to a computer, it often comes with a program called a *driver*. The driver tells the computer how to use the device. Many computer companies have the latest drivers available for download from the Internet.

Choosing Other Features

What do you need your computer to do? Do you intend to use your computer for routine e-mail, Web surfing, and word processing? Will you

Arts, A/V Technology & Communications

Video Graphics Designers

Video graphics designers plan, create, and analyze video communications. They also develop material for Web sites, interactive media, and multimedia projects. They must be able to use color, illustration, photography, and animation techniques to enhance communications.

use it for more complicated tasks such as downloading video files and editing photos? Do you need a connection to cell phones or other computers?

Assess your needs realistically before making choices. It is important to investigate thoroughly before you invest in a computer. This way, you will be sure you end up with what you need at a reasonable price. Additional features you may want on your computer include the following:

- *DVD and BD burners.* People use their computers to store and access data, video, and audio. DVDs and the newer Blue-ray Discs (BDs) are storage mediums. A burner is a device that can write to a DVD or a BD.

- *Universal serial bus (USB) ports.* Peripheral devices such as digital cameras and personal media players are plugged into USB ports. There are often multiple ports located on both the fronts and backs of computers.

- *Webcams.* A webcam is a type of camera that allows users to stream live video over the Internet. If two computer users have webcams on their computers, they can go online and see each other in real time. Some webcams are built into the computer. Others can be purchased separately.

New developments in computer hardware and software surface almost daily. You can review what is available and keep up-to-date by reading computer publications, manufacturers' literature online, and online articles. The more capabilities a computer offers, the more you will pay.

Cell Phones

Choosing a cell phone can be a complicated process. As electronic devices continue to converge, cell phones come packaged with other devices such as PDAs and personal media players. The variety of phones on the market can be confusing. Deciding on the best carrier or service provider and service plan are major decisions as well. Start with a careful look at how, when, and where you will use your cell phone, 20-7.

- Is it primarily for emergency calling, routine calling, or business?

- Will you use your phone frequently and during peak hours? Approximately how many minutes per month do you think you will use?

- Will you make long distance as well as local calls?

- What geographical areas do you want to cover—local, regional, and national? If international calling will be important for you, be sure to ask about it.

- Will you use a landline too, or depend only on your cell phone?

20-7

If text messaging is a feature you desire, make sure the phone you choose has that capability.

Central Ideas

- Evaluating your personal interests, aptitudes, abilities, values, and goals can help you form a career plan.

- The career clusters can help guide you to choose a career area of interest.

- Once you choose a career path, you can determine the education and training you will need to meet your career goals.

Most Americans enter the workforce at some point in their lives. People work primarily to earn money for life's necessities and a few extras. Most people begin working during their teens or early 20s and continue to retirement age. Because you will likely be working for many years, it pays to get the training and education that will lead to good jobs and good pay.

If you are like most young people, entering the world of work will be a major step. It calls for thoughtful choices. You will spend about one-third of your waking hours at the occupation you choose. Therefore, you will want to find work you can do well *and* enjoy. This can be a challenge.

Some people seem to know from an early age what they want to do with their lives. Most have to search out the jobs that will bring adequate income and job satisfaction. For high school students who plan to go on to college or enter a training program after graduation, the world of work may seem far away. However, it is not too early to begin thinking about your future and the career choices that will bring you satisfaction.

Case Study: Career Choices

Lee Goes from School to His Favorite Hobby

Lee loves computers. He works part-time at Compumart doing sales and service. Compumart offered him a full-time position when he graduates from high school. The money will be good and Lee already knows a lot about the business. The best part is the opportunity to develop new programs and work with the latest equipment.

Eventually, Lee might become a computer programmer or a systems analyst. Both careers require more schooling, so for the moment he just plans to enjoy his job.

Case Review

1. What are the advantages of being able to move right into the job you want from high school? Do you see any disadvantages for Lee?
2. Under what circumstances would Lee be smart to delay his computer job and go to college or enroll in an advanced training program?
3. What are some of the occupations that are open to high school graduates?
4. What other hobbies or activities can you think of that could lead to satisfying full-time employment?

Worker Protection Laws	
Law	**Key Provisions**
FLSA—Fair Labor Standards Act	Establishes fair minimum wage, overtime pay, child labor standards and other workplace conditions that affect workers
Family and Medical Leave Act	Requires employers to allow employees up to 12 weeks of unpaid job protected leave annually for birth or adoption and care of a child, care of a seriously ill family member, or a serious personal health condition
COBRA—Consolidated Omnibus Budget Reconciliation Act	Gives eligible workers who leave their place of employment the right to continue their employer-sponsored group health insurance, including coverage for preexisting conditions, for up to 18 months at their own expense
OSHA—Occupational Safety and Health Act	Promotes and enforces safety and health standards in the workplace
EEOC—Equal Employment Opportunity Act	Protects employees against discrimination based on race, color, disability, religion, sex, age, and national origin in hiring, promoting, firing, wages, testing, training, and all other terms and conditions of employment
ERISA—Employee Retirement Income Security Act	Outlines employees' rights as participants in an employer's pension and/ or profit-sharing plans

22-5

These federal laws protect the rights of workers.

Workplace Ethics

Ethics in the workplace have become a significant issue in the business world. *Ethics* are a set of moral values that guide a person's behavior. They help a person determine what is right and wrong in given situations. Ethics are based on traits such as trustworthiness, honesty, loyalty, respect, responsibility, and fairness. Over 90 percent of business schools now require ethics courses as part of their curriculum.

Companies differ in their approach to workplace behavior. Some simply assume that employees bring their own standards to the job, and management offers very little guidance. Some companies rely on an informal corporate culture that guides job-related decisions and actions. Other businesses follow a carefully developed program. This may include a statement of corporate values and a code of ethics to guide employees.

Today, more and more businesses are adopting clearly formulated ethics programs to guide behavior and decisions in the workplace. In companies that take ethics seriously, top management will project the value system that drives behavior. A company may convey its expectations for ethics on the job in different ways. These include employee handbooks, training sessions or seminars, or printed formal statements of company values and ethics.

Government & Public Administration

Equal Employment Opportunity Specialists

Equal employment opportunity specialists provide advice to management concerning how to prevent discriminatory practices in recruiting, hiring, promotions, pay, and benefits. They analyze workforce characteristics and organizational structure and make recommendations to ensure compliance with laws and requirements.

Case Study: Career Choices

Desiree Makes a Hard Choice

Desiree works at a local clothing store and gets a 20% employee discount. She spends a good share of her income on new outfits. Her best friend Lillea admires Desiree's clothes and wishes she could add to her wardrobe.

One Saturday, Lillea stops by the store to see the new fall clothes. The owner is at the bank and Desiree is in charge. Lillea tries on several outfits but can't afford everything she wants. Lillea asks Desiree to buy the outfits using her discount, and then Lillea will pay Desiree for the clothes.

Desiree is troubled by this suggestion. The owner of the shop made it clear the discount was for employees only—not family members or friends. It would be dishonest to use her discount this way and she could lose her job. On the other hand, Desiree doesn't want to lose Lillea's friendship.

Case Review

1. How do you think Desiree should resolve this dilemma?
2. How would you react if your best friend asked you to do something that compromised your values?
3. How do you think the store owner would react to this situation?
4. Why do you think Desiree should or should not let Lillea use her discount in this way?
5. How does this situation relate to ethics issues in the workplace?

The standards only have meaning when the message comes from management and is enforced by example. Stated codes of ethics generally address relationships of the business with employees, customers, suppliers, investors, creditors, competitors, and community. Business codes of ethics frequently relate to such issues as fair treatment of employees, teamwork, competition, and conflicts of interest. Other issues include use of business resources and assets, confidentiality, and environmental concerns.

When you apply for jobs, inquire about an employer's policies regarding employee decisions and behavior on the job. If ever in doubt about what is and is not acceptable, ask before you act.

Linking to... Science

Greenhouse Gases

Greenhouse gases include the following:

- **Carbon dioxide.** Mainly from the burning of substances: wood, solid waste, fossil fuels, etc.
- **Methane.** A by-product of fossil fuel production and the decay of organic material.

Common sources are landfills and agriculture. Animals also release methane gas.

- **Nitrous oxide.** The burning of fossil fuels and solid waste releases this gas.
- **Fluorinated gases.** Powerful gases released during industrial activities.

plants filter carbon dioxide from the air, using it and sunlight to grow. With fewer plants to absorb carbon dioxide, more remains in the atmosphere.

If carbon dioxide and other greenhouse gases continue to collect in the atmosphere, experts predict serious consequences, 23-1.

Waste Disposal

The average U.S. citizen generates about 4 pounds of garbage each day. All that waste must be disposed somehow. Some solid waste is disposed through burning, but most household waste is buried in a landfill. A **landfill** is a permanent waste disposal site for most solid, non-hazardous waste.

Special sites are devoted to the disposal of *hazardous waste.* **Hazardous waste** includes substances—liquids, solids, and gases—that are dangerous or potentially harmful to health or the environment. They are discarded by-products of agricultural, manufacturing, medical, national defense, and

23-1

Climate change could permanently alter weather and other conditions.

Possible Results of Climate Change

Rising sea levels and flooding. Ice in artic regions and high altitudes would melt faster if temperatures rise. This would release large volumes of water, possibly flooding many coastal areas.

Weather pattern changes. Some regions would suffer water shortages and drought. Warmer oceans would trigger more hurricanes that could cause flooding.

Famine. Extreme weather changes would threaten crop production in many regions, causing food shortages.

Animal and plant extinction. Weather would probably change faster than many plants and animals could adjust. In the short term, animals would probably try to migrate to more comfortable climates that supported familiar food supplies. Plants, however, would likely die off.

Human migrations. Flooded coastal areas plus shortages of food and safe water could force millions of people from their homes. This might lead to regional conflicts.

Science, Technology, Engineering & Mathematics

Hazardous Waste Technicians

Hazardous waste technicians identify, remove, package, transport, and dispose of various hazardous materials, including asbestos, radioactive and nuclear materials, arsenic, lead, and mercury. They often respond to emergencies where harmful substances are present. They transport and prepare materials for treatment or disposal.

other sources. Households discard hazardous waste, too. Some examples are paint, cleaners, auto products, pesticides, and flame-retardants. Also hazardous are fluorescent lamps, batteries, consumer electronics, and anything with mercury, such as fever thermometers.

Existing landfills are filling up, and building new landfills is costly. Few communities are willing to permit landfills in their area, so new sites are located further from the areas they serve. This requires transporting waste for long distances at considerable cost.

Improper disposal of waste poses serious threats to human health and the environment. If hazardous waste ends up in landfills, it can contaminate groundwater and cropland. Without proper controls, burning waste can release greenhouse gases that contribute to climate change.

Dwindling Resources

Natural resources—land, water, forests, fuel, and wildlife—are valuable economic assets. Everyone shares the challenge of making sure these resources continue to be available to future generations.

Fossil Fuels

Fossil fuels—coal, petroleum, and natural gas—are derived from the decomposed remains of animals and plants that lived in prehistoric times. Burning fossil fuels is the major source of greenhouse gases. Fossil fuels provide more than 85 percent of all energy consumed in the United States. This includes gas that powers cars and heats homes and coal that produces electricity.

Energy sources can be classified as renewable or nonrenewable. **Renewable energy** sources are those that are continually available or can be replenished. They include wind, water, solar (sun), and biofuels. **Biofuels** are fuels composed of or produced from biological raw material. An example is ethanol made from corn or sugar beets.

Nonrenewable energy sources are those that can be used up or cannot be used again, 23-2. Once they are gone, they cannot be replaced. Fossil fuels are nonrenewable energy sources. Nuclear energy is also a nonrenewable resource because it is created from uranium, a substance available in limited amounts.

At present, the United States depends on foreign sources for over 50 percent of its petroleum. This dependence is a big concern because the U.S. has little or no control over the supply or price of fuel imports. Achieving energy independence will require greater fuel efficiency and conservation. It will also require development of new energy sources that are renewable, affordable, and environmentally safe.

Clean Water

Most people in the United States take fresh, pure water for granted. In many parts of the country, water is plentiful and relatively cheap. This natural resource, which is vital to all forms of life, is becoming more precious. Many of the common items you buy require huge amounts of water to manufacture. For example, hundreds of gallons of water are used in the production of one pair of denim jeans.

Both the availability and quality of water are important environmental issues. Water scarcity creates severe problems. Demands for fresh water increase dramatically with population growth. In the years ahead, conserving water and keeping the water supply clean, will become vitally important.

Renewable Energy Source	Description	Disadvantages
Solar	The sun's radiation that reaches the earth. It can be converted to electricity and heat. Produces almost no undesirable side effects. Used most often and most effectively in warm climates. In cloudy areas, solar energy systems usually must be used with other forms of power.	• Cannot be concentrated into high-grade, usable fuel in large enough quantities. • Limited use at night and on cloudy days unless new storage systems are installed to absorb, store, and release energy as needed.
Wind	Large windmill-like turbines turn wind energy into electricity. A wind farm is a business that generates power from multiple turbines at one location.	• Many areas lack sufficient wind or space to set up wind turbines. • Not a constant or dependable source of energy. • Getting wind energy to places that need it requires creating a system of power lines across many miles. • The equipment to harness wind energy requires an investment. • People who live near wind farms complain about disturbances such as light deflection off turbine blades.
Hydro	Captures the power of ocean waves or water flowing over a dam to create electricity.	• Depends on the presence of enough water.
Geothermal	Uses hot water and steam produced deep inside the earth to create energy.	• Sources of geothermal energy are very limited.
Biofuels	Made of biological matter from plants and animals that can be converted to energy. Ethanol is made from grains—corn, sorghum, wheat, sugar cane, etc. It is usually mixed with gasoline. Biodiesel is made from plant and animal oils and fats.	• Not yet possible to produce adequate quantities of usable energy from any of these sources. • Depends on availability of farmland and forests. When land is used to grow sources of biofuels, it cannot be used to grow food.

(Continued.)

23-2

Dependence on nonrenewable energy sources will eventually use up remaining supplies.

Nonrenewable Energy Source	Description	Disadvantages
Petroleum, Natural Gas	Fossil fuels. Main forms of energy used in the United States today.	• Their use contributes to air pollution and climate change. • Oil spills foul water and kill wildlife. • U.S. is dependent on imports to meet demand. • Supplies (and prices) are controlled by other governments, including those hostile to the U.S.
Coal	Also a fossil fuel. A plentiful U.S. source of energy and a major export. Coal is likely to be a major source of energy well into the future.	• Difficult to transport. • Burning coal adds to climate change. • Strip-mining causes long-lasting damage to the land. • Converting coal to a gaseous or liquid form is a costly process.
Nuclear	Energy is produced from nuclear fission, or splitting apart, of uranium in nuclear power plants. Produces 20 percent of our electric power and 8 percent of our total energy production. Releases little greenhouse gas. Is used as the main source of energy in some countries, including France and Japan.	• Questions persist about plant safety and safe waste disposal. • Nonrenewable because uranium is scarce. • Nuclear waste, improperly handled, could cause catastrophic environmental damage.

23-2

(Continued.)

Urban Sprawl

Before the invention of cars, most people worked and went to school within walking distance of their homes. Everything a person needed was concentrated in a compact town center. If public transportation was available, most people used it.

Cars gave people more mobility. Homes and businesses were built along highways that led to and from city centers. Open land was converted into housing developments, roads, malls, and business parks. This dispersed development is described as *urban sprawl*. Many environmental groups oppose urban sprawl, especially when it replaces forests or prime farmland. They argue that sprawling areas require more roads, more driving, and more services than well-planned, concentrated business and residential developments.

While some areas of the country allow unchecked growth, others areas carefully plan new developments. Many towns and communities

What Government Can Do

In Chapter 2, you learned about the role of government in the U.S. economic system. Another important function of government is to ensure a safe and healthy environment for its citizens. Because both the environment and the economy are critical issues, the methods used to protect and conserve the environment and its resources need to be cost-effective.

Many environmental problems—climate change, deforestation, and water pollution, among others—are global. The government frequently pursues environmental interests at the international level.

Regulation and Legislation

In 1970, the federal government passed legislation creating the Environmental Protection Agency (EPA). The agency serves as the national watchdog and coordinating bureau for matters affecting the environment. The EPA focuses on air and water quality, noise, solid waste, hazardous waste, toxic substances, and other ecological issues.

Under a 1975 law, the Department of Energy (DOE) was required to set efficiency standards for major home appliances and several commercial products. The goal of the standards was to reduce the nation's energy use. Since then, the list of products under the DOE's review has grown. Besides setting minimum efficiency standards, it also sets maximum water-use standards for certain products. The DOE is charged with periodically reviewing opportunities for more energy- and water-savings from the items under its authority. These reviews involve input from manufacturers and consumers.

In addition, many state and local regulations govern environmental activities. To find out how your state is involved, go to your state Web site and look for the department or agency that deals with environmental issues.

Taxation

The use of taxes as a tool in fighting pollution is a recent concept. The so-called "green tax" offers a way to charge the cost of pollution to the polluter, whether producer or consumer. Examples of possible items subject to a green tax include excess household waste and auto emissions.

Green taxes could take the form of direct tax, fines, or user fees. They would provide greater incentive and pressure to find cost-effective ways of reducing and controlling pollution. Green taxes would also produce revenues that could be used to help clean up waste and pay for government pollution control services.

In some cases, government can use tax incentives to reward and encourage good environmental stewardship by both consumers and business. Examples include tax benefits for insulating homes, using solar energy, or purchasing fuel-efficient cars and appliances.

Transportation, Distribution & Logistics

Environmental Compliance Inspectors

Environmental compliance inspectors examine, evaluate, and investigate eligibility for or conformity with laws and regulations governing contract compliance of licenses and permits, and other compliance and enforcement inspection activities. They work to control and reduce the pollution of water, air, and land.

ECONOMICS in ACTION

Can Pollution Credits Work?

The U.S. government uses market incentives to tackle environmental problems. New programs create markets where "pollution credits" are bought and sold like stocks and bonds. The laws of supply and demand set credit prices.

For example, conservation banking programs reward landowners and local governments for preserving open space, endangered species, and habitats. They earn credits that can be sold. Other people or businesses must buy credits to offset environmental damage they cause. Having to buy credits is costly and discourages practices that are harmful to the environment.

Another example is a cap-and-trade program for greenhouse gas emissions. The government sets a cap, or maximum allowable amount, for GHG emissions. Businesses get an initial allowance of credits from the government.

They are awarded additional credits for good environmental stewardship, such as planting trees.

If a business exceeds the emissions cap, it must pay the government with credits. If a business doesn't have enough credits, it can buy them from other lower-polluting businesses. Having to purchase credits is like paying a fine.

These programs, especially the cap-and-trade program, are controversial. Program promoters say they minimize the cost of government regulation. Business owners, not government regulators, decide how to keep their emissions under the cap. However, some environmentalists say the programs don't do enough to curtail fossil fuel burning and other environmental damage. Other critics say they create undue hardship for businesses and will boost energy prices for consumers.

Clean Energy Development

Energy policies and choices affect jobs, prices, industries, the environment, and lifestyles here and around the world. It is clear that dependence on nonrenewable and polluting sources of energy must be severely curtailed. Harnessing the energy of the sun, wind, and water may provide a large share of the energy used in the future. Scientists and entrepreneurs are also developing other sources of energy. Government is heavily involved in these efforts both through its own laboratories and through funding of research in leading universities.

Other actions government could take on energy issues include the following:

- Tax fossil fuels to encourage greater efficiency and discourage excessive energy consumption.

- Provide incentives for industries to conduct comprehensive clean energy research.

- Work out a cooperative policy with other nations for the development, allocation, and efficient safe use of world energy resources.

Water Conservation

Areas experiencing water shortages can lower the system-wide operating pressure to reduce the flow of water. Government can also enact bans, restrictions, and rationing for different types of water usage. These normally are temporary measures taken during periods of severe shortages. More permanent conservation measures include

- local building codes that require water-efficient faucets, toilets, showerheads, and appliances in new construction

- utility billing that imposes higher rates for excess water usage

- increased recycling of industrial water

Case Study: Town Meeting

The Well Runs Dry

Two summers after Devon became town council president, a drought hit the area and the water table dropped substantially. The town needed to reduce its water usage.

Devon suggested raising water rates by 20 percent. A town council member recommended a ban on watering lawns, trees, shrubs, and gardens. Other council members advised limiting watering to evening and early morning hours.

Council members also suggested educating residents about taking shorter showers and finding ways to reduce water use. Another idea mandated low-flow toilets, showerheads, and appliances in new and remodeled bathrooms and kitchens. Members also discussed installing a water-rationing system to limit water usage in each household.

Case Review

1. What other steps can you think of for conserving water?
2. How would each of the council's suggestions affect you and your family?
3. Which idea do you think would be most effective? Why?
4. How would you be willing to change your own habits to help conserve water and other resources in a crisis situation?
5. What are some important considerations for government bodies to think about when passing laws and policies to deal with resource shortages?

- public education programs to encourage voluntary reductions in water usage

- water meter accuracy and leak detection

What Businesses Can Do

Manufacturers and retailers share responsibility for the environmental impact of the production, use, and disposal of their products. *Product stewardship* is an environmental concept that calls on businesses to take a leadership role in reducing the health and environmental impacts of consumer products. For example, producers should try to:

- design products to be upgraded instead of discarded

- incorporate energy-saving features

- use recycled materials in the product or its packaging, if feasible

- avoid excess packaging

- use renewable energy and recycled water in the manufacturing process

- upgrade machinery and vehicles to energy-saving models

- minimize the discharge of pollutants into the environment

Manufacturers and retailers can encourage recycling by providing free pickup of unused goods, such as old appliances. They can sponsor education programs to identify the efforts being made to preserve natural resources.

Some businesses are taking back products that reach end-of-life and offering free recycling to customers. Others are refurbishing used products for resale or donation. By planning for disposal during product design, producers can also minimize disposal problems.

Chapter Summary

Protecting the environment is one of the most pressing challenges of our day. It calls for the attention, participation, and best efforts of all of us—individuals, local communities, government, and businesses. Climate change, waste disposal, dwindling resources, and urban sprawl are some of the environmental challenges that need attention and action.

You can take an active role in protecting the earth. Stay informed about current environmental issues. Learn to conserve resources in your own life and participate in community environmental protection programs.

Government protects the environment with regulation, legislation, and tax policies that encourage and enforce conservation and sustainable practices. The government also supports research to find solutions for environmental challenges.

Manufacturers and retailers also play an important role in solving environmental challenges. Businesses can reduce the toll of manufacturing on the environment by minimizing waste, conserving resources, and recycling materials.

Review

1. Name three key environmental issues facing the United States and the world today.

2. What factors contribute to climate change?

3. Explain the difference between fossil fuels and biofuels and give an example of each.

4. Name three renewable energy sources.

5. What are the two main forms of energy used in the United States?

6. What are three drawbacks of using coal as an energy source?

7. List five ways to conserve energy in the home.

8. Name three ways to conserve water in the home.

9. List three ways to reduce waste.

10. What are three ways to use less gasoline in your car?

11. Which government agency was created to serve as the national watchdog and coordinating bureau for the environment?

12. What are green taxes?

13. Name three actions government can take regarding water conservation.

14. What steps can businesses take during the design process to reduce a product's environmental impact?

Critical Thinking

15. What are some of the problems that concern environmentalists today? What environmental problems concern you the most?

16. Investigate to find out where water shortages have been a serious problem in the United States. Find out how affected communities coped with the problem.

17. Why is it important for consumers to be informed about threats to the environment?

18. Name several steps you as an individual can take to preserve and protect our planet.

19. How can consumer spending habits and decisions serve as an environmental protection tool?

20. What are some environmental problems that exist in your community? How might they be solved? What are some things you personally can do to address environmental issues?

Academic Connections

21. **Research, writing, speech.** Visit the Web sites of the Environmental Protection Agency, the Department of Energy, or another government agency for facts and data you need to prepare a written or an oral report on one of the following:
    * climate change
    * ecosystems
    * urban sprawl versus smart growth
    * air quality
    * conservation
    * The Kyoto Accord
    * water shortages
    * Earth Day
    * recycling
    * pollution control regulations and costs
    Make an effort to present a balanced view covering both sides of controversial issues. Cite authorities, events, dates, figures, pros, and cons.

22. **Research, science.** Divide into research teams to investigate one of the following sources or types of energy: nuclear, natural gas, coal, solar, geothermal, petroleum, wind, water, or underwater technology. Prepare a report on its use, cost, safety, effectiveness, availability, and impact on the environment.

23. **Reading, speech, writing.** Select one of the current local, state, or federal laws or pending bills designed to protect the environment. Study it carefully to find out:
    A. Its main objectives and key provisions.
    B. Its costs and benefits.
    C. Its impact on different segments of society.
    D. Its effectiveness in achieving its purpose.
    E. The ease of enforcing it.
    Present your findings to the class in an oral report or a written report.

24. **Speech.** Debate the pros and cons of an energy tax to reduce pollution, conserve energy, and generate government revenues.

25. **Science.** Conduct an experiment to explore biodegradable materials. Bury the following items in soil in milk cartons (cut off the tops). Add a cup of water to each carton.
    * plastic utensil
    * apple slices
    * piece of trash bag marketed as biodegradable
    * piece of plastic trash bag
    * piece of newspaper
    * wood chip
    After three weeks, remove and examine the items. Rate each item high or low in terms of biodegradability.

26. **Writing.** Write a letter to an appropriate government agency, representative, or official at the federal, state, or local level regarding an environmental issue of concern to you. Define the issue, suggest possible solutions, and express your opinion with supporting arguments. Cite authorities and relevant publications or studies, if available.

MATH CHALLENGE

27. Suppose a car gets 20 miles per gallon (mpg) going 70 miles per hour (mph). If the car gets 20 percent better fuel economy going 55 mph, how much farther does it travel per gallon of fuel at the lower speed?

Tech Smart

28. Go to www.epa.gov/climatechange. Use the greenhouse gas household emissions calculator to estimate the amount of GHGs you create. You may need recent gas and electric bills to estimate utility use for your family's home. What are your total emissions?environmental issues.

GLOSSARY

A

abilities. Physical and mental skills developed through learning, training, and practice. (21)

abstract of title. A summary of the public records or history of the ownership of a particular piece of property. (18)

accessories. Items designed to go with an outfit. (16)

adjustable rate mortgage (ARM). A mortgage in which the interest rate is adjusted up or down periodically. (18)

advertising. A paid message touting the attributes of something in order to convince consumers to buy it. (13)

amortization. The process by which loan payments are applied to the principal, or amount borrowed, as well as to the interest on a loan according to a set schedule. (18)

annual percentage rate (APR). The annual cost of credit a lender charges. (9)

annual percentage yield (APY). The rate of yearly earnings from an account, including compound interest. (11)

annuity. A contract with an insurance company that provides income for a set period of time or for life. (12)

appraisal. An estimate of the current value of property. (10)

appreciation. An increase in the value of an investment. (12)

apprenticeship. A type of education that combines on-the-job training, work experience, and classroom-type instruction. (21)

aptitudes. Natural physical and mental talents. (21)

asset. An item of value that a person owns, such as cash, stocks, bonds, real estate, and personal possessions. (3)

ATM card. A card that allows customers to withdraw cash from and make deposits to their accounts using an ATM. (8)

automated teller machine (ATM). A computer terminal used to transact business with a financial institution. (8)

B

bait and switch. A fraudulent sales technique that involves advertising an attractive offer to bring the customer into the store. The item is either sold out or is undesirable. The seller then presents a more expensive substitute. (14)

balance of payments. An account of the flow of goods, services, and money coming into and going out of the country. (4)

bandwidth. The maximum amount of information that can be carried over an electronic cable or device at one time. (20)

bankruptcy. A legal state in which the courts excuse a debtor from repaying some or all debt. In return, the debtor must give up certain assets and possessions. (9)

bank statement. A record of checks, deposits, and charges on a checking account. (8)

bear market. Term for the market when investors feel insecure and stock prices fall. (12)

beneficiary. Person named by the policyholder to receive the death benefit of an insurance policy. (10)

binding arbitration. A method of settling disputes outside of court in which the parties involved agree to accept the decision of a third party. (14)

biodegradable. Describes a material that can be broken down naturally by microorganisms into harmless elements. (23)

biofuel. A fuel composed of or produced from biological raw material. (23)

blend. A yarn made by combining two or more fibers. (16)

bodily injury liability. Coverage that protects insured persons when they are liable for an auto accident that injured or killed others. (10)

body composition. The proportion of muscle, bone, fat, and other tissue that make up body weight. (17)

bond. A certificate of debt issued by a corporation or government that entitles the bondholder to a set rate of interest on the face value of the bond until it matures. (12)

bonus. Money added to an employee's base pay. It is usually a reward for performance or a share of business profits. (7)

brand name products. Products that have distinctive packaging and are identified with one manufacturer. (15)

broadband. High-speed Internet access that transmits data at speeds greater than 200 kilobits per second. (20)

budget. A spending plan for the use of money over time based on goals and expected income. (6)

bull market. Term for the market when investors are confident in the economy and stock prices are rising. (12)

business cycle. A cycle of economic activity with periods called *contraction, trough, recovery,* and *peak.* (2)

buying incentives. Trading stamps, coupons, store games, and prizes offered by sellers to help sell goods and services. (14)

C

capital. Money used to generate income or to invest in a business or asset. (4)

capital gain. Income earned from selling an asset for more than the purchase price. (12)

career clusters. Sixteen general groupings of occupational and career developed by a partnership among the states, educators, and employers. (21)

career ladder. An outline of jobs in a given career field that are available at different levels of education and training experience. (21)

career plan. An outline of steps or action you can take to reach a career goal, including required courses and training, job-related experiences, and extracurricular activities or projects. (21)

cartel. A group of countries or firms that control the production and pricing of a product or service. (4)

cash flow statement. A summary of the amount of money received as well as the amount paid out for goods and services during a specific period. (6)

cashier's check. A check drawn by a bank on its own funds and signed by an authorized officer of the bank. (8)

caveat emptor. A principle meaning the risk in the transaction is on the buyer's side; literally, *let the buyer beware.* (14)

certificate of deposit (CD). Money deposited for a set period of time that earns a set annual rate of interest. (11)

certified check. A personal check with a bank's guarantee the check will be paid. (8)

certified used car. A previously owned car that received a thorough mechanical and appearance inspection along with necessary repairs and replacements. (19)

chain letters. Letters or e-mails that generally promise big returns for sending something, such as a postcard or a dollar, to the first person on the list. (14)

class action lawsuits. Legal actions in courts of law brought by a group of individuals who have been similarly wronged. (14)

climate change. Shifts in measurements of climate—such as temperature, precipitation, or wind—that last decades or longer. (23)

closed-end credit. A loan that must be repaid with finance charges by a certain date. (9)

closing costs. Fees that must be paid before the sale of a home can be made final. (18)

coinsurance. A percentage the policyholder must pay for certain services. (10)

collateral. Property that a borrower promises to give up in case of default. (9)

collusion. When companies make illegal secret agreements, usually to engage in price fixing or to shut out smaller competitors. (2)

command economy. An economy in which a central authority, usually the government, controls economic activities. (1)

commercial bank. A bank owned by stockholders and organized to receive, transfer, and lend money to individuals, businesses, and governments. (8)

commission. Income paid as a percentage of sales made by a salesperson. (7)

common stock. Stock that pays dividends declared by the company and gives stockholders certain voting rights. (12)

community colleges. Two-year school offering both academic and occupational courses. (21)

comparative advantage. The benefit to the party that has the lower opportunity cost in pursuing a given course of action. (4)

comparison shopping. The process of gathering information about products and services to get the best quality or usefulness at the best price. (13)

compensation. Payment and benefits received for work. (7)

composting. A natural process that transforms materials like food waste, leaves, and grass into useful soil-like particles. (23)

compound interest. Interest figured on money deposited plus interest. (11)

condominium. A form of home ownership in which an individual owns his or her own unit and shares ownership and expenses of maintaining common areas such as halls, stairs, lobby, and grounds. (18)

conservation. The protection and management of the environment and valuable natural resources. (23)

consumer. The buyer or user of goods and services. Also, a person who provides the demand for goods and services at prices he or she can afford to pay. (1)

consumer advocates. Individuals or groups who promote consumer interests in areas such as health and safety, education, redress, truthful advertising, fairness in the marketplace, and environmental protection. (14)

consumer cooperative. A nonretail association owned and operated by a group of members for their own benefit rather than for profit. (13)

consumer electronic product. Devices that run on electric current or batteries and are used for communication, entertainment, education, or information gathering. (20)

consumer price index (CPI). A measurement of changes in the prices of selected consumer goods and services. (2)

contingency clause. An agreement that calls for certain requirements to be met before the contract is binding. (18)

continuing education. Learning pursued after a person completes formal education and training. (21)

contract. A legally binding agreement between a borrower and a creditor. (9)

convenience foods. Foods that are partially prepared or ready-to-eat. (15)

convergence. The merging of separate devices, technologies, or industries into one. (20)

cooperative. A form of home ownership in which an individual buys shares in a corporation that owns the property. In return, the buyer becomes a resident in a designated unit and a member of the cooperative. (18)

co-payment. A flat fee the policyholder must pay for certain services. (10)

corporation. A business that is a separate entity created and owned by the founder and shareholders. (22)

cosigner. A responsible person who signs a loan along with a borrower thereby agreeing to pay the obligation if the borrower fails to do so. (9)

cost-benefit principle. The idea that an action should be taken or a purchase made only if the benefits are at least as great as the costs. (5)

credit. An arrangement that allows consumers to buy goods or services and pay for them later. (9)

credit card. Allows consumers to make purchases or borrow money on a time-payment plan. (9)

creditor. The party that supplies money, goods, or services in a credit agreement. (9)

credit report. A record of a person's credit history and financial behavior. (9)

credit union. A nonprofit financial cooperative owned by and operated for the benefit of its members. It accepts deposits, makes loans, and provides other services. (8)

creditworthy. A credit applicant judged to have the assets, income, and tendency to repay debt. (9)

D

decision-making process. A method of choosing a course of action after evaluating information and weighing the costs and benefits of alternative actions and their consequences. (5)

deductible. The amount you will be required to pay before insurance pays for any services. (10)

default. When a borrower fails to pay the debt owed. (9)

deficit spending. When government spends more than it collects in tax revenues and must borrow money. (2)

demand. The amount of a product or service consumers are willing to buy. (1)

demographics. The statistical characteristics of the population. (6)

dependent. An individual who relies on someone else for financial support. (10)

depreciation. A decrease in the value of property as a result of age or wear and tear. (10)

depression. An extended period of economic recession. (2)

dial-up. Internet access through a telephone line using a modem in the computer. (20)

Dietary Guidelines for Americans. Suggestions for choosing nutritious foods and maintaining a healthful lifestyle developed by the U.S. Departments of Agriculture and Health and Human Services. (14)

dietary supplement. A product that is intended to enhance a person's diet. It contains ingredients such as vitamins, minerals, herbs, or amino acids and other substances. (17)

digital subscriber line (DSL). Internet access that uses a digital frequency that does not interfere with telephone service. (20)

direct broadcast satellite (DBS). A type of television and Internet service that works by bouncing transmissions off orbiting satellites directly to receivers on customers' homes. (20)

direct mail advertising. Advertising circulars, catalogs, coupons, and other unsolicited offers that arrive through mail or another delivery service. (14)

disability. A limitation that affects a person's ability to function in major life activities. (7)

distance learning. Education or training delivered to the student online, by mail, or on television, offering many choices in both individual courses and total program options. (21)

diversification. Spreading risk by putting money in a variety of investments. (12)

dividend. A portion of a company's earnings paid to stockholders. (12)

dollar-cost averaging. A strategy of investing a fixed dollar amount at regular intervals. (12)

dual-career family. A family where both spouses have careers outside the home. (22)

durable goods. Products that have lasting value, such as furniture, appliances, and cars. (3)

E

earned income. Income from employment. (7)

earnest money. The deposit you make when you sign a purchase agreement to show that your offer is serious. (18)

easy-access credit. A short-term, high-interest loan granted to borrowers regardless of credit history. (9)

ecology. The study of the relationship between living things and their environment. (23)

e-commerce. Buying and selling goods and services online. (13)

economic globalization. The flow of goods, services, labor, money, innovative ideas, and technology across borders. (4)

economic system. The structure in which resources are turned into goods and services to address unlimited needs and wants. (1)

economies of scale. The concept that cost of producing one unit of something declines as the number of units produced rises. (4)

e-learning. Internet education and training programs. (21)

electronic funds transfer (EFT). The movement of money electronically from one financial institution to another. (8)

employee benefit. A form of nonmonetary compensation received in addition to a wage or salary. (7)

endorse. To sign one's name on the back of a check in order to cash or deposit the check. (8)

endowment insurance. Insurance that pays the face value of the policy to beneficiaries if the insured dies before the endowment period ends. It also pays the face amount to the insured if he or she lives beyond the endowment period. (10)

EnergyGuide label. A label that lists the estimated annual cost of operating an appliance. (20)

ENERGY STAR label. A program that is a voluntary partnership of the U.S. Department of Energy and the Environmental Protection Agency, product manufacturers, local utilities, and retailers. Its purpose is to encourage the purchase of energy-efficient consumer electronics and appliances. (20)

entitlement. A government payment or benefit promised by law to eligible citizens, such as Social Security and Medicare benefits, unemployment benefits, veterans' services, food stamps, and housing assistance. (7)

entrepreneur. A person who owns, operates, and assumes the risk for a business. (22)

environmentalist. A person concerned with the quality of the environment and how to maintain it. (23)

escrow account. An account used to hold money until it can be paid to the party that is owed. (18)

estate. The possessions, such as property, savings, investments, and insurance benefits, a person leaves when he or she dies. (12)

ethic. A moral principle or belief that directs a person's actions. (5)

euro. A common currency used in Europe among the nations participating in the European Union (EU). (4)

European Union (EU). A group of nations joined together to form a trade sector, most of which use a common currency called the euro. (4)

exchange rate. The value of one currency compared to another. (4)

exclusions. The services that are not covered in an insurance plan. (10)

exclusive buyer agent. A real estate agent who works for the buyer, not the seller. (18)

executor. A person appointed to carry out the terms outlined in a will. (12)

exemption. A tax benefit that reduces the amount of income a person is taxed on. (7)

expense. The cost of a good or service a person buys. (6)

expiration date. The last day a product should be used. (15)

exports. The goods and services grown or made in a particular country and then sold in world markets. (4)

extended warranty. A contract that provides for the servicing of a product, if needed, during the term of the contract. (13)

F

fabric finish. A treatment applied to a fabric to achieve certain characteristics. (16)

fad. A fashion style that stays popular for only a short time. (16)

family crisis. A major problem that impacts the future of the family and its lifestyle. (6)

family life cycle. The stages of change a family passes through from formation to aging. (6)

Federal Deposit Insurance Corporation (FDIC). A U.S. government agency that protects bank customers by insuring deposits as well as examining and supervising financial institutions. (8)

Federal Reserve System. The U.S. government system that regulates the nation's money supply and banking system. It is comprised of the Federal Reserve Board, 12 Federal Reserve Banks, and the Federal Open Market Committee. (2)

fee-for-service. A health insurance plan that pays for covered medical services after treatment is provided. (10)

FHA-insured loan. A loan in which the Federal Housing Administration insures the lender against the borrowers' possible default or failure to pay. (18)

fiber. The indigestible or partially indigestible part of foods that helps move food and digestive byproducts through the large intestine for healthy digestion. (15)

fiber optics. Glass strands as narrow as a human hair that carry data at the speed of a laser light beam. (20)

FICA (Federal Insurance Contributions Act). The law that requires the collection of social security payroll taxes. (7)

financial literacy. The understanding of the basic knowledge and skills needed to manage financial resources. (6)

firewall. A protection system to block unwanted e-mail, offensive Web sites, and potential hackers. (20)

fiscal policy. The government's taxing and spending decisions. (2)

fixed expense. A set cost that must be paid each budgeted period. (6)

fixed rate mortgage. A mortgage that guarantees a fixed or unchanging interest rate for the life of the loan. (18)

floor plan. A drawing that shows the size and shape of a room on a scale of ¼ inch to a foot. (18)

food grades. An indication of how well a food meets quality standards. (15)

foreclosure. The forced sale of a property. (9)

Form W-2. A Wage and Tax Statement that states the amount an employee was paid in the previous year. It also gives the amounts of income, Social Security, and Medicare taxes withheld from an employee's income during the year. (7)

Form W-4. The Employee's Withholding Allowance Certificate that tells the employer how much tax to withhold from an employee's paycheck. (7)

fossil fuel. A fuel derived from the decomposed remains of animals and plants that lived in prehistoric times. (23)

franchise. An agreement that permits the franchisee to market and sell goods and services in a given area that the franchiser provides. (22)

free enterprise system. An economy in which privately owned businesses operate and compete for profits with limited government regulation. Also called *market economy* or *capitalism* (1)

free trade. A policy of limited government trade restrictions. (4)

freshness date. The last day a product should be expected to have peak quality. (15)

full warranty. Provides for free repair or replacement of the warranted item or part if any defect occurs while the warranty is in effect. (13)

G

garnishment. A legal procedure requiring a portion of a debtor's pay to be set aside by the person's employer to pay creditors. (9)

GDP per capita. The market value of final goods and services produced per person. (3)

generic drug. A drug sold by its common name, chemical composition, or class. Generally costs less than a similar brand-name drug. (17)

generic products. Plain-labeled, no-brand grocery products. (15)

global warming. The steady rise in average temperatures near the earth's surface. (23)

goal. An objective a person wants to attain. (5)

good. A physical item that is produced, such as food or clothing. (1)

grace period. The time between the billing date and the start of interest charges. (9)

graduated payment mortgage. A mortgage that allows the buyer to pay low monthly payments at first and higher payments in the future. (18)

gross domestic product (GDP). The value of all goods and services produced by a nation during a specified period. (2)

gross income. A worker's earnings before deductions. (7)

H

hazardous waste. Substances—liquids, solids, and gases—that are dangerous or potentially harmful to health or the environment. (23)

health savings account (HSA). A tax-advantaged savings account available to people enrolled in qualified High Deductible Health Plans (HDHPs). (10)

high-definition TV (HDTV). Televisions that receive digital signals and display them as crisp images. (20)

home appliances. Major or small devices that run on gas or electric current and perform a specific function in the home. (20)

home equity loan. A loan in which home owners borrow the money they paid on a mortgage. (18)

human resource. A quality or characteristic a person has within himself or herself. (1)

hypoallergenic. A type of product that does not contain ingredients likely to cause allergic reactions. (17)

I

identity theft. The crime of stealing someone's credit cards, bank and investment account numbers, or social security number and using the information to commit theft or fraud. (14)

implied fitness. An unwritten warranty that guarantees a product is fit for any performance or purpose promised by the seller. (13)

implied merchantability. An unwritten warranty that guarantees a product is what it is called and does what its name implies. (13)

imports. Goods and services that come into a country from foreign countries. (4)

impulse spending. Unplanned or "spur of the moment" purchases. (15)

income. Any form of money a person receives from various sources. (6)

income tax. A tax on the earnings of individuals and corporations levied by the federal government and most state governments. (3)

inflation. An overall increase in the price of goods and services. (2)

infomercial. A program-length form of paid television programming designed to sell a service, product, or idea. (14)

innovation. The process of creating something, such as new or improved products and new ways to do things and solve problems. (1)

inpatient. A person whose care requires a stay in the hospital. (10)

inspection stamps. Stamps indicating foods are wholesome and safe to eat. (15)

interest. Payments from financial institutions, businesses, and government to use customers' money. (7)

interest only mortgage. A mortgage in which monthly payments are applied only to the interest, not the principal, for a certain number of years. (18)

interests. Activities, subjects, ideas, sports, or hobbies a person enjoys. (21)

international trade. The buying and selling of goods and services across national borders and among the people of different nations. (4)

internship. A short-term position with a sponsoring organization to gain experience in a certain field of study. (21)

interview. A meeting in which a prospective employer or an admissions officer of a school talks with an applicant. (22)

investment. An asset bought to increase wealth over time, but that carries the risk of loss. (3)

investment portfolio. The collection of securities and other assets a person owns. (12)

K

knit fabrics. Fabrics made by looping yarns together. (16)

L

labor force. Composed of people, age 16 and over, who are employed or looking for and able to work. (2)

INDEX